# ROMANS

## VOLUME 1
### CHAPTERS 1 - 5

# THE

# TEACHER'S

# OUTLINE & STUDY

# BIBLE

# ROMANS

## VOLUME 1
### CHAPTERS 1 - 5

# THE

# TEACHER'S

# OUTLINE & STUDY

# BIBLE

NEW TESTAMENT

KING JAMES VERSION

Leadership Ministries Worldwide
PO Box 21310
Chattanooga, TN 37424-0310

The Teacher's Outline & Study Bible is written for God's people to use both in their personal lives and in their teaching. Leadership Ministries Worldwide wants God's people to use The Teacher's Outline & Study Bible.  The purpose of the copyright is to prevent the reproduction, misuse, and abuse of the material.

May our Lord bless us all as we live, preach, teach, and write for Him, fulfilling His great commission to live righteous and godly lives and to make disciples of all nations.

Please address all requests for information or permission to:
Leadership Ministries Worldwide
PO Box 21310
Chattanooga TN  37424-0310
Ph.# (423) 855-2181   FAX (423) 855-8616   E-Mail 74152.616@compuserve.com
http://www.outlinebible.org

Library of Congress Catalog Card Number: 94-073070
International Standard Book Number: 1-57407-052-5

PRINTED IN THE U.S.A.

PUBLISHED BY LEADERSHIP MINISTRIES WORLDWIDE

# H O W   T O   U S E
## THE TEACHER'S OUTLINE AND STUDY BIBLE (TOSB)

*To gain maximum benefit,* here is all you do. Follow these easy steps, using the sample outline below.

**1 STUDY TITLE**

**2 MAJOR POINTS**

**3 SUB-POINTS**

**4 COMMENTARY, QUES-
TIONS, APPLICATION,
ILLUSTRATIONS**
(Follows Scripture)

**B. The Steps to Peace
(Part II): Prayer
& Positive Think-
ing, 4:6-9**

1. **Peace comes through prayer**
   a. The charge: Do not worry or be anxious
   b. The remedy: Prayer
      1) About everything
      2) With requests
      3) With thanksgiving
   c. The promise: Peace
      1) Peace that passes all understanding
      2) Peace that keeps our hearts & minds
2. **Peace comes through positive thinking**
   a. The charge: Think & practice things that are...
      1) True
      2) Honest
      3) Just
      4) Pure

6 Be careful for nothing; but in every thing by prayer and supplication with thanksgiving let your requests be made known unto God.

7 And the peace of God, which passeth all understanding, shall keep your hearts and minds through Christ Jesus.

8 Finally, brethren, whatsoever things are true, whatsoever things are honest, whatsoever things are just, whatsoever things are pure, whatsoever things are lovely, what-

1. First: Read the **Study Title** two or three times so that the subject sinks in.
2. Then: Read the **Study Title** and the **Major Points** (Pts.1,2,3) together quickly. Do this several times and you will quickly grasp the overall subject.
3. Now: Read both the **Major Points** and **Sub-Points**. Do this slower than Step 2. Note how the points are beside the applicable verse, and simply state what the Scripture is saying—in Outline form.
4. Read the **Commentary**. As you read and re-read, pray that the Holy Spirit will bring to your attention exactly what you should study and teach. It's all there, outlined and fully developed, just waiting for you to study and teach.

## <u>TEACHERS, PLEASE NOTE</u>:

⇒ Cover the **Scripture** and the **Major Points** with your students. Drive the **Scripture** and **Major Points** into their hearts and minds.

(Please continue on next page)

⇒ Cover *only some of the commentary* with your students, not all (unless of course you have plenty of time). Cover only as much commentary as is needed to get the major points across.

⇒ Do NOT feel that you must...
- cover all the commentary under each point
- share every illustration
- ask all the questions

An abundance of commentary is given so you can find just what you need for...
- your own style of teaching
- your own emphasis
- your own class needs

**PLEASE NOTE**: It is of utmost importance that you (and your study group) grasp the Scripture, the Study Title, and Major Points. It is this that the Holy Spirit will make alive to your heart and that you will more likely remember and use day by day.

---

<u>MAJOR POINTS</u> include:

<u>APPLICATIONS:</u>
Use these to show how the Scripture applies to everyday life.

<u>ILLUSTRATIONS:</u>
Simply a window that allows enough light in the lesson so a point can be more clearly seen. A suggestion: Do not just "read" through an illustration if the illustration is a story, but learn it and make it your own. Then give the illustration life by communicating it with *excitement & energy*.

<u>QUESTIONS:</u>
These are designed to stimulate thought and discussion.

<u>A CLOSER LOOK:</u>
In some of the studies, you will see a portion boxed in and entitled: "A Closer Look." This discussion will be a closer study on a particular point. It is generally too detailed for a Sunday School class session, but more adaptable for personal study or an indepth Bible Study class.

<u>PERSONAL JOURNAL:</u>
At the close of every lesson there is space for you to record brief thoughts regarding the impact of the lesson on your life. As you study through the Bible, you will find these comments invaluable as you look back upon them.

---

*Now, may our wonderful Lord bless you mightily as you study and teach His Holy Word. And may our Lord grant you much fruit: many who will become greater servants and witnesses for Him.*

# REMEMBER!

The Teacher's Outline & Study Bible is the only study material that actually outlines the Bible verse by verse for you right beside the Scripture. As you accumulate the various books of The Teacher's Outline & Study Bible for your study and teaching, you will have the Bible outlined book by book, passage by passage, and verse by verse.

The outlines alone makes saving every book a must! (Also encourage your students, if you are teaching, to keep their student edition. They also have the unique verse by verse outline of Scripture in their version.)

Just think for a moment. Over the course of your life, you will have your very own personalized commentary of the Bible. No other book besides the Bible will mean as much to you because it will contain your insights, your struggles, your victories, and your recorded moments with the Lord.

> **"Study to show thyself approved unto God, a workman that needeth not to be ashamed, rightly dividing the word of truth" (2 Tim.2:15).**

> **"All scripture is given by inspiration of God, and is profitable for doctrine, for reproof, for correction, for instruction in righteousness: that the man of God may be perfect, throughly furnished unto all good works" (2 Tim.3:16-17).**

*** All direct quotes are followed by a Superscript Footnote number. The credit information for each Footnote is listed at the bottom of the page.

## MISCELLANEOUS ABBREVIATIONS

| | | |
|---|---|---|
| & | = | And |
| Bckgrd. | = | Background |
| Bc. | = | Because |
| Circ. | = | Circumstance |
| Concl. | = | Conclusion |
| Cp. | = | Compare |
| Ct. | = | Contrast |
| Dif. | = | Different |
| e.g. | = | For example |
| Et. | = | Eternal |
| Govt. | = | Government |
| Id. | = | Identity or Identification |
| Illust. | = | Illustration |
| K. | = | Kingdom, K. of God, K. of Heaven, etc. |
| No. | = | Number |
| N.T. | = | New Testament |
| O.T. | = | Old Testament |
| Pt. | = | Point |
| Quest. | = | Question |
| Rel. | = | Religion |
| Resp. | = | Responsibility |
| Rev. | = | Revelation |
| Rgt. | = | Righteousness |
| Thru | = | Through |
| V. | = | Verse |
| Vs. | = | Verses |

Publisher &
Distributor

## DEDICATED:

To all the men and women of the world
who preach and teach the Gospel of our
Lord Jesus Christ
and
To the Mercy and Grace of God.

———————— & ————————

- Demonstrated to us in Christ Jesus our Lord.

  "In whom we have redemption through His
  blood, the forgiveness of sins, according to the
  riches of His grace." (Eph. 1:7)

- Out of the mercy and grace of God His Word has
  flowed. Let every person know that God will have
  mercy upon him, forgiving and using him to fulfill
  His glorious plan of salvation.

  "For God so loved the world, that he gave his only
  begotten Son, that whosoever believeth in him should
  not perish, but have everlasting life. For God sent not
  his Son into the world to condemn the world; but that
  the world through him might be saved." (Jn 3:16-17)

  "For this is good and acceptable in the sight of God
  our Saviour; who will have all men to be saved, and to
  come unto the knowledge of the truth." (I Tim. 2:3-4)

———————— & ————————

## The Teacher's Outline and Study Bible™
is written for God's people to use
in their study and teaching of God's Holy Word.

# ACKNOWLEDGMENTS

Every child of God is precious to the Lord and deeply loved. And every child as a servant of the Lord touches the lives of those who come in contact with him or his ministry. The writing ministry of the following servants have touched this work, and we are grateful that God brought their writings our way. We hereby acknowledge their ministry to us, being fully aware that there are so many others down through the years whose writings have touched our lives and who deserve mention, but the weaknesses of our minds have caused them to fade from memory. May our wonderful Lord continue to bless the ministry of these dear servants, and the ministry of us all as we diligently labor to reach the world for Christ and to meet the desperate needs of those who suffer so much.

## THE GREEK SOURCES

1    Expositor's Greek Testament, Edited by W. Robertson Nicoll. Grand Rapids, MI: Eerdmans
Publishing Co., 1970

2.   Robertson, A.T. Word Pictures in the New Testament. Nashville, TN: Broadman Press, 1930.

3.   Thayer, Joseph Henry. Greek-English Lexicon of the New Testament. New York: American Book Co.

4.   Vincent, Marvin R. Word Studies in the New Testament. Grand Rapids, MI: Eerdmans Publishing Co., 1969.

5.   Vine, W.E. Expository Dictionary of New Testament Words. Old Tappan, NJ: Fleming H. Revell Co.

6.   Wuest, Kenneth S. Word Studies in the Greek New Testament. Grand Rapids, MI: Eerdmans Publishing Co., 1953.

## THE REFERENCE WORKS

7.   Cruden's Complete Concordance of the Old & New Testament. Philadelphia, PA: The John C. Winston Co., 1930.

8.   Josephus' Complete Works. Grand Rapids, MI: Kregel Publications, 1981.

9.   Lockyer, Herbert, Series of Books, including his Books on All the Men, Women, Miracles, and Parables of the Bible. Grand Rapids, MI: Zondervan Publishing House.

10.  Nave's Topical Bible. Nashville, TN: The Southewstern Co.

11.  The Amplified New Testament. (Scripture Quotations are from the Amplified New Testament, Copyright 1954, 1958, 1987 by the Lockman Foundation. Used by permission.)

12.     The Four Translation New Testament (Including King James, New American Standard, Williams - New Testament In the Language of the People, Beck - New Testament In the Language of Today.) Minneapolis, MN: World Wide Publications.

13.     The New Compact Bible Dictionary, Edited by T. Alton Bryant. Grand Rapids, MI: Zondervan Publishing House, 1967.

14.     The New Thompson Chain Reference Bible. Indianapolis, IN: B.B. Kirkbride Bible Co., 1964,

## THE COMMENTARIES

15.     Barclay, William. Daily Study Bible Series. Philadelphia, PA: Westminster Press.

16.     Bruce, F.F. The Epistle to the Colossians. Westwood, NJ: Fleming H. Revell Co., 1968.

17.     Bruce, F.F. Epistle to the Hebrews.Grand Rapids, MI: Eerdmans Publishing Co., 1964.

18.     Bruce, F.F. The Epistles of John. Old Tappan, NJ: Fleming H. Revell Co., 1970.

19.     Criswell, W.A. Expository Sermons on Revelation. Grand Rapids, MI: Zondervan Publishing House, 1962-66.

20.     Greene, Oliver. The Epistles of John. Greenville, SC: The Gospel Hour, Inc., 1966.

21.     Greene, Oliver. The Epistles of Paul the Apostle to the Hebrews. Greenville, SC: The Gospel Hour, Inc., 1965.

22.     Greene, Oliver. The Epistles of Paul the Apostle to Timothy & Titus. Greenville, SC: The Gospel Hour, Inc., 1964.

23.     Greene, Oliver. The Revelation Verse by Verse Study. Greenville, SC: The Gospel Hour, Inc., 1963.

24.     Henry, Matthew. Commentary on the Whole Bible. Old Tappan, NJ: Fleming H. Revell Co.

25.     Hodge, Charles. Exposition on Romans & on Corinthians. Grand Rapids, MI: Eerdmans Publishing Co., 1972-1973.

26.     Ladd, George Eldon. A Commentary On the Revelation of John. Grand Rapids, MI: Eerdmans Publishing Co., 1972-1973.

27.     Leupold, H.C. Exposition of Daniel. Grand Rapids, MI: Baker Book House, 1969.

28.  Newell, William R. _Hebrews, Verse by Verse_. Chicago, IL: Moody Press.

29.  Strauss, Lehman. _Devotional Studies in Philippians_. Neptune, NJ: Loizeaux Brothers.

30.  Strauss, Lehman. Colossians _& 1 timothy_. Neptune, NJ: Loizeaux Brothers.

31.  Strauss, Lehman. _The Book of the Revelation_. Neptune, NJ: Loizeaux Brothers.

32.  _The New Testament & Wycliffe Bible Commentary_, Edited by Charles F. Pfeiffer & Everett F. Harrison. New York: The Iverson Associates, 1971. Produced for Moody Monthly. Chicago Moody Press, 1962.

33.  _The Pulpit Commentary_, Edited by H.D.M. Spence & Joseph S. Exell. Grand Rapids, MI: Eerdmans Publishing Co., 1950.

34.  Thomas, W.H. Griffith. _Hebrews, A Devotional Commentary_. Grand Rapids, MI: Eerdmans Publishing Co., 1970.

35.  Thomas, W.H. Griffith. _Studies in Colossians & Philemon_. Grand Rapids, MI: Baker Book House, 1973.

36.  _Tyndale New Testament Commentaries_. Grand Rapids, MI: Eerdmans Publishing Co., Began in 1958.

37.  Walker, Thomas. _Acts of the Apostles_. Chicago, IL: Moody Press, 1965.

38.  Walvoord, John. _The Thessalonian Epistles_. Grand Rapids, MI: Zondervan Publishing House, 1973.

## OTHER SOURCES

39.  Anderson, Leith. _A Church for the 21st Century_. Minneapolis, MN: Bethany House Publishers, 1992.

40.  Green, Michael P. _Illustrations for Biblical Preaching_. Grand Rapids, MI: Baker Books, 1996.

41.  Hybels, Bill & Wilkins, Rob. _Descending Into Greatness_. Grand Rapids, MI: Zondervan Publishing House, 1993.

42.  _INFOsearch Sermon Illustrations_. Arlington, TX: The Computer Assistant, 1-888-868-9029, 1986-1996.

43.   Knight, Walter B. <u>Knight's Master Book of 4,000 Illustrations</u>. Grand Rapids, MI: Eerdmans Publishing Company, 1994.

44.   Kyle, Ted & Todd, John. <u>A Treasury of Bible Illustrations</u>. Chattanooga, TN: AMG Publishers, 1995.

45.   Knight, Walter B. <u>Knight's Treasury of 2000 Illustrations</u>. Grand Rapids, MI: Eerdmans Publishing Company, 1963.

46.   Larson, Craig B., Editor. <u>Illustrations for Preaching and Teaching</u>. Grand Rapids, MI: Baker Books, 1993

47.   Rowell, Edward K., Editor. <u>Quotes & Idea Starters for Preaching & Teaching</u>. Grand Rapids, MI: Baker Books, 1996.

48.   Thomas, Cal. <u>The Things That Matter Most</u>. New York, NY: Harper Collins Publishers, 1994.

49.   Zodhiates, Spiros, Th.D. <u>Illustrations of Bible Truths</u>. Chattanooga, TN: AMG Publishers, 1995.

PUBLISHER & DISTRIBUTOR

Materials Published & Distributed by **LEADERSHIP MINISTRIES WORLDWIDE:**

- *THE PREACHER'S OUTLINE & SERMON BIBLE®* — DELUXE EDITION
  - Volume 1 . . . . . . . . . . . . St. Matthew I (chapters 1-15)     3-Ring, looseleaf binder
  - Volume 2 . . . . . . . . . . . . St. Matthew II (chapters 16-28)
  - Volume 3 . . . . . . . . . . . . St. Mark
  - Volume 4 . . . . . . . . . . . . St. Luke
  - Volume 5 . . . . . . . . . . . . St. John
  - Volume 6 . . . . . . . . . . . . Acts
  - Volume 7 . . . . . . . . . . . . Romans
  - Volume 8 . . . . . . . . . . . . 1, 2 Corinthians (1 volume)
  - Volume 9 . . . . . . . . . . . . Galatians, Ephesians, Philippians, Colossians (1 volume)
  - Volume 10 . . . . . . . . . . . 1,2 Thessalonians, 1,2 Timothy, Titus, Philemon (1 volume)
  - Volume 11 . . . . . . . . . . . Hebrews -James (1 volume)
  - Volume 12 . . . . . . . . . . . 1,2 Peter, 1,2,3 John, Jude (1 volume)
  - Volume 13 . . . . . . . . . . . Revelation
  - Volume 14 . . . . . . . . . . . Master Outline & Subject Index
  - FULL SET — 14 Volumes

- *THE PREACHER'S OUTLINE & SERMON BIBLE®* — OLD TESTAMENT
  - Volume 1 . . . . . . . . . . . Genesis I (chapters 1-11)
  - Volume 2 . . . . . . . . . . . Genesis II (chapters 12-50)
  - Volume 3 . . . . . . . . . . . Exodus I (chapters 1-18)
  - Volume 4 . . . . . . . . . . . Exodus II (chapters 19-40)    New volumes release periodically

- *THE PREACHER'S OUTLINE & SERMON BIBLE®* — SOFTBOUND EDITION
  Identical content as Deluxe above. Lightweight, compact, and affordable for overseas & traveling.

- The Minister's Personal Handbook - What the Bible Says...to the Minister
  12 Chapters — 127 Subjects — 400 Verses *OUTLINED* — Standard, Deluxe, 3-ring
  * More than 400 verses from OT and NT dealing with God's minister and servant; all assembled in
  the unique *Outline* style. Features God's Word for His chosen and called servants who minister the Word.

- Translations of N.T. Volumes and Minister's Handbook: <u>Limited Quantities</u>
  Russian — Spanish — Korean • *Future: Portuguese, Hindi, Chinese + others*
  — *Contact us for Specific Language and Prices* —

- *THE TEACHER'S OUTLINE & STUDY BIBLE*™ • New Testament Books •
  Average 17 lessons/book & 205 pages • Verse-by-Verse Study •• Also: Student Journal Guides

- CD-ROM New Testament - (Windows/STEP) - WORD*Search* 4™

**All these great Volumes & Materials are also available at affordable prices in quantity orders, particularly for overseas ministry, by contacting:**

LEADERSHIP MINISTRIES WORLDWIDE      *Your OUTLINE Bookseller*
PO Box 21310
Chattanooga, TN 37424-0310
**(423) 855-2181 (8:30 - 5:00 ET) • FAX (423) 855-8616 (24 hrs)**
**E•Mail - outlinebible@compuserve.com.**
    ↦ **FREE Download Sample Pages — www.outlinebible.org**

• *Equipping God's Servants Worldwide with OUTLINE Bible Materials* •
— LMW is a 501(c)3 nonprofit, international nondenominational mission agency — 8/97

# LEADERSHIP MINISTRIES WORLDWIDE

## OUR FIVEFOLD MISSION & PURPOSE:

- To share the Word of God with the world.
- To help the believer, both minister and layman alike, in his understanding, preaching, and teaching of God's Word.
- To do everything we possibly can to lead men, women, boys, and girls to give their hearts and lives to Jesus Christ and to secure the eternal life which He offers.
- To do all we can to minister to the needy of the world.
- To give Jesus Christ His proper place, the place which the Word gives Him. Therefore — No work of Leadership Ministries Worldwide will ever be personalized.

This material, like similar works, has come from imperfect man and is thus susceptible to human error. We are nevertheless grateful to God for both calling us and empowering us through His Holy Spirit to undertake this task. Because of His goodness and grace, *The Preacher's Outline & Sermon Bible®* - New Testament is complete in 14 volumes as well as the single volume of **The Minister's Handbook**.

God has given the strength and stamina to bring us this far. Our confidence is that, as we keep our eyes on Him and grounded in the undeniable truths of the Word, we will continue working through the Old Testament Volumes and introduce a new series known as *The Teacher's Outline & Study Bible.* Future materials will include CD-ROM, The Believer's *Outline* Bible, and similar *Outline* and **Handbook** materials.

To everyone, everywhere who preaches and teaches the Word, we offer this material firstly to Him in whose name we labor and serve, and for whose glory it has been produced.

Our daily prayer is that each volume will lead thousands, millions, yes even billions, into a better understanding of the Holy Scriptures and a fuller knowledge of Jesus Christ the incarnate Word, of whom the Scriptures so faithfully testify.

As you have purchased this volume, you will be pleased to know that a portion of the price you paid goes to underwrite providing similar volumes at affordable prices in other languages (Russian, Korean, Spanish and others yet to come) to a preacher, pastor, church leader, or Bible student somewhere around the world, who will present God's message with clarity, authority, and understanding beyond their own.
*Amen.*

• *Equipping God's Servants Worldwide with OUTLINE Bible Materials* •
— LMW is a 501(c)3 nonprofit, international nondenominational mission agency —    8/97

LEADERSHIP
MINISTRIES
WORLDWIDE

P.O. Box 21310, 515 Airport Road, Suite 107
Chattanooga, TN 37424-0310
(423) 855-2181  FAX (423) 855-87616
E-Mail - outlinebible@compuserve.com
www.outlinebible.org [Free download samples]

*Go ye therefore, and teach all nations*

" (Mt. 28:19)

## A SPECIAL NOTE FOR THE BIBLE STUDY LEADER, PASTOR OR MINISTER OF EDUCATION

The teaching material you have before you gives your church the *maximum flexibility* in scheduling for the church year or for any Bible study program. If you prefer not to follow a self-paced schedule, please note:

# To Begin Your Exciting Study, Follow These Simple
# LESSON PLANS FOR ROMANS,
## VOLUME 1, CHAPTERS 1 - 5
# QUARTER #1

I.  **GREETING AND THEME: THE GOSPEL AND GOD'S RIGHTEOUSNESS, 1:1-17**

| WEEK # | LESSON TITLE | SCRIPTURE TEXT | PAGE NUMBER |
|--------|--------------|----------------|-------------|
| 1 | *"Paul's Credentials: Enslavement to Christ"* | 1:1-7 | 15 |
| 2 | *"Paul's Interest & Boldness: A Man Who Was Enslaved & Unashamed of the Gospel"* | 1:8-15 1:16-17 | 29 39 |

II.  **SIN AND CONDEMNATION: THE WORLD'S NEED TO GET RIGHT WITH GOD, 1:18-3:20**

| WEEK # | LESSON TITLE | SCRIPTURE TEXT | PAGE NUMBER |
|--------|--------------|----------------|-------------|
| 3 | *"God's Case Against All Ungodliness & Unrighteousness of Men: Why & How God Shows Wrath"* | 1:18-23 1:24-32 | 49 59 |
| 4 | *"God's Case Against the Moralist: Judgment"* | 2:1-16 | 73 |
| 5 | *"God's Case Against the Religionist"* | 2:17-29 3:1-8 | 88 99 |
| 6 | *"God's Case Against All Men"* | 3:9-20 | 107 |

## III. FAITH AND JUSTIFICATION: THE WAY FOR THE WORLD TO BE RIGHT WITH GOD, 3:21-5:21

# OUTLINE OF ROMANS

## Volume 1, Chapters 1 - 5

**THE TEACHER'S OUTLINE & SERMON BIBLE** is *unique*. It differs from all other Study Bibles and Lesson Resource Materials in that every Passage and Subject is outlined right beside the Scripture. When you choose any *Subject* below and turn to the reference, you have not only the Scripture, but you discover the Scripture and Subject *already outlined for you--verse by verse*.

*For a quick example*, choose one of the subjects below and turn over to the Scripture, and you will find this marvelous help for faster, easier, and more accurate use.

*A suggestion*: For the quickest overview of Romans, Volume 1, first read *all the major titles* (I, II, III, etc.), then come back and read the sub-titles.

# OUTLINE OF ROMANS

## Volume 1, Chapters 1 - 5

# THE EPISTLE OF PAUL THE APOSTLE TO THE
# ROMANS

## INTRODUCTION

**AUTHOR**: Paul, the Apostle. Paul clearly states that he is the author (Ro.1:1), and the personal references and facts given in Chapter 15 tell us beyond any doubt that Paul is the author.

**DATE**: A.D. 55-58.
Paul says, "Now I go unto Jerusalem to minister unto the saints" (Ro.15:25). This journey to Jerusalem was the trip made necessary by the extreme poverty of the believers in the Jerusalem church. Paul had taken a collection from the Gentile churches and felt compelled to deliver the offering himself. This occurred on his third missionary journey.

**TO WHOM WRITTEN**: "To all that be in Rome, beloved of God, called to be saints."
Several manuscripts have been found with the personal and local touches of chapters 15-16 omitted and the doxology included. This would definitely point to there being several churches. The place of writing seems to be Corinth, for Paul recommended Phoebe to the Romans. Phoebe was a deaconess from Cenchrea, the eastern seaport of Corinth.

**PURPOSE**: Paul had several reasons for writing.
1.    Paul wished to evangelize Spain (Ro.15:25). To do so he needed a local church from which to launch his ministry--a church that would be much closer to Spain than Antioch. Antioch had been his home base up until now. By writing Romans, he was preparing the Roman church for the day when he would reveal his vision to them. He was making them familiar with his name, his mission, and his love.
2.    Paul had a personal compulsion to visit and witness in Rome itself. His life-long strategy had been to evangelize the great metropolitan cities along the route that stretched from Jerusalem to Rome. He knew that a route so greatly traveled and cities so actively engaged in commerce would assure the spread of the Gospel. Rome was the capital, the center of the world; it provided the greatest strategic opportunity for world evangelism. A Rome conquered for Christ could mean a world conquered for Christ.
3.    Paul was not sure he would ever reach Rome personally. He was going to Jerusalem and knew the danger. There was a chance he might be killed in Jerusalem. He requested the Roman church to pray for him: "I beseech you, brethren...strive together with me in your prayers to God for me, that I may be delivered from them that do not believe in Judea" (15:30-31). Yet despite the danger, Paul was a master strategist: he knew the strategic importance of Rome for the spread of the Gospel worldwide. The church had to be rooted and grounded in the faith; therefore he sat down and wrote this great letter. The message of the letter is what Paul would hammer into the believers' hearts if he ever did get to stand before them.

**SPECIAL FEATURES**:
1.    The church at Rome. The church was strong. Five factors show its strength.

First, Rome was a *lay church*. A writer of the fourth century said that some Roman citizens "had embraced the faith of Christ...without any sign of mighty works or any of the apostles" (Ambrosiaster, a Latin Father, in his <u>Epistle to the Romans</u>. Quoted by F.F. Bruce. *The Epistle of Paul to the Romans*. "The Tyndale New Testament Commentaries," ed. by RVG Tasker. Grand Rapids, MI: Eerdmans, 1963, p.13). The content of the epistle shows a people of great spiritual depth and maturity. But how did the gospel reach Rome? Who founded the church? The only thing known for sure is that there was a great and flourishing church in the capital. But just when the church was founded is unknown. There are several possibilities.

    a. At Pentecost there were "strangers from Rome, both Jews and proselytes" (Acts 2:10). Were any converted during Pentecost? There is no specific mention of converts among the Romans, but Romans are the only group identified among the European pilgrims.

    b. Many of the members of the Roman church were known by Paul personally. He had met them elsewhere, sometime long ago. The church could have been founded by these. He greets Aquila and Priscilla (16:3; cp. Acts 18:2-3). He also greets some well-known believers whom he says were "in Christ" even before himself: Andronicus and Junia (16:7). Rufus, perhaps the son of Simon of Cyrene who carried the cross of Christ, is also greeted (see note--16:13; cp. Mk.15:21). Paul may have known Rufus and his mother in Antioch.

    c. The lay followers of Christ were probably among the first to carry the gospel to Rome. This was Paul's great strategy as God's chief commander for world evangelization. Paul had penetrated the great cities of the world with the glorious gospel, and he did all he could to establish a strong church in each of the major cities. Each of these cities lay along the world's great roads that led right into the heart of the world's capital, Rome itself. In all the hustle and bustle of business and traveling to and fro, some men, racing throughout the world and carrying on their affairs, were bound to be reached for Christ and to become lay missionaries themselves. It was only inevitable that Rome be penetrated. A church was bound to be founded right in the heart of Rome.

Second, Rome had a *worldwide reputation*. Its faith was strong (1:8). It was spiritually mature, able to digest the *meat* of the Word. Practically every page covers a major doctrine or theological discussion.

Third, Rome was a *Gentile church*. The Gentiles, who comprised a vast majority of the membership, were reminded of the fact that Christianity had come from Jewish roots. Therefore, the Jews were to be deeply respected--even if they were outnumbered (11:18).

Fourth, Rome was a *persecuted church*. The church was severely persecuted seven years after Paul wrote this great letter to the believers. Nero had burned the older section of the great city in a fit of madness, and he blamed the burning of Rome upon the Christians. Believers were also charged with such crimes as cannibalism, immoral practices, and with being enemies of the state. They were actually charged with any other crime that could be connived. However, the blood of the church proved to be its seed (Tertullian, Apology 50. Quoted by F.F. Bruce. *The Epistle of Paul to the Romans*. "The Tyndale New Testament Commentaries," p.17). Believers, fleeing the persecution, spread all over the world; and wherever they went they shared the glorious news of eternal life in Christ Jesus. In addition, the citizens of Rome grew tired of so much savagery and eventually demanded that the savagery against the Christians stop. The church was left alone and the glorious news of salvation was allowed to be freely proclaimed.

Fifth, Rome was a *triumphant church*. The church was unashamed of its life and witness. It was willing to stand up and be counted by the side of those who suffered. When Paul was being escorted into the city as a Roman prisoner, while still some thirty to forty miles away, the Christian church marched forward to meet and give him a triumphant processional over those thirty to forty miles. The sight of these dear believers filled Paul with a sense of glory seldom experienced by men. (See note--Acts 28:13-15.)

    2.    Romans is *The Great Epistle of Theology*. It is a statement of what Paul believed, a statement of his theology. Paul was not writing to meet a special problem or danger or error. He was writing primarily to root and ground the Roman believers in the faith as deeply as he could, for they lived in the great strategic center with explosive potential for

world evangelization. He was completely free to set forth what he saw to be the essential theology for a living faith.

3. Romans is *The Epistle Written for Every Man*. It is the Gospel of God (1:1). It is a book for the world (1:4-2:16; etc.); a book for the church (see 1:1-7; etc.); a book for theologians (see 3:1-5:21; etc.); a book for philosophers (see 1:1-2:16; etc.); a book for legalists (see 7:1f; etc.); a book for immature believers (see 6:1-8:30); a book for mature believers (see 8:12-14; etc.); a book for sufferers (see 7:1-8:39; etc.); a book for unbelievers (see 1:1-2:16; etc.); a book for religionists (see 2:17-5:21; etc.). Romans is the truth desperately needed by every man, whoever or wherever he may be.

4. Romans is *The Church's Last Testament*. Although one of the driving forces of Paul's heart was to visit the Roman church, he was not sure he would ever get to see them face to face (See Purpose, point 3). Yet, the church's strategic importance necessitated that he do what he could to assure that they use their explosive potential for Christ. Thus, he was forced to write--just in case. And write he did. In the Book of Romans the church has what Paul wished to say to the church--just in case he never got there. In a sense it is *The Church's Last Testament*--just what the church needs to hear. Romans comes closest to being the one written possession a church needs, the most comprehensive statement of Christian truth.

5. Romans is *The Gospel's Main Truth*. This is evident from Special Features, points 1 and 2.

6. Romans is *God's WorldWide Plan for Israel and the Gentiles*. More clearly than any other book, Romans shows God's glorious plan for the ages in Israel and the Gentile nations. A panoramic view of history is given from a Christian perspective. This is quickly grasped by a study of the Outline, chapters 9-11.

# THE EPISTLE OF PAUL THE APOSTLE TO THE

# ROMANS

**CHAPTER 1**

**I. GREETING AND THEME: THE GOSPEL AND GOD'S RIGHTEOUSNESS, 1:1-17**

**A. Paul's Credentials: Enslavement to Christ, 1:1-7**

**1. He was a slave of Christ**

**2. He was an apostle of God**

**3. He was set apart to the gospel of God**
   a. The gospel promised long ago
   b. The gospel that concerns God's Son, Jesus Christ,

**P**aul, a servant of Jesus Christ, called to be an apostle, separated unto the gospel of God,

2 (Which he had promised afore by his prophets in the holy scriptures,)

3 Concerning his Son Jesus Christ our Lord, which was made of the seed of David according to the flesh;

4 And declared to be the Son of God with power, according to the spirit of holiness, by the resurrection from the dead:

5 By whom we have received grace and apostleship, for obedience to the faith among all nations, for his name:

6 Among whom are ye also the called of Jesus Christ:

7 To all that be in Rome, beloved of God, called to be saints: Grace to you and peace from God our Father, and the Lord Jesus Christ.

becoming a Man

   c. The gospel that declares Jesus Christ to be the Son of God
      1) By the Spirit of holiness
      2) By the resurrection

**4. He had received God's grace & God's mission**

**5. He acknowledged the enslavement of others**
   a. They too were called
   b. They too were beloved
   c. They too were saints
   d. They too were recipients of grace & peace

---

**Section I**

## GREETING AND THEME: THE GOSPEL AND GOD'S RIGHTEOUSNESS
### Romans 1:1-17

**Study 1: Paul's Credentials: Enslavement to Christ**

**Text:** Romans 1:1-7

**Aim:** To willingly become a slave to Christ; to serve Christ with no reservation.

**Memory Verse:**
> "If any man serve me, let him follow me; and where I am, there shall also my servant be: if any man serve me, him will [my] Father honour" (John 12:26).

**INTRODUCTION:**
People today are enslaved to many different things, things like...
- money
- power
- food
- fame
- sex
- alcohol
- drugs
- pornography
- work

With a little bit of imagination, you could probably add many more items to this list. As you may have experienced, when you become enslaved to one thing, you give up rights in other areas. For instance, if you are enslaved to food, you sacrifice health and weight. If you are enslaved to drugs, you give up control of your mind and body. If you are enslaved to fame, you lose your privacy and humility. And on and on. You become bound to that which controls you. When you give in and give up to evil masters, you are doomed to a life of bitter slavery.

But it does not have to be that way. You can be enslaved to a good master,

⇒ to someone who will save you, save you from all the bondages and enslavements of life

⇒ to someone who will give you life, a life that overflows with abundance, with all the good things of life

⇒ to someone who will meet your every need

⇒ to someone who will guide you and teach you how to conquer and live victoriously over all the trials and problems of life

Is it possible to be a slave to both good and evil? No! You cannot have it both ways. You cannot be a slave to the things of the world and a slave of Christ. You cannot enjoy an intimate relationship with the world and still love Christ. No person is a true follower of Jesus Christ unless he is *enslaved by Christ*. In fact, it is *impossible* for a person to *belong* to Christ unless he is *enslaved by Christ*. This is the shocking message Paul wants to get across to the believers at Rome.

**OUTLINE:**
1. He was a slave of Christ (v.1).
2. He was an apostle of God (v.1).
3. He was set apart to the gospel of God (v.1-4).
4. He had received God's grace and God's mission (v.5).
5. He acknowledged the enslavement of others (v.6-7).

---

**A CLOSER LOOK:**

(1:1-7) **Gospel--Christianity**: in these verses Paul gives the raw outline of the gospel he preached (v.1-4). It is a penetrating look at primitive Christianity. Note the gospel's close agreement with the Apostle's Creed.

### The Apostle's Creed

*I believe in God the Father Almighty, Maker of Heaven and Earth,*
*And in Jesus Christ, His only Son, our Lord, Who was conceived by the Holy Ghost,*
*Born of the Virgin Mary, Suffered under Pontius Pilate,*
*Was crucified, dead, and buried; He descended into Hell.*
*The third day he rose again from the dead,*
*He ascended into Heaven, and sitteth on the right hand of God the Father Almighty;*
*from hence He shall come to judge the quick and the dead.*
*I believe in the Holy Ghost, the holy Catholic [or universal] Church; the communion of the saints; the forgiveness of sins; the resurrection of the body; and the life everlasting. Amen*

### The Apostle Paul
1. Paul's view of the Old Testament.
   a. It comes from God.
   b. It is given "through His prophets."
   c. It is "holy" Scripture.

> 2. Paul's view of the Lord Jesus Christ.
>    a. He is God's Son: "concerning His Son."
>    b. He is the promised Savior: "Christ," the Messiah.
>    c. He is Lord: "our Lord."
>    d. He is man: "born of the seed of David according to the flesh."
>    e. He is declared to be the very Son of God: "declared to be the Son of God with power."
>    f. He is divine or holy: "according to the Spirit of holiness."
>    g. He is risen from the dead: "by the resurrection from the dead."
> 3. Paul's view of the gospel.
>    a. It is of God: "the Gospel of God" (cp. Ro.1:1, 17; 3:21).
>    b. It was prophesied: "he had promised...."
>    c. It agrees with the Old Testament: "promised afore...in the holy scriptures."
>    d. It concerns God's very own Son: "concerning His Son."
>    e. It concerns the divine Savior: "Jesus Christ, our Lord...declared to be the Son of God with power, according to the spirit of holiness [sinlessness]."
>    f. It concerns the human Savior: "made of the seed of David...."
>    g. It concerns the risen Savior: "the resurrection from the dead."

**QUESTIONS:**
1. How important is it to study the Scriptures on a regular basis?
2. Do you know what you believe as solidly as Paul did? Do you know the simple facts of the gospel? Would it be useful for you to memorize the Apostle's Creed? Why or why not?


## 1. HE WAS A SLAVE OF CHRIST (v.1).

The word *slave* means far more than just a servant. It means a slave totally possessed by the master. It is a *bond-servant* bound by law to a master.

A look at the slave market of Paul's day shows more clearly what Paul meant when he said he was a "slave of Jesus Christ."

1. The slave was owned by his master; he was totally possessed by his master. This is what Paul meant. Paul was purchased and possessed by Christ. Christ had looked upon him and had seen his degraded and needful condition. And when Christ looked, the most wonderful thing happened: Christ loved him and bought him; therefore, he was now the possession of Christ.

2. The slave existed for his master and he had no other reason for existence. He had no personal rights whatsoever. The same was true with Paul: he existed only for Christ. His rights were the rights of Christ only.

3. The slave served his master and he existed only for the purpose of service. He was at the master's disposal any hour of the day or night. So it was with Paul: he lived only to serve Christ--hour by hour, day by day, and night by night.

4. The slave's will belonged to his master. He was allowed no will and no ambition other than the will and ambition of the master. He was completely subservient to the master and owed total obedience to the will of the master. Paul belonged to Christ. In fact, he said that he fought and struggled to bring every thought into captivity to the obedience of Christ (2 Cor.10:5).

5. There is a fifth and most precious thing that Paul meant by "a slave of Jesus Christ." He meant that he had the highest, most honored and kingly profession in all the world. Men of God, the greatest men of history, have always been called "the servants of God." It was the highest title of honor. The believer's slavery to Jesus Christ is no cringing, cowardly, or shameful subjection. It is the position of honor--the honor that bestows

upon a man the privileges and responsibilities of serving the King of kings and Lord of lords.

⇒ Moses was the slave of God (Dt.34:5; Ps.105:26; Mal.4:4).
⇒ Joshua was the slave of God (Josh.24:29).
⇒ David was the slave of God (2 Sam.3:18; Ps.78:70).
⇒ Paul was the slave of Jesus Christ (Ro.1:1; Ph.1:1; Tit.1:1).
⇒ James was the slave of God (Jas.1:1).
⇒ Peter was the slave of Jesus Christ (2 Pt.1:1).
⇒ Jude was the slave of God (Jude 1).
⇒ The prophets were the slaves of God (Amos 3:7; Jer.7:25).
⇒ Christian believers are said to be the slaves of Jesus Christ (Acts 2:18; 1 Cor.7:22; Eph.6:6; Col.4:12; 2 Tim.2:24).[1]

**"If any man serve me, let him follow me; and where I am, there shall also my servant be: if any man serve me, him will my Father honour" (Jn.12:26; cp. Ro.12:1; 1 Cor.15:58).**

**ILLUSTRATION:**
Have you ever thought what it would be like to be a slave? If you were to retrace your family tree, there is a very good chance that one of your ancestors was a slave to someone.

*"Many years ago a well-to-do Christian paid a very high price for a particular slave. Actually, the man abhorred the practice of slavery, and his sole purpose was to set at liberty the one he had purchased. When the two met for the first time, the wealthy man said, 'It is true, I bought you, but I did it only to free you from the terrible bondage you have known.' Then he handed the other man some papers that guaranteed freedom.*
*"The slave looked at him in sheer amazement. 'Am I truly free? Am I my own? May I go where I wish?' 'Yes,' said the Christian, 'that's why I bought you, so you could be loosed from those chains forever.' Overwhelmed by these words, the slave fell at his feet and said with heartfelt devotion, 'Then my greatest joy and freedom will be to stay with you and serve you gladly for the rest of my life.'"[2]*

We are all slaves to someone or something. Who is your master? What kind of master do you serve? Remember: the believer's slavery to Jesus Christ is no cringing, cowardly, or shameful subjection. It is a position of honor--the honor that bestows upon a man the privileges and responsibilities of serving the King of kings and Lord of lords.

**QUESTIONS:**
1. To what degree do you consider yourself to be a bond-servant to Christ?
   ⇒ I am totally committed.
   ⇒ I tend to flee when things get tough.
   ⇒ I often find myself struggling between two masters.
2. Describe in your own words what it means to be a slave to Christ.
3. What hinders men from wanting to be slaves to Christ? How can these factors be overcome?

---

[1] This point is built upon what William Barclay says. *The Letter to the Romans*. "The Daily Study Bible." (Philadelphia, PA: The Westminster Press, 1955), p.2.
[2] *INFOsearch Sermon Illustrations* (Arlington, TX: The Computer Assistant, 1-888-868-9029, 1986-1996).

## 2. HE WAS AN APOSTLE OF GOD (v.1).

The word *apostle* means either a person who is sent out or a person who is sent forth. An apostle is a representative, an ambassador, a person who is sent out into one country to represent another country. Three things are true of the apostle: (1) he belongs to the One who has sent him out; (2) he is commissioned to be sent out; and (3) he possesses all the authority and power of the One who sends him out.

Note three forceful lessons.

1. Paul said he was "called" to be an apostle. He was not in the ministry because he...
- chose to be
- had the ability
- had been encouraged by others to choose the *ministerial profession*
- enjoyed working with people

He was an apostle, a minister of the gospel, for one reason only: God had called him.

> "And I thank Christ Jesus our Lord, who hath enabled me, for that he counted me faithful, putting me into the ministry" (1 Tim. 1:12).

2. Paul had heard and answered God's call. God did not override Paul's will--He wanted Paul in the ministry, so He called Paul. But note: it was up to Paul to hear and respond.

3. Paul was called to be an apostle, that is, to be a minister. He was not called to occupy a position of authority or to be honored by men.

### APPLICATION:
Every servant of God is called for two primary purposes:

1) To serve and minister.

> "And whosoever will be chief among you, let him be your servant: Even as the Son of man came not to be ministered unto, but to minister, and to give his life a ransom for many" (Mt.20:27-28).
> "As we have therefore opportunity, let us do good unto all men, especially unto them who are of the household of faith" (Gal.6:10).

2) To go forth and bear fruit.

> "Bring forth therefore fruits meet for repentance" (Mt.3:8).
> "Ye have not chosen me, but I have chosen you, and ordained you, that ye should go and bring forth fruit, and that your fruit should remain" (Jn.15:16).
> "And he shall be like a tree planted by the rivers of water, that bringeth forth his fruit in his season; his leaf also shall not wither; and whatsoever he doeth shall prosper" (Ps.1:3).

### QUESTIONS:
1. Men serve God for a lot of reasons. What *should* motivate men to serve God?
2. What role does the believer play in the call of God?
3. Why did God call you to serve Him? How faithful have you been to that call today? This week? This year?

## 3. HE WAS SET APART TO THE GOSPEL OF GOD (v.1-4).

This is the reason God called Paul: that Paul might be separated or marked and set apart to the gospel of God. The word *gospel* simply means the *good news of God*.

⇒ Paul did not say he was called and set apart to a man-made religion, denomination, or sect; nor was he called primarily to a gospel of social justice and welfare, as important as these calls are.

⇒ Paul said he was set apart to the gospel, the good news of God (cp. 1 Th.2:2-13).

Note what the gospel is.

1. The gospel of the New Testament is the *same good news* of God which was promised in the Old Testament Scriptures. Jesus Christ is the Subject and the Author of the gospel, but the gospel *began long before* the birth of Jesus. The gospel began long, long ago in the *mind and plan* of God, and God foretold the coming of the gospel (His Son) through the prophets of old. Mark says what Paul was later to say:

> "The beginning of the gospel of Jesus Christ, the Son of God; as it is written in the prophets, behold, I send my messenger before thy face, which shall prepare thy way before thee. The voice of one crying in the wilderness, Prepare ye the way of the Lord, make his paths straight" (Mk.1:1-3).
> "Search the scriptures; for in them ye think ye have eternal life: and they are they which testify of me" (Jn.5:39).

2. The gospel is the incarnation of "God's Son, Jesus Christ our Lord" (see **A CLOSER LOOK**, Gospel--Ro.1:1-7). Note how Paul takes the names and titles of Jesus Christ and stacks them one upon another, and note the verses that clearly support Paul's declaration.

⇒ God's Son

> "And I saw, and bare record that this is the Son of God" (Jn.1:34).

⇒ Jesus

> "And she shall bring forth a son, and thou shalt call his name JESUS: for he shall save his people from their sins" (Mt. 1:21).

⇒ Christ

> "Now the birth of Jesus Christ was on this wise: When as his mother Mary was espoused to Joseph, before they came together, she was found with child of the Holy Ghost" (Mt. 1:18).

⇒ Our Lord

> "Therefore let all the house of Israel know assuredly, that God hath made that same Jesus, whom ye have crucified, both Lord and Christ" (Acts 2:36).

The gospel concerns "God's Son, Jesus Christ our Lord." He is both the *Subject* and the *Author* of the gospel. By Him and through Him the gospel is created and proclaimed.

He brings the *good news* of God to man. He is the very embodiment of the good news of God Himself.

The gospel concerns two glorious truths.

    a. The first glorious truth is that God's Son became a man. He was made of the seed of David; that is, he was born as a man, as a descendant of David. David was the greatest ruler of Israel; he was one of the greatest ancestors of Jesus. (See Lk.3:24-31.)

        The point is this: God sent His Son into the world in human flesh. The words *was made* mean to become. God's Son *became* a man--flesh and blood-- just like all other men. He had a human nature, and because He had a human nature...

- He suffered all the *trials of life* which we suffer.
- He is *able to succor* us through all the trials of life.

      **"The Word [God's Son] was made flesh, and dwelt among us, (and we beheld his glory, the glory as of the only begotten of the Father,) full of grace and truth" (Jn.1:14).**

    b. The second glorious truth is both profound and critical, for it proclaims the divine nature of Jesus Christ. Jesus Christ was the Son of God *before He came into the world*. (See Jn.1:1-2; 1:3; Ph.2:6; 2:7.) However, since coming, He is declared to be the Son of God by two things.

      ⇒ The Spirit of holiness that dwelt in Him declares Jesus to be the Son of God. He was the very embodiment of holiness, of purity and morality and justice. His life upon earth proves the fact. He lived as a man for thirty some years and *never sinned*.

      **"For he hath made him to be sin for us, who <u>knew no sin</u>; that we might be made the righteousness of God in him" (2 Cor.5:21).**

      ⇒ The resurrection from the dead declares that Jesus is the Son of God.

      ⇒ All other men are dead and gone. The proof is demonstrated by one simple question: "Where are they? Where are our mothers, our fathers, our sisters, our ancestors?" Once they have left this world, they are gone and the earth never sees them again. But not Christ. He died, but He arose and walked upon the earth again. And today Jesus Christ lives forever in the presence of God. Death could not hold Him because He was the Son of God and possessed the perfect spirit of holiness.

      **"Whom God hath raised up, having loosed the pains of death: because it was not possible that he should be holden of it" (Acts 2:24).**

<u>**QUESTIONS:**</u>
1. How would your life change if you were more set apart to the gospel of our Lord Jesus Christ, that is, if you committed yourself more and more to share the good news of Jesus Christ? What kinds of things would you need to change?
2. Using the simplest terms, define the gospel.
3. God's Son came to earth as a man. Why is this an important part of the gospel? How does this fact help you when you are going through trials?
4. Jesus Christ was the Son of God before He came to earth. What difference does it make to the gospel that Christ is God?

## 4. HE HAD RECEIVED GOD'S GRACE AND GOD'S MISSION (v.5).

Note the word *we*. Paul now speaks of all believers, not only of himself.

1.    We have received God's glorious grace: His favor, His mercy, His love, His salvation. (See Tit.2:11-15.) Grace includes all that God has done for us and all the wonderful blessings He showers upon us. Very simply, God's grace includes...

    a. His love for us from all eternity past.

> **"Blessed be the God and Father of our Lord Jesus Christ, who hath blessed us with all spiritual blessings in heavenly places in Christ: according as he hath chosen us in him before the foundation of the world, that we should be holy and without blame before him in love" (Eph.1:3-4).**

    b. His saving us freely, without any cost to us whatsoever.

> **"Being justified freely by his grace through the redemption that is in Christ Jesus" (Ro.3:24).**

    c. His care and looking after us day by day.

> **"But my God shall supply all your need according to his riches in glory by Christ Jesus" (Ph.4:19).**

    d. His glorious promise of eternal redemption: of our being transformed and being made perfect, and being given the glorious privilege of living with Him forever in worship and service.

> **"In whom we have redemption through his blood, the forgiveness of sins, according to the riches of his grace" (Eph.1:7).**

2.    We have received apostleship, that is, God's mission. The idea is that we have received a special mission, God's very own special task in the world. What is that mission? Paul said it is *"obedience to the faith"* (see **A CLOSER LOOK**, Obedience--Ro.1:5 for discussion).

### ILLUSTRATION:
God has given each believer a special mission to accomplish in his lifetime. Can you imagine how displeasing and harmful it would be if you decided to pursue *your own mission* instead of God's?

> *Throughout his adult life, Don had focused on one mission. It was a mission to destroy anything or anyone who got in his way. A businessman with a knack for making a profit, Don found himself living a life that was the envy of many. Life had been good and the prospects for the future looked even better.*
> *But lately, the more money Don made, the more empty he felt inside. It did not make any sense. Everything he could ever want was his, but he could not escape the haunting voice that echoed in his mind: "Lay it all down and follow Me." Don knew that God was speaking to his heart. He had made a profession of faith when he was a young boy, but that seemed like such a long time ago. He had forgotten a lot of what he had learned in church about God. But one thing*

*he did not forget was that God was able to speak to His children. And God was speaking to him now.*

*"God, what do you want me to do? Sell all I have and become a missionary to Africa?" The very thought sent cold chills down Don's back. "God, anything but that!" Desperate for relief, Don began to read his Bible again. He started to go back to church when he was in town. One day at church he asked one of the older men for some advice. "Mr. Billy, what kind of advice would you give a fellow like me who wants to do what's best for himself?" Mr. Billy was a treasure in the community, a godly man respected by all. The old gentleman looked Don right in the eye and said, "Don, God has blessed you with the gift of being able to make a lot of money. The best thing you could do for yourself is to invest it in God's work. Why don't you pray about sponsoring some folks who are going to become missionaries to Africa?"*

*That was good enough for Don. After holding back from doing God's will for so long, Don finally gave in and allowed God to have His way. It was not much longer before Don was sponsoring short-term mission trips into the heart of Africa--and he was leading the way!*

It is so important for the believer to be consumed by God's mission, to be obedient to the faith. Any other mission will become a lost cause. Are you willing to do God's will no matter what it is?

**QUESTIONS:**
1. What practical benefits does God's grace provide for you? What is life like when these benefits of grace are not used?
2. What can any man do to earn more grace?
3. God has given you a mission. Do you know what it is? Are you consciously seeking to be obedient to your mission?

---

**A CLOSER LOOK:**

(1:5) **Obedience**: the Scripture clearly says that God saves us for two specific purposes...
- to obey Him
- to lead other persons to obey Him--persons from all nations

What God is after is for mankind to become His family: for men to freely choose to live together with Him and with all other believers in a perfect world. God wants mankind living together in perfect love, joy, peace, worship, praise, and service as the family of God. He wants men living soberly, righteously, and godly before Him. He wants men obeying Him as His dear children.

Therefore, when God saves us, He saves us primarily to obey Him and to carry the glorious message of obedience to a rebellious and corrupt world. God calls us to obey the faith and to proclaim obedience to all the nations.

Note several facts about obedience.
1. There is a massive difference between *forced obedience* and *free obedience*.
    a. Forced obedience has no choice and reveals...
       - fear of rebellion
       - lack of control
       - weakness of purpose
       - selfishness and self-centeredness
       - low self-esteem
       - no sense of godliness
    b. Free obedience has a choice and can choose to obey or not to obey. Therefore, free obedience reveals...
       - love and trust
       - interest and care
       - a sense of godliness
       - a sense of brotherhood
       - strength of purpose and will
       - knowledge of self and confidence in self

2. Scripture says the following about obedience.
  a. Obedience demonstrates several things.
    ⇒ Obedience demonstrates that a person is wise.

> **"Therefore whosoever heareth these sayings of mine, and doeth them, I will liken him unto a wise man, which built his house upon a rock" (Mt.7:24).**

    ⇒ Obedience demonstrates love.

> **"He that hath my commandments, and keepeth them, he it is that loveth me: and he that loveth me shall be loved of my Father, and I will love him, and will manifest myself to him" (Jn.14:21).**

    ⇒ Obedience demonstrates that God is worthy.

> **"Then Peter and the other apostles answered and said, We ought to obey God rather than men" (Acts 5:29).**

    ⇒ Obedience demonstrates that Christ is of God.

> **"If any man will do his will, he shall know of the doctrine, whether it be of God, or whether I speak of myself" (Jn.7:17).**

  b. Obedience assures several things.
    ⇒ Obedience assures a prosperous life and success.

> **"This book of the law shall not depart out of thy mouth; but thou shalt meditate therein day and night, that thou mayest observe to do according to all that is written therein: for then thou shalt make thy way prosperous, and then thou shalt have good success" (Josh.1:8).**

    ⇒ Obedience assures entrance into the kingdom of heaven.

> **"Not every one that saith unto me, Lord, Lord, shall enter into the kingdom of heaven; but he that doeth the will of my Father which is in heaven" (Mt.7:21; cp. Lk.8:21).**

    ⇒ Obedience assures the mercy of God.

> **"And showing mercy unto thousands of them that love me, and keep my commandments" (Ex.20:6).**

    ⇒ Obedience assures that a person is a member of God's family.

> **"For whosoever shall do the will of my Father which is in heaven, the same is my brother, and sister, and mother" (Mt.12:50; cp. Mk.3:35).**

⇒ Obedience assures being blessed.

"**But he said, Yea rather, blessed are they that hear the word of God, and keep it**" (Lk.11:28; cp. Dt.11:27).

⇒ Obedience assures that we know the truth.

"**If any man will do his will, he shall know of the doctrine, whether it be of God, or whether I speak of myself**" (Jn.7:17).

⇒ Obedience assures the abiding presence of the Father and of Christ.

"**Jesus answered and said unto him, If a man love me, he will keep my words: and my Father will love him, and we will come unto him, and make our abode with him**" (Jn.14:23).

⇒ Obedience assures deliverance from enemies.

"**But if thou shalt indeed obey his voice, and do all that I speak; then I will be an enemy unto thine enemies, and an adversary unto thine adversaries**" (Ex.23:22).

⇒ Obedience assures that God will be our God and that all things will work out for our good.

"**But these things commanded I them, saying, Obey my voice, and I will be your God, and ye shall be my people: and walk ye in all the ways that I have commanded you, that it may be well unto you**" (Jer.7:23).

⇒ Obedience assures being loved by God and by Christ.

"**If ye keep my commandments, ye shall abide in my love; even as I have kept my Father's commandments, and abide in his love**" (Jn.15:10).

⇒ Obedience assures a good and a longer life.

"**Thou shalt keep therefore his statutes, and his commandments, which I command thee this day, that it may go well with thee, and with thy children after thee, and that thou mayest prolong thy days upon the earth, which the LORD thy God giveth thee, for ever**" (Dt.4:40).

⇒ Obedience assures being a friend of Christ.

"**Ye are my friends, if ye do whatsoever I command you. Henceforth I call you not servants; for the servant knoweth not what his lord doeth: but I have called you friends**" (Jn.15:14-15).

> ⇒ Obedience assures eating the good of the land.

**"If ye be willing and obedient, ye shall eat the good of the land" (Is.1:19).**

c. Obedience is better than sacrifice, even the sacrifice of all one has.

**"Hath the LORD as great delight in burnt offerings and sacrifices, as in obeying the voice of the LORD? Behold, to obey is better than sacrifice, and to hearken than the fat of rams" (1 Sam.15:22).**
**"Wherefore when he cometh into the world, he saith, Sacrifice and offering thou wouldest not, but a body hast thou prepared me: in burnt offerings and sacrifices for sin thou hast had no pleasure. Then said I, Lo, I come (in the volume of the book it is written of me,) to do thy will, O God" (Heb.10:5-7).**

**QUESTIONS:**
1. In what area of your life is obedience the hardest? Why? What practical steps can you take today that will help you be more obedient?
2. Why do you think God is so concerned about His people obeying Him?
3. Think of the difference between forced obedience and free obedience. What is God's preference for you? Why does your attitude make a difference to God?

## 5. HE ACKNOWLEDGED THE ENSLAVEMENT OF OTHERS (v.6-7).

Paul said four things about believers.

1. Believers are the *called* of Jesus Christ, called just as Paul was.
   ⇒ Believers are called to be saved, to be "of Jesus Christ."

   **"Who will have all men to be saved, and to come unto the knowledge of the truth. For there is one God, and one mediator between God and men, the man Christ Jesus; who gave himself a ransom for all, to be testified in due time" (1 Tim.2:4-6).**

   ⇒ Believers are called to the mission and task of Jesus Christ.

   **"Then said Jesus to them again, Peace be unto you: as my Father hath sent me, even so send I you" (Jn.20:21).**

2. Believers are "beloved of God," held ever so close to His heart, counted precious and dear to Him and deeply loved.

   **"The Lord hath appeared of old unto me, saying, Yea, I have loved thee with an everlasting love: therefore with lovingkindness have I drawn thee" (Jer.31:3).**

3. Believers are called to be "saints."

   **"But as he which hath called you is holy, so be ye holy in all manner of conversation; Because it is written, Be ye holy; for I am holy" (1 Pt.1:15-16).**

"Unto the church of God which is at Corinth, to them that are sanctified in Christ Jesus, called to be saints, with all that in every place call upon the name of Jesus Christ our Lord, both theirs and ours" (1 Cor.1:2).

4.  Believers are recipients of God's grace and peace (See previous note Ro.1:5).

"The LORD will give strength unto his people; the LORD will bless his people with peace" (Ps.29:11).

## ILLUSTRATION:
As believers, we often forget what a blessing it is to serve the Lord. What is your attitude as you serve Him?

*There once were two servants who lived and worked in the king's court. The competition between these two servants was often spirited. A day did not go by without an argument about who had the greatest right to serve the king. "It's my duty to serve the king by bringing him his meals" said the first servant. "After all, if I did not bring the king his food, he would get hungry. It is my right to serve him." The second servant said, "That is nothing. I cook the king's meals. If I did not cook for him, you would have nothing to serve him. It is my right to serve him also!"*

*Overhearing their conversation was one of the king's oldest and wisest servants. Motioning for them to come to him, the wise servant said, "You are both wrong when you say you have a right to serve our king. You will learn that the more you serve the king, the less rights you can claim. To serve our king is the greatest of privileges; it is never a right."*

## QUESTIONS:
1. Do you ever feel all alone in your walk with the Lord? That no one else understands? What comfort can be gained from verses 6 and 7?
2. What kind of mission has God sent you on? Are you currently serving Him by being totally committed to that mission? What adjustments do you need to make in your life and your priorities today?

## SUMMARY:

Do you really know what it is like to be enslaved by Jesus Christ? Remember that you cannot have it both ways. You cannot be a slave of the world and a slave of Christ. Like the apostle Paul, you must...

1.  Become a slave of Christ only.
2.  Become an apostle (or messenger) of God.
3.  Become set apart for the gospel of God.
4.  Receive God's grace and God's mission.
5.  Acknowledge the enslavement of others.

# ROMANS 1:1-7

## PERSONAL JOURNAL NOTES
### (Reflection & Response)

1. The most important thing that I learned from this lesson was:

2. The area that I need to work on the most is:

3. I can apply this lesson to my life by:

4. Closing Statement of Commitment:

| | | |
|---|---|---|
| | **B. Paul's Interest in the Church: Enslavement to the Gospel, 1:8-15** | unto you some spiritual gift, to the end ye may be established; |
| | | establish them |
| **1. The gospel produced a great church** | 8 First, I thank my God through Jesus Christ for you all, that your faith is spoken of throughout the whole world. | 12 That is, that I may be comforted together with you by the mutual faith both of you and me. |
| a. A cause for thanksgiving | | b. To be encouraged together with them |
| b. The reason: A worldwide testimony | | |
| **2. The gospel subjected his spirit to God's Son** | 9 For God is my witness, whom I serve with my spirit in the gospel of his Son, that without ceasing I make mention of you always in my prayers; | 13 Now I would not have you ignorant, brethren, that oftentimes I purposed to come unto you, (but was let hitherto,) that I might have some fruit among you also, even as among other Gentiles. |
| **3. The gospel stirred him to pray without ceasing** | | c. To bear fruit among them |
| **4. The gospel stirred him to seek people personally** | 10 Making request, if by any means now at length I might have a prosperous journey by the will of God to come unto you. | 14 I am debtor both to the Greeks, and to the Barbarians; both to the wise, and to the unwise. |
| | | **5. The gospel stirred him with a deep sense of indebtedness & a readiness to reach all men** |
| a. To impart some spiritual gift to | 11 For I long to see you, that I may impart | 15 So, as much as in me is, I am ready to preach the gospel to you that are at Rome also. |
| | | a. His indebtedness to reach all |
| | | b. His readiness to reach all |

**Section I**

# GREETING AND THEME: THE GOSPEL AND GOD'S RIGHTEOUSNESS
## Romans 1:1-17

### Study 2: Paul's Interest in the Church: Enslavement to the Gospel

**Text:**   **Romans 1:8-15**

**Aim:**   To understand what *total commitment* to the gospel means; to strive to live a life of total commitment.

**Memory Verse:**

> **"I am debtor both to the Greeks, and to the Barbarians; both to the wise, and to the unwise. So, as much as in me is, I am ready to preach the gospel to you that are at Rome also" (Romans 1:14-15).**

**INTRODUCTION:**

When is the last time you took a *commitment test*? This test is given every time you have to choose between one thing and another. Every day you must chose between such things as the following:

| | | |
|---|---|---|
| ⇒ keeping your promises | or | ⇒ breaking your promises |
| ⇒ honoring your family | or | ⇒ dishonoring your family |
| ⇒ being honest & hardworking | or | ⇒ doing as little work as you can |
| ⇒ helping the poor | or | ⇒ ignoring the needs of the poor |
| ⇒ boldly sharing the gospel | or | ⇒ being ashamed of the gospel |

# ROMANS 1:8-15

A Christian who has been transformed, truly changed by the power of the gospel, will make a passionate commitment to live for Christ. He will also make an unswerving commitment to share the gospel. Like many others, the apostle Paul was required to take the commitment test, a test which he passed with flying colors!

Paul had never visited the Roman church, and he had never seen the believers at Rome; yet here he is writing to them. How could he best reach them and express his purpose for writing them? How could he arouse their interest to such a peak that they would read what he was writing and heed it? This is the subject of the present passage. Paul wanted the Roman believers to know his great interest in them; therefore, to the best of his ability he shared why he was writing to them. Simply stated, he said he was writing because he could do nothing else; he was compelled to share the gospel with the whole world including the capital of the world, Rome itself. In fact he was enslaved by the gospel.

**OUTLINE:**
1. The gospel produced a great church (v.8).
2. The gospel subjected his spirit to God's Son (v.9).
3. The gospel stirred him to pray without ceasing (v.9).
4. The gospel stirred him to seek people personally (v.10-13).
5. The gospel stirred him with a deep sense of indebtedness and a readiness to reach all men (v.14-15).

## 1. THE GOSPEL PRODUCED A GREAT CHURCH (v.8).

The church at Rome was a great church--so great that Paul thanked God for the church "always" (v.2). The word *always* shows that the church held a very special place in Paul's heart. This is significant, for Paul had never been to the church. He did not know the church personally; he only knew what he had heard about it. But note: the church's testimony for Christ was so strong it was being talked about throughout *the whole world*. It had a phenomenal testimony, and wherever Paul traveled he heard about the strength of the church. What made the church at Rome so strong? Two significant things can be gleaned from Scripture.

    1. The believers were living pure lives in the midst of an immoral, base, and unjust society. The citizens of Rome were known for their...

| | | |
|---|---|---|
| • immorality | • extravagance | • license |
| • fleshliness | • hoarding | • indulgence |
| • drunkenness | • materialism | • idolatry |
| • partying | • greed | • pride |
| • gluttony | • selfishness | • sin and wickedness |

Nevertheless, the believers were standing firm for Christ and living pure lives, proclaiming the gospel of Jesus Christ and the need for morality and justice among men.

    2. The believers were serving Christ faithfully and laboring ever so diligently for the Lord. Wherever they were, at home or away traveling, they were sharing Christ and ministering to people--so much so that some of them were known by name all around the world. Paul himself apparently had run across quite a few of them as they were traveling about and ministering. (See Ro.16:3-16.)

    <u>**APPLICATION 1:**</u>
The Roman church stands as a testimony for every church.
1) No matter how immoral and base, polluted and corrupt a society is, we are to stand firm for Christ.

**"And be not conformed to this world: but be ye transformed by the renewing of your mind, that ye may prove what is that good, and acceptable, and perfect, will of God" (Ro.12:2).**

2) No matter where we are, at home or away, on business or pleasure, we are to be witnessing and ministering for Christ.

**"But ye shall receive power, after that the Holy Ghost is come upon you: and ye shall be witnesses unto me both in Jerusalem, and in all Judaea, and in Samaria, and unto the uttermost part of the earth" (Acts 1:8).**

## APPLICATION 2:

Every church and every believer should have a strong testimony, a testimony so strong that it is talked about everywhere.

**"[Timothy] which was well reported of by the brethren that were at Lystra and Iconium" (Acts 16:2).**
**"For your obedience is come abroad unto all men. I am glad therefore on your behalf: but yet I would have you wise unto that which is good, and simple concerning evil" (Ro.16:19).**
**"For by it [faith] the elders obtained a good report" (Heb.11:2).**

## ILLUSTRATION:

When the gospel is lived out, it affects every member of the church. Instead of begging people to get involved in the mission of the church, members have a deep passion to do something for the Lord. If the gospel is not taken seriously, the results are obvious as noted in this story.

*"There is a story about four people in the church whose names were Everybody, Somebody, Anybody, and Nobody.*
*"The church had financial responsibilities and Everybody was asked to help. Everybody was sure that Somebody would do it. Anybody could have done it. But you know who did it? Nobody. It ended up that Everybody blamed Somebody when Nobody did what Anybody could have done.*
*"Then the church grounds needed some work, and Somebody was asked to help. But Somebody got angry about that, because Anybody could have done it just as well and, after all, it was really Everybody's job. In the end the work was given to Nobody, and Nobody did a fine job.*
*"On and on this went. Whenever work was to be done, Nobody could always be counted on. Nobody visited the sick. Nobody gave liberally. Nobody shared his faith. In short, Nobody was a faithful member.*
*"Finally the day came when Somebody left the church and took Anybody and Everybody with him. Guess who was left. Nobody!"*[1]

Are you working to make your church great? Or are you leaving it up to everybody else?

---

[1]  Michael P. Green. *Illustrations for Biblical Preaching.* (Grand Rapids, MI: Baker Books, 1996), p.64-65.

# ROMANS 1:8-15

**QUESTIONS:**
1. What would it be like to belong to a local church that was well known? Known far and wide? What would be your ministry, your service, if you were a member of this kind of church?
2. You live in an immoral culture just like the first believers of Rome. How hard is it for you to stand up for the gospel? What challenges do you regularly face?
3. Is it easy or difficult for you to share the gospel with others? How can you have a more effective witness?

## 2. THE GOSPEL SUBJECTED HIS SPIRIT TO GOD'S SON (v.9).

Every man should subject, submit, or yield his spirit to God's Son. Why? Because of the gospel, the glorious salvation that is in Christ Jesus: the deliverance from sin, death, and hell. When a person considers that he is enslaved by sin and that he is actually going to die and have to give an account to God, he is most foolish...
- not to accept the salvation that is in God's Son
- not to subject his spirit to God's Son
- not to serve in the gospel of God's Son

**QUESTIONS:**
1. What is the greatest challenge a believer faces when yielding his spirit to Christ? What motivated you to submit your spirit to Christ? What did you gain from doing this?
2. Given the difference between being enslaved by sin and being enslaved by Christ, why do so many people choose to continue in sin?

---

**A CLOSER LOOK:**

(1:9) **Serve**: labor of hire, service that is bought. Paul says, "I serve with my spirit in the gospel of His Son." Note three points.
    1.    The believer's labor and service are bought and paid for by the precious blood of Christ.

> **"What? know ye not that your body is the temple of the Holy Ghost which is in you, which ye have of God, and ye are not your own? For ye are <u>bought</u> with a price: therefore glorify God in your body, and in your spirit, which are God's" (1 Cor.6:19-20).**

    2.    The believer owes his labor and service to the Lord. Once he has surrendered to the gospel, he has no choice. He is to diligently serve and work for Christ.

> **"Bear ye one another's burdens, and so fulfil the law of Christ" (Gal.6:2).**

    3.    The believer is to serve God in his spirit and in his body. The spirit controls the body. What the spirit does, the body does. Therefore, if the believer is serving God in spirit, he is serving God in body. If a man's spirit is right, then his body will be right. For example, a man may feel bad; he may be down, depressed, and oppressed; but if his spirit is strong, he arises and conquers his feelings. He controls and overcomes the oppressing circumstances, and he lives a victorious day. But if his spirit is weak--whether at work or at play--he often wallows around in self-pity, grumbling and griping, and living a defeated day. And too often the day stretches into weeks and months until a person's life is down more than it is up--all because the spirit is too weak to conquer.

---

### APPLICATION:

The point is this: the believer is to serve God in his spirit and in his body. He is...

- to keep his spirit strong
- to conquer his emotions
- to overcome his weaknesses, the ups and downs of his body

When a believer does this, then he can serve God to the fullest extent possible.

> "I beseech you therefore, brethren, by the mercies of God, that ye present your bodies a living sacrifice, holy, acceptable unto God, which is your reasonable service. And be not conformed to this world: but be ye transformed by the renewing of your mind, that ye may prove what is that good, and acceptable, and perfect, will of God" (Ro.12:1-2).

### QUESTIONS:

1. As a believer, what right does Christ have to require you to serve Him?
2. How willing are you to serve Christ?
   ⇒ When I find it convenient within my personal schedule.
   ⇒ When it seems to be the popular thing to do.
   ⇒ When it does not cost me anything.
   ⇒ Anytime, anyplace, anywhere.
3. How strong is your testimony in your local church? How strong is your testimony where you work? What can you do to strengthen your testimony in both of these places?


## 3. THE GOSPEL STIRRED HIM TO PRAY WITHOUT CEASING (v.9)

Paul was a man of intercessory prayer, a man who always prayed *for others*. Note two points.

1.    Paul called upon God to bear witness that he prayed. He did not...
- just talk about praying
- just tell people he was praying for them as a courtesy
- just pretend to pray
- just spend a few minutes in a *religious exercise* of prayer

Paul really prayed; he took time to ask God to strengthen and help others. (See Eph.3:14-21 below for the specifics of what Paul prayed. Also see Mt.6:9-13 below for what Christ tells us to pray daily. These two passages taken together tell us what we should be praying every day, both for ourselves and for others.)

> "For this cause I bow my knees unto the Father of our Lord Jesus Christ, Of whom the whole family in heaven and earth is named, That he would grant you, according to the riches of his glory, to be strengthened with might by his Spirit in the inner man; That Christ may dwell in your hearts by faith; that ye, being rooted and grounded in love, May be able to comprehend with all saints what *is* the breadth, and length, and depth, and height; And to know the love of Christ, which passeth knowledge, that ye might be filled with all the fulness of God. Now unto him that is able to do exceeding abundantly above all that we ask or think, according to

the power that worketh in us, Unto him *be* glory in the church by Christ Jesus throughout all ages, world without end. Amen" (Eph. 3:14-21).

"After this manner therefore pray ye: Our Father which art in heaven, Hallowed be thy name. Thy kingdom come. Thy will be done in earth, as *it is* in heaven. Give us this day our daily bread. And forgive us our debts, as we forgive our debtors. And lead us not into temptation, but deliver us from evil: For thine is the kingdom, and the power, and the glory, for ever. Amen" (Mt. 6:9-13).

2. Paul even prayed for believers and churches whom he did not know. Remember he knew only a few of the believers in the Roman church; he had never met most of them. They were totally unfamiliar and unknown to him; yet he prayed for the church.

## APPLICATION:
Scripture is strong in its charge to us. We are to pray constantly and we are to pray for all believers throughout the world. Our prayers are not to be limited to a few minutes each day nor to our loved ones and close friends.

"Seek the LORD and his strength, seek his face continually" (1 Chron.16:11).

## ILLUSTRATION:
How many of you tend to worry first or to act first or to give up hope before you think to pray? Each believer is charged by God to pray: to pray before, during, and after. We are to pray morning, noon, and night. We are always to pray.

*"While very ill, John Knox, the founder of the Presbyterian Church in Scotland, called to his wife and said, 'Read me that Scripture where I first cast my anchor.' After he listened to the beautiful prayer of Jesus recorded in John 17, he seemed to forget his weakness. He began to pray, interceding earnestly for his fellowmen. He prayed for the ungodly who had thus far rejected the Gospel. He pleaded in behalf of people who had been recently converted. And he requested protection for the Lord's servants, many of whom were facing persecution. As Knox prayed, his spirit went Home to be with the Lord. The man of whom Queen Mary had said, 'I fear his prayers more than I do the armies of my enemies,' ministered through prayer until the moment of his death."*[2]

Does Satan, your greatest enemy, fear your prayers?

## QUESTIONS:
1. How important do *you* consider prayer to be? Does your prayer life back up your belief in prayer? Or are you too busy to spend time praying? How much time do you honestly spend in prayer each day?
2. What habits have you developed that have enhanced your prayer life? What can you do to bring growth to your prayer life?

---

[2] *INFOsearch Sermon Illustrations* (Arlington, TX: The Computer Assistant, 1-888-868-9029, 1986-1996).

## 4. THE GOSPEL STIRRED HIM TO SEEK PEOPLE PERSONALLY (v.10-13).

Paul did not leave the ministry and the sharing of the gospel up to others. He became personally involved, so much so that he begged God to give him opportunity after opportunity--even to the point of letting him travel to the capital of the world itself to share Christ with its citizens. Note how deeply he was stirred: he made a request--if by any means, now at last--that he might be allowed to preach the gospel at Rome.

The point is forceful: Paul was stirred to seek people, for he longed to reach people for Christ.

1. Paul wished to *impart some spiritual gift* to the believers. Why? So they might be more deeply established in the faith. The term spiritual gift (*charisma*) means a gift of grace. The term often refers to specific gifts given by the Holy Spirit (Ro.12:6-8), but here it means *the truths* of the grace of God, of His spiritual blessings to man revealed in Christ Jesus our Lord. Very simply, Paul longed to share the truths of the gospel with the believers at Rome. God's spiritual blessings were overflowing in his heart, and he was aching to share the gift of God's blessings.

### APPLICATION:
What an indictment against us! How many of us are so full of the gospel that we are aching to share it? How many of us even know the gospel that well, know God's gifts and blessings well enough to be overflowing with them?

> **"Blessed be the God and Father of our Lord Jesus Christ, who hath blessed us with all spiritual blessings in heavenly places in Christ" (Eph.1:3).**

Note that God's spiritual gift establishes the believer. The word *established* means to fix, set, make fast, strengthen. Note the descriptive picture behind each word.

2. Paul wished to be *comforted or encouraged together* with other believers. The word *comforted* means to be strengthened and consoled together. Paul expected to be taught and strengthened by the believers as well as to teach and to strengthen them. There was to be a mutual sharing among all. Paul expected all believers to be actively sharing the gospel. He even expected them to share with him so that he might grow and be more firmly rooted in the faith.

### APPLICATION:
How many believers are actively grounded enough in the faith to share with Paul? What an indictment! Yet the *expectation* is that we are to be deeply rooted, continuously studying the Word and learning. How much we need to awaken and arise from our slumber.

> **"Rooted and built up in him, and stablished in the faith, as ye have been taught, abounding therein with thanksgiving" (Col.2:7).**

3. Paul wished to bear fruit among them (see Jn.15:1-8). Paul wished to bear the fruit of...
- converts (Ro.1:13)
- righteousness (Ro.6:21-23)
- Christian character, the fruit of the Spirit (Gal.5:22-23)

Note Paul's worldwide vision. He wished to bear fruit among the citizens of Rome as well as "among other Gentiles."

## APPLICATION:

How desperately God needs men, women, boys and girls with a worldwide vision!

"Say not ye, There are yet four months, and then cometh harvest? behold, I say unto you, Lift up your eyes, and look on the fields; for they are white already to harvest" (Jn.4:35).

## QUESTIONS:

1. It is far easier to give money to fund evangelism and allow others to do the work than it is to get personally involved in the lives of the lost. How can you know exactly what part God wants you to play in reaching the lost?
2. What benefits can you gain from sharing the blessings in your life with other believers? What do others gain if you do this?
3. Being a Christian believer involves both giving and receiving. Who does God use in your life to comfort and strengthen you? In whose life are you being used by God?

## 5. THE GOSPEL STIRRED HIM WITH A DEEP SENSE OF INDEBTEDNESS AND A READINESS TO REACH ALL MEN (v.14-15).

Note two points.

1. The word *debtor* means to owe, to be obligated, to be bound by duty. The Greek is impossible to translate into English, for two ideas are being expressed by Paul. He was a *debtor*...
   - because Christ had done so much for him (saved him).
   - because Christ had called him to preach (given him a task to do).

The *indebtedness* was deeply felt by Paul. The idea is that it was intense, unwavering, relentless, powerful. The sense of debt just would not let Paul go. He was compelled to preach the gospel; therefore, he could do nothing else. He was obligated and duty-bound to preach it. He actually felt that he owed the gospel to the world; therefore, if he kept quiet, it would be worse than knowing the cure for the most terrible disease of history and refusing to share it.

Note how Paul declared his indebtedness to the whole world. He made a contrast between the Greeks and the Barbarians. He meant that he owed the gospel to all nationalities and cultures, to all the peoples of the earth whether civilized or uncivilized, industrialized or primitive, rich or poor. (The Greeks considered everyone a barbarian who did not speak the Greek language and adopt Greek culture.) He made a contrast between the wise and the unwise. He meant that he owed the gospel to the educated and the uneducated, the learned and the unlearned, the motivated and the unmotivated, the seeking and the complacent.

## APPLICATION:

If you knew someone who had cancer and you had access to the cure, you wouldn't hesitate to tell the person about the cure, would you? Although the cure would only be as long-lasting as life on this earth, you would feel indebted to tell the individual. Likewise, Paul sensed a *deep indebtedness* to share the glorious news of salvation with the world. The *answer* to eternal life is now known and must be proclaimed to the whole world. To keep the message to yourself is the most inexcusable and criminal act in all of human history. The glorious news that death has been conquered and that man can now live eternally must be proclaimed. We who know the wonderful news are *indebted* to get the news out to the world.

"For God so loved the world, that he gave his only begotten Son, that whosoever believeth in him should not perish, but have everlasting life" (Jn.3:16).

2.    The word *ready* means an *urgent willingness*. Paul experienced both a willingness and an urgency to preach the gospel. Note the words, "as much as in me is." Paul wanted to take all that was in him and pour it into people--all the energy and effort, all the truth and knowledge of the gospel. There was nothing that could keep him from sharing the gospel, not if he had a chance to share it. He *allowed* no hindrance to enter his life that would affect his message. He was possessed and obsessed with a readiness to preach the glorious message of the living Lord.

"For though I preach the gospel, I have nothing to glory of: for necessity is laid upon me; yea, woe is unto me, if I preach not the gospel!" (1 Cor.9:16).
"And as ye go, preach, saying, The kingdom of heaven is at hand" (Mt.10:7).

## APPLICATION:

How quickly and easily we share the unimportant things of life with friends, neighbors, loved ones, even with strangers! If you have discovered a great new restaurant, heard the outcome of an exciting ballgame, read a good book, seen a good movie, shopped in a great store, or met a fascinating new friend, you cannot wait to pick up the phone, write a letter, or even drop what you are doing to inform someone of your 'good news.' Yet all these things are passing fads or fancies. None of them have a lasting impact on people's lives. How much more should we as believers be excited about spreading the good news of the gospel! When you think of the value of the gospel, you should feel an urgency and willingness to share the good news with everyone you know and meet.

## QUESTIONS:

1. As a believer, you are a debtor to Christ and also a debtor to the world. Why is this so?
2. As a debtor, what is your obligation to Christ and the world? If you do not feel indebted, what element is missing in your life?
3. Do you exclude some people from hearing the gospel, exclude them because of their status, culture, color, or education?
4. What is the key to having an "urgent willingness" to make the gospel known?

## SUMMARY:

How committed are you to share the gospel of Jesus Christ? Do you have a passion to share Christ, the same passion God gave the apostle Paul? The only way to have this passion is to be enslaved by the gospel. What does the gospel do in your life as a believer?

1.    The gospel produces a great church.
2.    The gospel subjects their spirit to God's Son.
3.    The gospel stirs them to pray without ceasing.
4.    The gospel stirs them to seek people personally.
5.    The gospel stirs them with a deep sense of indebtedness and a readiness to reach all men.

# ROMANS 1:8-15

## PERSONAL JOURNAL NOTES
### (Reflection & Response)

1. The most important thing that I learned from this lesson was:

2. The area that I need to work on the most is:

3. I can apply this lesson to my life by:

4. Closing Statement of Commitment:

| | C. Paul's Boldness for Christ: Un-ashamedness of the Gospel, 1:16-17 | salvation to every one that believeth; to the Jews first, and also to the Greek. | a. All who believe<br>b. All nationalities, both Jew & Greek |
|---|---|---|---|
| | | 17 For therein is the righteousness of God | 3. It is the revelation of God's righteousness |
| 1. It is the "good news" from God Himself | 16 For I am not ashamed of the gospel of Christ: for it is the power of God unto | revealed from faith to faith: as it is written, The just shall live by faith. | a. The problem: man's unrighteous-ness |
| 2. It is the power of God to save | | | b. The answer: Faith |

**Section I**

## GREETING AND THEME: THE GOSPEL AND GOD'S RIGHTEOUSNESS
### Romans 1:1-17

**Study 3: Paul's Boldness for Christ: Unashamedness of the Gospel**

**Text:** **Romans 1:16-17**

**Aim:** To fully share the gospel without any shame or embarrassment.

**Memory Verse:**
> "For I am not ashamed of the gospel of Christ: for it is the power of God unto salvation to every one that believeth; to the Jew first, and also to the Greek" (Romans 1:16).

## INTRODUCTION:

How open are you with your Christian faith? Are you the same in public as you are in private? Many believers find it awkward to share their faith in public places--to really share what is in their heart. Careful not to offend, they choose to say nothing about the gospel. Every day in the world people miss opportunities...

- to share Christ at their workplace
- to share Christ with their neighbors
- to share Christ with friends and family
- to share Christ with perfect strangers

How can this be? How is it that people who love Jesus Christ can come up empty-handed when it comes to leading the lost to Christ? Donald McGavran, one of the greatest experts on world missions, says:

> *"The world has more winnable people than ever before...but it is possible to come out of a ripe field empty-handed."*[1]

What is the key to leading people to Christ? The key is being able to share the gospel without any shame or embarrassment. All over the world God is raising up men and

---

[1] Edward K. Rowell, Editor. *Quotes & Idea Starters for Preaching & Teaching.* (Grand Rapids, MI: Baker Books, 1996), p.53.

women who are not ashamed of the gospel. Like the Apostle Paul, these believers are convinced of the gospel's power to save the most unlikely of characters...including themselves.

These two verses contain one of the greatest summaries of the gospel ever written. It is a clear declaration of God's power to save all who believe, no matter their nationality or condition. It is a clear explanation of why Paul was never ashamed of the gospel.

**OUTLINE:**
1.    It is the *good news* from God Himself (v.16).
2.    It is the power of God to save (v.16).
3.    It is the revelation of God's righteousness (v.17).


## 1. IT IS THE "GOOD NEWS" FROM GOD HIMSELF (v.16).

The gospel is the news that God has given to the world and wants proclaimed to the world. The fact that the gospel had been given by God Himself made Paul unashamed of the gospel. No man should ever be ashamed of anything concerning the Sovereign Majesty of the universe. (See note--Ro.1:1-4 for discussion.) However, Paul had every reason to be ashamed.

1.    Paul's day was a day of moral degeneracy, the hideous days of Nero. Rome was a moral sewer, a cesspool of detestable and inconceivable wickedness. Such a day stood diametrically opposed to the moral righteousness of the gospel.

2.    Paul was by nationality a Jew, a race that was thought by many of that day to be a despicable sub-human race, worthy only to be cursed, ill-used, and enslaved. Naturally, Paul would be apprehensive among non-Jews. In the flesh he would be tempted to shy away from them.

3.    The gospel Paul preached was almost unbelievable. A male member of the despicable Jewish race was said to be the Savior of the world, and not only was He said to be a Jew, He was said to be a mere man like all other men. But not only that, His death was said to be different from the death of other men. He was said to have died "for all other men," that is, in their place, as a substitute for them. And then to top it all, He was said to have risen from the dead. His resurrection was said to be the proof that He was the very Son of God. Such unbelievable claims made the gospel a contemptible thing in the minds of many. A natural man would shrink from making such phenomenal claims.

4.    Paul was often rejected, not by just a few persons, but by whole communities. The authorities imprisoned him in Philippi (Acts 16:19-23). The religionists ran him out of Thessalonica and threatened his life in Berea (Acts 17:5-15). The intellectuals laughed him out of Athens (Acts 17:32; cp. 16-32). His message was considered foolishness to the intellectuals (the Greeks) and a stumbling block to his own people (the Jews). There were several times in Paul's life when he could have given up in shame and fled to some part of the earth to begin life all over again.

**APPLICATION:**
Many people are ashamed of the gospel. They are ashamed because they fear ridicule, rejection, and loss of recognition, position, and livelihood. They fear two things in particular.

1) There is the fear of intellectual shame. This is the fear that the gospel does not measure up intellectually. It is judged not to be for the scholar or philosopher. Note: this feeling is common to those who do not understand the philosophy of the gospel. No greater philosophy exists; no greater reasoning has ever been worked through. A man holds either to the philosophy and thought of the world, or to the philosophy and thought of God's Son, the gospel of Jesus Christ and His

redemption. There is no question which philosophy and intellectual thought is greater.

**"The foolishness of God is wiser than men; and the weakness of God is stronger than men" (1 Cor.1:25; cp. Ro.1:18-31).**

2) There is the fear of social shame. Many fear if they accept and proclaim the gospel, they will be...
- ridiculed and mocked
- rejected and ignored
- passed over and cut off
- left without job and livelihood
- left without family and friends
- abused and killed

**"The fear of man bringeth a snare: but whoso putteth his trust in the LORD shall be safe" (Pr.29:25).**

**ILLUSTRATION:**
The unbeliever considers you to be a fool if you believe the gospel. The Bible clearly states that those who reject the gospel are the foolish ones.

*"Dwight Moody was preaching when someone passed a note to him through the usher. It had only one word: 'Fool.' Moody looked at it and said, 'I've often received notes that weren't signed. This is the first time I've received a note that someone forgot to write, but signed.'"*[2]

Do not be intimidated by people who speak or write in ignorance or denial. Remember: you have the truth on your side.

**QUESTIONS:**
1. The gospel of Jesus Christ is not just *Good* News; it is the *best* news! Why are some believers ashamed of sharing the Good News?
2. How hard is it for you to take a stand for morality? What difference can a believer make in a culture that is wicked?
3. Do you ever feel like a social outcast because of your Christian beliefs? What encouragement can you find from God's Word that will help you overcome this challenge?
4. Many people take rejection personally when their presentation of the gospel is not received by the lost. What does God want you to do when someone rejects the gospel you have shared?

## 2. IT IS THE POWER OF GOD TO SAVE (v.16).

Note four significant facts.

1. The word *power* means the might, energy, force, and strength that is *within* God. The power is "of God," of His very nature. As God, He is the embodiment of power; He possesses all power, that is, omnipotent power, within His Being. He can do and act as He chooses.

The point is this: God has chosen to use His power in a loving way by sending men the "good news," the gospel of salvation. Being all powerful, God could wipe men off the face of the earth, but instead He has chosen to give men the good news of salvation. This tells us a critical truth: God's nature is love. He is full of compassion and grace. He is the

---

[2] Ted Kyle & John Todd. *A Treasury of Bible Illustrations.* (Chattanooga, TN: AMG Publishers, 1995), p.102.

God of salvation; therefore, He sent the "gospel of Christ" to the world that men might be saved.

2.     The word *salvation* must be understood and grasped by every person upon earth. The hope of the world is God's salvation (see **A CLOSER LOOK**--Ro.1:16 for discussion).

3.     God saves all who believe. Belief is the one condition for salvation, *but* we must always remember that a person who really believes *commits himself* to what he believes. If a man does not commit himself, he does not really believe. God saves the person who believes, that is, who really commits his life to the gospel of Christ (see Ro.10:16-17; Jn.2:24).

4.     God saves all nationalities, both Jew and Greek. Note the word "first." This does not mean favoritism, but *first in time*. God does not have favorites, favoring the Jew over the Gentile. It simply means the gospel was to be carried to the Jew first. They had been the channel through whom God had sent His Word and His prophets and eventually His Son into the world. Therefore, they were to be reached first; then the gospel was to be carried to the Greeks, that is, to all nationalities. The point is twofold.

    a. The gospel is God's power, and it can reach any nationality and any person, no matter who they are.

    b. No one is to be exempt from the gospel.

        ⇒ No messenger is to *exempt anyone* from the gospel.

        ⇒ No person is to *exempt himself* from the gospel. The gospel is for everyone, no matter his race, color, condition, circumstance, or depravity.

> **"And the Spirit and the bride say, Come. And let him that heareth say, Come. And let him that is athirst come. And whosoever will, let him take the water of life freely" (Rev.22:17).**

**QUESTIONS:**

1. God has chosen to use His Almighty power for good not evil.  How should this make you feel?  How can you use this fact to help you share the gospel with others?
2. What is the key to making the power of God a part of your life?
3. God has offered His salvation to all who believe.  As you look at your own circle of influence, who presents the greatest challenge for you to lead to Christ?  Is it a family member, a friend, a neighbor?  In what way can God use you to bring them to a saving knowledge of Jesus Christ?

---

**A CLOSER LOOK:**

(1:16) **Salvation**: means deliverance, made whole, preservation. From what does man need to be saved and delivered and preserved? Scripture paints five descriptive pictures of salvation, showing man's great need.

1.     Salvation means *deliverance from being lost*. Man is pictured as wandering about in the forest of life trying to go someplace, but unable to find his way. He is lost, and if he continues to stumble about through the forest of life, the underbrush and thorns of the forest will sap his strength and prick him to the point that he lies down and dies. His only hope is for someone to notice that he is lost and to begin seeking for him. This is where the glorious gospel of salvation comes in. God sees that man is lost and He sends His Son to seek and to save man.

Salvation means that Christ...

• seeks and saves man from his lost condition.
• sets man on the right road that leads him to eternal life.

> **"For the Son of man is come to save that which was lost. How think ye? if a man have an hundred sheep, and one of them be gone astray, doth he not leave the ninety and nine, and goeth into the mountains, and seeketh that which is gone astray?" (Mt.18:11-12; cp. Lk.15:4).**

2.    Salvation means *deliverance from sin*. It means deliverance from mistakes, from corrupt ideas and thoughts, from moral impurity and from a crooked and perverse generation. Sin is like...

- an infection, a disease for which man has no cure.
- a master that enslaves and will not let go.
- a crooked and perverse world that man cannot straighten out.

Man's only hope is for someone to discover a cure, someone with the intelligence and power to do it. This is where God steps in with His glorious salvation. God knows all about man's infection and enslavement by sin, all about his crooked and perverse world; so He sends His Son to save man, to cure him and liberate him and straighten out his world. Salvation means that Christ saves man from the terrible tyranny of sin, from...

- the infection of sin.
- the enslavement of sin.
- the crooked and perverse world of sin.

Salvation also does something else. It frees man from the pricking and burden of guilt and shame, and it plants within man's soul a deep sense of health and peace with God.

> **"Thou shalt call his name JESUS: for he shall save his people from their sins" (Mt.1:21).**

3.    Salvation means *deliverance in the future from all evil and corruption*: from aging and wasting away, deterioration and decay, death and hell. It is the complete redemption of man's spirit and body at the end of the world. It is salvation from the wrath of God--salvation that saves a man from being separated from God eternally. It is the life and exaltation which believers will receive at the final triumph of Jesus Christ. It is the salvation that will keep a man safe and preserve him both in time and eternity.

Man and his world are pictured as having a *seed of corruption* within their very nature, a seed of corruption that eats away, causing them to...

- age and waste away
- deteriorate and decay
- suffer and die

Again, man is hopeless. He cannot stop himself and his world from death and destruction, but God can. God can save both man and his world; God can deliver them from the terrible fate of death and destruction. This is the message of salvation. God loves man and his world and wants to save them, so He sent His Son into the world to save them. Salvation is...

- the complete redemption of man's body and soul in the future: a redemption that saves man from the process of aging and wasting away, deteriorating and decaying, dying and being condemned to hell.
- the perfect deliverance from the wrath of God: a salvation that saves man from being separated from God eternally.
- the gift of life and exaltation: a salvation that will be given to believers at the final triumph of Jesus Christ.
- the presence of perfect assurance: a salvation of security and preservation both in time and eternity.

> "We ourselves groan within ourselves, waiting for the
> adoption, to wit, the redemption of our body. For we are saved
> by hope" (Ro.8:23-24).

4. Salvation means *deliverance from enemies and dangers*. Man is pictured as walking in a world lurking with many enemies and countless dangers. Man has to confront all kinds of enemies and dangers that attack both his body and soul, his mind and spirit. He faces all kinds of problems and difficulties, trials and temptations. No matter how much he may long for peace and security, he is forced to combat...

- a hostile environment
- a savage world of nature
- an unknown universe
- an uncertain future
- unregulated urges
- inevitable aging and dying
- a lust for more and more (possessions, fame, wealth, power)
- an evil pride and ego
- greed and covetousness
- unpreventable accidents
- dreadful diseases

Man is seen as helpless in overcoming all the enemies and dangers that lurk in the shadows of this world. But God is not helpless--God can *save* man; He can gloriously deliver man as he journeys along the road of life. This is exactly what salvation means. God delivers man from the enemies and dangers that war against him. But note the next paragraph, a crucial point.

Salvation does not mean that God delivers man *from* experiencing difficulty and danger, not in this present world. God does not give a life free from the nature and circumstances of this world. What salvation does is deliver one _through_ the difficulties and dangers of life.

Salvation means that...
- God gives *security and peace* of soul, no matter what happens.
- God gives *safety* independent of circumstances and environment.
- God gives *inward strength and courage* to bear the onslaught and attacks of danger.

> "And his disciples came to him, and awoke him, saying, Lord,
> save us: we perish. And he saith unto them, Why are ye fearful, O
> ye of little faith? Then he arose, and rebuked the winds and the sea;
> and there was a great calm. But the men marvelled, saying, What
> manner of man is this, that even the winds and the sea obey him!"
> (Mt.8:25-27).

5. Salvation means to *make well, to heal, to restore to health, to make whole* both physically and mentally. Man is pictured as a suffering creature, a creature who...
- gets sick
- becomes diseased
- has accidents
- wears out from aging
- suffers infirmities
- struggles against deformities

Salvation declares that Christ is concerned with man's suffering. Christ saves and delivers man, rescues and restores man in body as well as in spirit. He takes a man who suffers and makes him whole.

"And, behold, a woman, which was diseased with an issue of blood twelve years, came behind him, and touched the hem of his garment: for she said within herself, If I may but touch his garment, I shall be whole. But Jesus turned him about, and when he saw her, he said, Daughter, be of good comfort; thy faith hath made thee <u>whole</u>. And the woman was made whole from that hour" (Mt.9:20-22).

**QUESTIONS:**
1. If an unbeliever asks you what it means to be saved, what can you tell him?
2. Salvation means deliverance from being lost. How does a lost sinner come to realize he is lost? What does it mean, in very practical words, to be lost?
3. Salvation means deliverance from sin. In today's culture, the word sin is an offensive term. Words like "mistake," "error," "poor choice," or "oversight" have replaced the use of sin. But sin is still sin. What is the world's solution for sin? What is God's solution for sin?
4. Believers and unbelievers are all aging and dying every day. How can you explain what difference salvation makes in that process? What hope can you offer a believer who has struggled with destructive addictions? (like drugs, alcohol, immorality, etc.)
5. God does not promise to save you *from* trials and troubles, but *through* them. What does this mean? Have you experienced such deliverance?
6. How concerned do you think God is when His people are suffering? Does God physically heal every believer who asks? Why or why not? Which is more important--physical deliverance or eternal deliverance?

## 3. IT IS THE REVELATION OF GOD'S RIGHTEOUSNESS (v.17).

Note two points.
1.  Man has a serious problem--that of thinking he is righteous. The problem is easily seen by picturing the following:
⇒  Man thinks he is good enough and that he does enough good to be acceptable to God.
⇒  Man thinks he is righteous and that he walks righteously enough to be acceptable to God.

However, there is one problem with man's thinking: man is not perfect. But God is perfect, and He is perfectly righteous. Therefore, He cannot allow an unrighteous and imperfect being to live in His presence, not even man. Man just cannot live with God, not in his imperfect and unrighteous condition, for he would pollute the perfect world of God, the very ground and atmosphere and nature of heaven, of the spiritual world and dimension.
The only way man can live with God is to be made righteous, perfectly righteous. How can man be made perfectly righteous? The gospel gives the answer. The gospel is the revelation of God's righteousness and reveals how man can be made righteous and reconciled to God. (See note, <u>Righteousness</u>--Ro.3:21-22. This notes should be read for a clear understanding of what Scripture means by righteousness and justification.)

"For I say unto you, That except your righteousness shall exceed the righteousness of the scribes and Pharisees, ye shall in no case enter into the kingdom of heaven" (Mt.5:20).

2.    The answer to man's problem is faith. When a person believes the gospel--really believes that Christ saves him--God takes that person's faith and *counts it* for righteousness. The person is not righteous; he is still imperfect, still corruptible, and still short of God's glory as a sinful human being. But he does believe that Jesus Christ saves him. Such belief honors God's Son, and because of that, God accepts and counts that person's faith as righteousness. Therefore, he becomes acceptable to God. This is *justification*; this is what is meant by being justified before God.

But note a most critical point: a person must *continue* to believe. A person must continue to live by faith from the very first moment of belief to the last moment of life on this earth, for it is his faith that God takes and counts as righteousness.

What is meant by the two statements...
- "from faith to faith,"
- and, "the just shall live by faith"?

Very simply, the whole life of the believer is to be a life of faith, from beginning faith to ending faith, from faith to faith. Therefore, the righteousness of God is revealed *continuously* through all of life, from the beginning of a person's faith to the ending of a person's faith. As Scripture says:

**"And by him all that believe are justified from all things, from which ye could not be justified by the law of Moses" (Acts 13:39).**

### ILLUSTRATION:

What a great promise for the Christian believer: God takes your faith and counts it as righteousness. It is not made possible because of *your* righteousness or *your* power or *your* being good enough. The believer is counted as righteous because of the righteousness of God. Belief comes a whole lot easier when you keep your eyes upon Him and not upon yourself.

> *"While an English farmer was walking through his field one day with a friend, he suddenly remarked, 'You know, I was saved by my good looks.' He explained that he had attended a gospel meeting where he heard an evangelist preach on Isaiah 45:22. The farmer said, 'He pictured Jesus on the cross in a general way as the divine substitute bearing the sin of the world. Then the preacher pointed us to Hebrews 12:2 and told us to look again unto Jesus, the author and finisher of our faith, who saves to the uttermost (Heb. 7:25) all that come to Him. He said that everyone has to accept this personally. When I saw the Lord in this way, I received Him as MY Savior.' The farmer's friend was impressed. 'Now I know what you mean,' he said. 'It was your good looks at Christ and His cross that resulted in your conversion.'"* [3]

Is your faith causing you to continually look at Christ or do you have your eyes upon yourself?

### QUESTIONS:

1. In what ways are men tempted to believe *their own righteousness* is sufficient?
2. When are you most tempted to trust in your own righteousness?
3. Can you honestly say you walk by faith, that you trust Jesus Christ to take care of you and to deliver you through all the trials of life day by day, that you trust Him to deliver you right up until the very day He is to take you into heaven? If not, what can you do to grow in faith?

---

[3]    *INFOsearch Sermon Illustrations* (Arlington, TX: The Computer Assistant, 1-888-868-9029, 1986-1996).

---

**A CLOSER LOOK:**

(1:17) **Justification—Faith**: this verse is used three times in the new Testament. A different point is emphasized each time it is used. It tells how a man can be just with God (cp. Hab.2:3-4).

    1.    "The just shall live by faith" (Ro.1:17). Who can live by faith? Only the just. People make two claims to justification. The man who says "I am justified by doing the best I can" is simply saying that he expects God to excuse his sin. But God does not excuse sin; God forgives sin. Excusing sin is nothing more than license—allowing man to go on living as he wishes and always coming up short. Therefore, a man is not justified by doing the best he can—by living after the law. He is justified by faith, by trusting God to forgive him. Once a man has really trusted God, he is just. And the just then begins to live by faith. The former man, whether a legalist or a man of fleshly indulgence, has no opportunity to live by faith. Why? Simply because he never started the life of faith. It is the just, not the legalist or the man of sinful indulgence, who lives by faith.

    2.    "The just shall live by faith" (Gal.3:11). By what rule does a person live? By the principle of faith, not by the principle of works. The person declared just by faith shall live apart from works. The believer is saved by faith, and the believer lives by faith (Gal.3:11).

    3.    "The just shall live by faith" (Heb.10:38). By what power does a person live? By the power that is given him by God because of faith. The Christian believes God, believes in the promises God has made. Therefore, the believer does what God says. The power of faith energizes him to live a just life. Works have nothing to do with making him just nor with keeping him just.

---

**SUMMARY:**

The charge to the believer is clear and striking: do not be ashamed of the gospel. You should never be ashamed of telling the Good News, of telling about the greatest story that has ever been told. Use God's power. Tell the lost about God's love. Be bold and courageous and do not be ashamed. The gospel...

1.    Is the *good news* from God Himself.
2.    Is the power of God to save.
3.    Is the revelation of God's righteousness.

**PERSONAL JOURNAL NOTES**
**(Reflection & Response)**

1. The most important thing that I learned from this lesson was:

2. The area that I need to work on the most is:

3. I can apply this lesson to my life by:

4. Closing Statement of Commitment:

| | | | |
|---|---|---|---|
| | **II. SIN AND CONDEMNATION: THE WORLD'S NEED TO GET RIGHT WITH GOD, 1:18-3:20**<br><br>**A. God's Case Against All Ungodliness and Unrighteousness of Men: Why God Shows Wrath, 1:18-23** | things of him from the creation of the world are clearly seen, being understood by the things that are made, even his eternal power and Godhead; so that they are without excuse: | **without them: The signs of creation**<br>a. God's eternal power & nature are clearly seen in creation<br>b. Men are without excuse |
| **1. Men are the subjects of God's wrath**<br>a. Men of ungodliness & unrighteousness<br>b. Men who suppress the truth | 18 For the wrath of God is revealed from heaven against all ungodliness and unrighteousness of men, who hold the truth in unrighteousness; | 21 Because that, when they knew God, they glorified him not as God, neither were thankful; but became vain in their imaginations, and their foolish heart was darkened. | **4. Men do not honor God nor give thanks**<br>a. Result 1: Their imaginations become vain (empty)<br>b. Result 2: Their hearts are darkened |
| **2. Men reject that within them: Conscience & thoughts** | 19 Because that which may be known of God is manifest in them; for God hath showed it unto them. | 22 Professing themselves to be wise, they became fools, | **5. Men become prideful & turn away from God**<br>a. They imagine & create their own ideas of God<br>b. They exchange the |
| **3. Men reject that** | 20 For the invisible | 23 And changed the glory of the uncorruptible God into an image made like to corruptible man, and to birds, and fourfooted beasts, and creeping things. | incorruptible God for corruptible idols |

## Section II

## SIN AND CONDEMNATION: THE WORLD'S NEED TO GET RIGHT WITH GOD
### Romans 1:18-3:20

**Study 1: God's Case Against All Ungodliness and Unrighteousness of Men: Why God Shows Wrath**

**Text:**    **Romans 1:18-23**

**Aim:**    To understand _why_ God pours out His wrath on unrighteous men.

**Memory Verse:**

"For the wrath of God is revealed from heaven against all ungodliness and unrighteousness of men, who hold the truth in unrighteousness" (Romans 1:18).

## SECTION OVERVIEW

The teaching of this whole passage can be summarized into three points.

1.    Men who sin bring upon themselves the judgment of God, and they need God's righteousness (Ro.1:18-2:16).

2.    Men without the law, the heathen, are taught by nature and conscience. However, they have sinned by falling short of the standard of righteousness given to them (Ro.1:18-32). Similarly, the moralist and self-righteous who have the law have sinned by falling short of their standard of righteousness, that is, the law (Ro.2:1-3:8).

3.    Therefore, all the world becomes guilty before God (Ro.3:19) and needs God's righteousness (Ro.3:9-20).

## INTRODUCTION:

*Would a loving God send someone to hell who was innocent...*
- who has never heard the gospel?
- who has never seen a Bible?
- who has never had a missionary come to his remote village?
- who was born and raised in a country that closed its borders to the Christian faith?

What do you think? Would a loving God do this? As you think about your answer, would God pour out His wrath on anyone...
- who has an evil, sinful heart?
- who was an enemy of God?
- who consistently ignored the truth?
- who has never trusted in Jesus Christ and His completed work on the Cross?

The answer to all of these questions is a resounding YES! The fall of man knows no borders. Sin is not just a problem for men who live in a civilized hemisphere. Sin is a worldwide problem that has been a point of vulnerability for every man since Adam. This passage declares that mankind--every person, everywhere--is without excuse. It is time to quit making excuses for the circumstances of the lost; it is time for us to fully understand why God's wrath is to be feared.

The message of this passage is perfectly clear: Why God reveals and executes wrath upon men.

## OUTLINE:
1.    Men are the subjects of God's wrath (v.18).
2.    Men reject that *within* them--conscience and thoughts (v.19).
3.    Men reject that *without* them--the signs of creation (v.20).
4.    Men do not honor God nor give thanks (v.21).
5.    Men become prideful and turn away from God (v.22-23).

## 1. MEN ARE THE SUBJECTS OF GOD'S WRATH (v.18).

Note three points.

1.    The wrath of God is a reality (see **A CLOSER LOOK, God's Wrath**--Ro.1:18 for discussion).

2.    God's wrath is revealed from heaven. God reveals and shows wrath in four ways. (See note, God's Wrath--Ro.1:24-32 for discussion.)

3.    The subjects of God's wrath are twofold. God shows His wrath and becomes angry with two classes of men:

    a.    Men who are ungodly and unrighteous.

        ⇒ The ungodly fail to love and obey God. They are those who do not live as God lives. They are not like God, not holy and righteous and pure. They do not work at developing a godly nature, do not honor God by word or deed, do not worship and obey God as the only living and true God, do not reverence Him by doing what He says. On the contrary, the ungodly are those who do what they want when they want, who may give lip-service to God, but who ignore Him in their day-to-day lives.

⇒ The unrighteous fail to love others. They are those who do not live with men as they should. They act against men: cheating, stealing, lying, abusing, enslaving, destroying, and taking advantage of them.

The point is clear: God is angry with such men--men who are ungodly and unrighteous--men who...
- do not love and obey God
- do not love and treat others as they should

b. Men who hold the truth in unrighteousness. The word *hold* means to hold down, suppress, repress, stifle, hinder. Men know the truth from three sources:
⇒ from nature (cp. Ro.1:20)
⇒ from reason and conscience (cp. Ro.1:18; 2:15)
⇒ from Scripture (Jn.5:39; 2 Tim.3:16)

Yet despite having access to the truth, they ignore, neglect, and even push the truth aside, doing all they can to avoid and get rid of it. Why? Because they want to live as *they* wish and not as God says. They want to live unrighteous lives, to taste and feel and see and have all the stimulating things they want.

But note what Scripture says: they "hold the truth in unrighteousness"; that is, they know the truth while they go about living in unrighteousness. They are without excuse.

> **"And with all deceivableness of unrighteousness in them that perish; because they received not the love of the truth, that they might be saved" (2 Th.2:10).**

Again the point is clear: God is angry with men...
- who are ungodly, who do not love and obey God
- who are unrighteous, who do not love and treat others as they should
- who hold or suppress the truth while they live ungodly and unrighteous lives

> **"For the grace of God that bringeth salvation hath appeared to all men, teaching us that, denying ungodliness and worldly lusts, we should live soberly, righteously, and godly, in this present world; looking for that blessed hope, and the glorious appearing of the great God and our Saviour Jesus Christ; who gave himself for us, that he might redeem us from all iniquity, and purify unto himself a peculiar people, zealous of good words" (Tit.2:11-14).**

**ILLUSTRATION:**
The wrath of God is often ridiculed and mocked. Ridiculous statements and pictures are made such as God being somewhat like an old man with a gray beard who is flinging thunderbolts at so-called sinful people. Be assured: the wrath of God is not ridiculous: it will be the execution of justice, the straightening out of all the injustices ever committed by men. It will be payday, the day when every man will receive exactly what he deserves, nothing more and nothing less.

> *"A little Scottish boy wouldn't eat his prunes, so his mother sent him off to bed saying, 'God is angry at you.'*
> *"Soon after the boy went to his room a violent storm broke out. Amidst flashes of lightning and peals of thunder, the mother looked into the boy's room,*

*worried that he would be terrified. When she opened the door she found him looking out the window muttering, 'My, such a fuss to make over a few prunes.'*[1]

The wrath of God does not concern little boys who have an aversion to prunes. God stores up His wrath for those who curse His name; who lie, steal, and kill; who reject and rebel against Him--all who insist on living ungodly and unrighteous lives.

**QUESTIONS:**
1. Even believers are ungodly and unrighteous at times. Does that mean God will pour His wrath out on us? Why or why not?
2. Why do ungodly and unrighteous people deserve God's wrath?
3. What motives cause people to suppress the truth? In what way have you attempted to ignore the truth in your life?

---

**A CLOSER LOOK:**

(1:18) **God's Wrath**: anger, not an agitated outburst of violence. It is not the anger that quickly blazes up and just as quickly fades away, not the anger that arises solely from emotion. Rather, it is decisive anger. It is an anger that has arisen from a thoughtful decision, an anger that arises from the mind much more than from the emotions. When used of God, it is always an anger that is *righteous and just and good*. It is an anger that stands against the sin and evil, violence and slaughter, immorality and injustices of men. It is an anger that abhors and hates sin and evil and that dishes out a just revenge and equal justice. However, it is an anger that is *deeply felt*; in fact, it must be felt, for evil and corruption must be opposed and erased from the face of the earth if there is to be a "new heavens and a new earth." And God has promised a new heavens and a new earth where righteousness and perfection dwell forever.

1. There is God's anger in judgment.

   **"But when he saw many of the Pharisees and Sadducees come to his baptism, he said unto them, O generation of vipers, who hath warned you to flee from the wrath to come?" (Mt.3:7).**

2. There is God's anger with those who disobey the Lord Jesus.

   **"He that believeth on the Son hath everlasting life: and he that believeth not the Son shall not see life; but the wrath of God abideth on him" (Jn.3:36).**

3. There was God's anger with Israel in the wilderness.

   **"So I sware in my wrath, They shall not enter into my rest" (Heb.3:11).**

4. There was the anger of the Lord Jesus at man's hardness of heart.

   **"And when he had looked round about on them with anger, being grieved for the hardness of their hearts, he saith unto the man, Stretch forth thine hand. And he stretched it out: and his hand was restored whole as the other" (Mk.3:5).**

---

[1] Michael P. Green. *Illustrations for Biblical Preaching*, p.173.

ROMANS 1:18-23

## 2. MEN REJECT THAT *WITHIN* THEM: CONSCIENCE AND THOUGHTS (v.19).

Note three clearly stated facts.
⇒ God can be known. There are *some things* that "may be known of God."
⇒ These things are manifest (evident, made clear and plain) "*in*" men. Men know about God; they know some things about God *within* their hearts, minds, and consciences.
⇒ How? "God has shown [made evident, clear and plain]" these things to men.

Now note.
1. There is a great deal *about* God that men cannot know (Job 11:7), but there is a great deal that men can know. Men can know enough to be led to God. This is the whole point of this passage: men know about God, but they do not worship Him as God. They have a sense of God, but they suppress the sense, trying to get rid of it.
2. Man's inner sense, or *innate awareness*, and *instinctive knowledge* of God are strong. Man is a very capable creature. He has enormous power and mental capacity. Man can reason and grasp that "God is [exists] and that He rewards those who diligently seek Him" (Heb.11:6). Man can "know God" (v.19), even the "invisible things" of God (v.20); he can know to such a degree that he is "without excuse" (v.20).
However, man chooses not to know God. He even chooses to take the truth that is *within* him and suppress it. Man rejects the knowledge of God that is *within* him. This is the first reason why God reveals and shows His wrath.

**QUESTIONS:**
1. God has given every man a conscience. In man's conscience, God reveals Himself. What causes a man to ignore his conscience?
2. Why is it impossible to know everything about God? Should you strive to know God more and more, despite your limitations? What benefits are there to learning more and more about God?
3. Do you know someone who has heard the truth but ignores it? How can you reach someone like that?

## 3. MEN REJECT THAT *WITHOUT* THEM: THE SIGNS OF CREATION (v.20).

Creation reveals God. The whole universe, its presence and its nature, declares God. However, note something often overlooked. Men can look at nature and see *more* than the simple fact that God is the great Creator. Men can see *more* than a Supreme Being behind the creation of the universe. They can see "the invisible things" of God. This means at least two things.
1. Man can see the "*eternal power*," the Supreme Intelligence and Force (or Energy), of God. Man can look at the creation of the earth and outer space, of plants and animals, of man and woman; he can look and clearly see their...
• bodies and structure, variety and beauty
• arrangement and order, purpose and laws

When man looks at such things and reasons with an *honest spirit*, he sees clearly that the world was made by a Creator. But, as stated above, he sees much more. He sees that the Creator is a God of supreme...
• Life & Being
• Intelligence & Knowledge
• Energy & Power (the Supreme Force)
• purpose & meaning
• design & order (law)
• beauty & majesty
• glory & honor
• value & worth (morality)
• mystery (things not understood; secrets undiscovered)

53

2.   Man can see the "*Godhead*," that is, the deity of God. When he looks at nature and reasons with an *honest spirit*, he sees clearly that the Creator is a God who...
- cares and provides for what He has created
- gives life and has interest in life
- regenerates, replenishes, and carries things on
- deserves worship and obedience (being the Creator of life and purpose, and being the Supreme Person of law and order demands that all his subjects serve and obey Him)

Note what Scripture says: man is without excuse. The point is shocking. Man has every evidence imaginable within creation directing him toward God, yet man rejects the knowledge of God within creation. This is the second reason why God reveals and shows His wrath. Man is without excuse. Man has no defense, no answer, no reason that can justify his rejection of God.

> "Nevertheless he left not himself without witness, in that he did good, and gave us rain from heaven, and fruitful seasons, filling our hearts with food and gladness" (Acts 14:17).
> "The heavens declare his righteousness, and all the people see his glory" (Ps.97:6).

QUESTIONS:
1. When you look at God's creation, what do you see that reveals God?
2. What should your attitude be in preserving God's creation?
3. How can you reason with a scientist or unbeliever who attempts to explain away the facets of creation?

## 4. MEN DO NOT HONOR GOD NOR GIVE HIM THANKS (v.21).

Note that Paul shifted to the past tense in this verse. He was speaking of what men had done in the past; and, of course, men still do the same today. Two serious charges are made against men. Men can clearly know God both...
- within themselves: in their own thoughts, reasonings, consciences
- without themselves: in creation and nature, in the earth and outer space

They can know that God gives them life and cares and provides for them, and that God runs everything in an orderly and lawful way, giving purpose and meaning to life. Men can see that God is great and good; therefore, God deserves to be glorified and given thanks. But men...
- did not glorify Him: did not worship, obey, or serve Him as God
- did not give thanks to Him: did not praise, magnify, or express appreciation to Him

What happens when men reject God is tragic. Two severe things happen when they push God out of their minds.
1.   Men's imaginations become vain.
   ⇒ The word *imaginations* means thoughts, reasonings, deliberations, conclusions, speculations.
   ⇒ The word *vain* means, empty, futile, unsuccessful, senseless, worthless.

## APPLICATION:

When men push God out of their minds, their minds are void and empty of God. God is not in their thoughts. (Cp. Ps.10:4.) Their minds are ready to be *filled* with some other *god* or *supremacy*.

> **"And God saw that the wickedness of man was great in the earth, and that <u>every imagination of the thoughts</u> of his heart was only evil continually" (Gen.6:5).**

2. Man's "foolish heart is darkened."
   ⇒ The word "foolish" means senseless, without understanding, unintelligent.
   ⇒ The word "darkened" means blinded, unable to see.

   > **"They know not, neither will they understand; they walk on in darkness: all the foundations of the earth are out of course" (Ps.82:5).**
   > **"Ever learning, and never able to come to the knowledge of the truth" (2 Tim.3:7).**

Note a critical point. Men suffer empty imaginations and darkened hearts because they...
   • do not glorify God
   • do not offer thanks to God

This is the third reason why God reveals and shows wrath toward men.

> **"And every one that heareth these sayings of mine, and doeth them not, shall be likened unto a foolish man, which built his house upon the sand: and the rain descended, and the floods came, and the winds blew, and beat upon that house; and it fell: and great was the fall of it" (Mt.7:26-27).**
> **"Therefore to him that knoweth to do good, and doeth it not, to him it is sin" (Jas.4:17).**

## QUESTIONS:

1. What are the horrible consequences a person faces when he rejects God's revelation?
2. What are some modern-day examples of "vain imaginations"?
3. There are any examples in the Bible of men and women who had foolish hearts that had been darkened. Can you think of some? What became of them? What lessons can you glean from the error of their ways?

## 5. MEN BECOME PRIDEFUL AND TURN AWAY FROM GOD (v.22-23).

This scene is one of the greatest tragedies in all of human history, and it is repeated every time a man turns away from God. The scene is man rejecting God and claiming that he is...
   • too wise to believe in God
   • too intelligent to depend upon the *fables* of the Bible
   • too capable not to look to self
   • too resourceful not to create his own world and future
   • too masterful not to trust his own *humanistic* ideas
   • too reasonable and rational not to create his own standards and laws to control life

But note what Scripture says: in denying God, men make two gross mistakes.

1. Men profess themselves to be wise, but in so doing they become fools. Why? For one simple reason.

⇒ God does exist, and He has clearly revealed Himself both within men's thoughts and through creation. Therefore, when men's hearts and minds are emptied of God, men have to fill their hearts and thoughts with something else. They have to have some other god, some other *guiding light* or *principle* to give purpose and meaning and direction to their lives. They have to replace God with something else. They have to have something--some standard, some law, some rule, some person, some god--by which they can guide their lives.

⇒ Therefore, when men dethrone and erase God from their lives, they imagine and create their own *god* within their minds. Men reason and speculate about the ultimate source of life, and whatever they come up with is that to which they give their lives.

> **"Therefore, behold, I will proceed to do a marvellous work among this people, even a marvellous work and a wonder: for the wisdom of their wise men shall perish, and the understanding of their prudent men shall be hid" (Is.29:14).**
>
> **"For the wisdom of this world is foolishness with God. For it is written, He taketh the wise in their own craftiness. And again, The Lord knoweth the thoughts of the wise, that they are vain" (1 Cor.3:19-20).**

2. Men exchange the incorruptible God for some corruptible idol. Note four facts.

  a. God is said to be *incorruptible*, which means non-decaying, imperishable, unchanging, and unaging. Incorruptible means that God is not subject to passing away; He is eternal. God *always has been* and *always will be*: *God will always exist*.

  b. Men swap and exchange God for "*corruptible man*," that is, for the image, the idea, the thought that man is his own god. Men swap God for *humanism*. They make themselves and mankind...

  • the gods of life
  • the masters of the world
  • the makers of their own destiny
  • the law-givers of their own laws
  • the determiners of their own morality
  • the standard by which their lives are to be governed

  Note that *humanism* makes an idol out of man and worships man as the "god" of his own destiny. This is usually the sin of *scientific and industrialized societies*--societies where a healthy and strong man, both mentally and physically, is essential--societies where good self-images and healthy bodies are necessary for the advancement of society.

  c. Men swap God for *corruptible creatures*. This is usually the worship followed by non-industrialized and non-scientific societies--societies where grotesque images of men and animals are actually constructed out of wood, stone, or metal.

  Now note: men create their own humanistic gods, whether mental images and thoughts or some grotesque image, because of pride and conceit. Men want to control their own lives, to do as they wish, to be recognized and honored, and to receive the credit and acknowledgment themselves. Therefore, they turn from God and make their own gods...

  • in their own image
  • as they conceive and wish their god to be

This is the fourth reason why God--the only living and true God--reveals and shows his wrath toward men.

> **"Behold, I set before you this day a blessing and a curse; a blessing, if ye obey the commandments of the LORD your God, which I command you this day: and a curse, if ye will not obey the commandments of the LORD your God, but turn aside out of the way which I command you this day, to go after other gods, which ye have not known" (Dt.11:26-28).**

### ILLUSTRATION:
The world has been contaminated by an infectious desire to enthrone men as gods of their own destiny. One would think that after thousands of years of failure, mankind would give up and bow its knee to Almighty God.

How could educated, spiritually literate people wind up in such dire circumstances? Who would believe such insane things? Christian columnist Cal Thomas sheds light on these questions:

> *"'The danger when men stop believing in God,' said G. K. Chesterton, 'is not that they will believe in nothing, but that they will believe in anything.' This summarizes the point at which our modern culture has arrived."*[2]

### QUESTIONS:
1. What kinds of circumstances can turn a person away from God? What can you do to guard your life in this area?
2. How do you know that God exists? What proof can you offer to those who are seeking spiritual reality?
3. What corruptions does modern man swap in exchange of God?
4. Why is humanism such a strong force in the world today? What can you do, as one person, to fight humanism's influence in the church, the schools, the communities?

### SUMMARY:

God is love. But He is also a God of wrath. Contrary to popular opinion, God's wrath has not become too outdated for the cultures of today. It is important that every believer know exactly why God pours out His wrath on certain men. This passage teaches that...

1. Men are the subjects of God's wrath.
2. Men reject that *within* them--conscience and thoughts.
3. Men reject that *without* them--the signs of creation.
4. Men do not honor God nor give thanks.
5. Men become prideful and turn away from God.

---

[2] Cal Thomas. *The Things That Matter Most*. (New York, NY: Harper Collins Publishers, 1994), p.108.

# ROMANS 1:18-23

## PERSONAL JOURNAL NOTES
### (Reflection & Response)

1. The most important thing that I learned from this lesson was:

2. The area that I need to work on the most is:

3. I can apply this lesson to my life by:

4. Closing Statement of Commitment:

| B. God's Case Against All Ungodliness and Unrighteousness of Men: How God Shows Wrath, 1:24-32 | | |
|---|---|---|
| **1. God gave men up to do as they willed** | selves that recompence of their error which was meet. | |
| **2. God gave men up to uncleanness** | 24 Wherefore God also gave them up to uncleanness through the lusts of their own hearts, to dishonour their own bodies between themselves: | **4. God gave men up to reprobate, depraved minds** |
| a. The reason: The lusts in their hearts | | a. The reason: They rejected God |
| b. The result: Gross idolatry | 28 And even as they did not like to retain God in their knowledge, God gave them over to a reprobate mind, to do those things which are not convenient; | b. The result: Depraved, unsuitable behavior |
| | 25 Who changed the truth of God into a lie, and worshipped and served the creature more than the Creator, who is blessed for ever. Amen. | |
| **3. God gave men up to vile, unnatural affections** | 26 For this cause God gave them up unto vile affections: for even their women did change the natural use into that which is against nature: | |
| a. The reason: They gave in to unnatural passion & homosexuality | 29 Being filled with all unrighteousness, fornication, wickedness, covetousness, maliciousness; full of envy, murder, debate, deceit, malignity; whisperers, | |
| b. The result: A burning, passionate bondage | 30 Backbiters, haters of God, despiteful, proud, boasters, inventors of evil things, disobedient to parents, | |
| 1) Women with women | 27 And likewise also the men, leaving the natural use of the woman, burned in their lust one toward another; men with men working that which is unseemly, and receiving in them- | 31 Without understanding, covenantbreakers, without natural affection, implacable, unmerciful: |
| 2) Men with men | | **5. God assures final judgment: Death** |
| | 32 Who knowing the judgment of God, that they which commit such things are worthy of death, not only do the same, but have pleasure in them that do them. | a. Because men do such things |
| | | b. Because men approve such things |

## Section II

## SIN AND CONDEMNATION: THE WORLD'S NEED TO GET RIGHT WITH GOD
### Romans 1:18-3:20

**Study 2:** God's Case Against All Ungodliness and Unrighteousness of Men: How God Shows Wrath

**Text:** Romans 1:24-32

**Aim:** To understand *how* God reveals His wrath to men.

**Memory Verse:**

"And even as they did not like to retain God in their knowledge, God gave them over to a reprobate mind, to do those things which are not convenient" (Romans 1:28).

# ROMANS 1:24-32

**INTRODUCTION:**

The wrath of God is usually a most unpopular subject--it makes people feel uncomfortable. It is far easier to talk about the love of God. But what kind of love would express no wrath at all the evil and injustices of the world, all the...

- holocausts
- murder
- assaults
- slavery

- hatred
- abuse
- immorality
- greed

Just like a parent who always indulges his child without ever correcting or disciplining him, God's love not balanced by God's wrath is both aimless and absurd. Scripture declares that "the wrath of God is revealed from heaven" (Ro.1:18). This particular passage discusses the four ways that God reveals and shows His wrath. Note three things.

1. All four ways concern judgments that come upon man. That is, the wrath of God is exercised and falls upon man because of his ungodliness and unrighteousness.

2. All four ways have to do with history, with human experience, with a moral universe. That is, God's wrath is revealed from heaven day by day...

- throughout history
- in man's experience
- within a moral universe

3. Three of the judgments are present judgments; they take place today in the lives of men (v.24-31). The fourth judgment is future and is to be the final judgment upon men (v.32).

How does God reveal and execute His wrath upon man?

**OUTLINE:**

1. God gave men up to do as they willed (v.24).
2. God gave men up to uncleanness (v.24-25).
3. God gave men up to vile, unnatural affections (v.26-27).
4. God gave men up to reprobate, depraved minds (v.28-31).
5. God assures final judgment: death (v.32).

## 1. GOD GAVE MEN UP TO DO AS THEY WILLED (v.24).

This is said three times in this passage, and each time was due to a serious sin of man (v.24, 26, 28). Man's sin forced God to give man up and to abandon him. The scene was terrible and frightening, for to be abandoned and left without God in this world leads to the worst possible life imaginable.

There are two strong reasons why God gives man up, and each issues a loud warning to man.

1. Man chooses sin over God, and when he does, two things happen.
   a. Man becomes enslaved to sin. Sin actually stirs more and more sin. The more a man sins the easier it is for him to sin again. At first he may ponder the wisdom of committing the sin; but later on, after committing the sin over and over, he seldom gives the sin a second thought. Sin looks good, tastes good, and feels good. It is attractive and it satisfies the human flesh and urges of man. It satisfies so much that man is naturally attracted to it. By sinning, he steadily makes himself a slave to sin. He becomes addicted. Sin becomes the terrible master and subjects man to its cruel habits and enticements that are almost impossible to break.

b. Sin *always* lies. This needs to be remembered. Sin entices, claiming to bring pleasure, stimulation, and happiness; but in reality it destroys a person's...

|     |     |     |
| --- | --- | --- |
| • body | • profession | • values |
| • family | • mind | • future |
| • friends | • will | • life |
| • soul | • hope | |

A terrible tragedy that is so often forgotten is this: we are not islands unto ourselves. Our sin involves others; therefore, our sin destroys others--both their lives and their souls. Sin may look, taste, and feel good to us; but it always involves and influences others. It hurts and dooms our children, spouses, friends and society.

**ILLUSTRATION:**
There is no such thing as a *private* sin. When we sin, we are not the only ones affected. Usually, our sin holds others back from doing God's will. Just think for a moment.

⇒ When a person cheats on his taxes, others will lose the benefits of what that tax money was designated to pay for.

⇒ When a person commits adultery, the other spouse and their children suffer deep emotional wounds.

⇒ When a person spies against his own country, the security of his fellow countrymen is placed at risk.

We *are not* islands unto ourselves. This humorous story illustrates how our sin entangles, how it violates others and keeps them from doing God's will.

> *"In addition to being one of the most successful baseball manager[s] of his day, John J. McGraw may have been responsible for there being a third-base umpire. Long before he became a famous manager of the New York Giants, as a young third baseman with the old Baltimore Orioles the intensely competitive McGraw had a habit of hooking his finger in the belt of a base runner who was tagging up to score after a long fly ball. This trick usually slowed the runner enough so that he was thrown out at home plate.*
> *"Despite violent protests, McGraw got away with his ploy for some months-- until one base runner secretly unbuckled his belt. When the runner dashed for home, he left his belt dangling from McGraw's finger. The need for a third-base umpire could hardly have been made clearer."*[1]

It is one thing for a person to be called out at home plate because you cheated and held him back. It is a far more serious thing to cause someone to miss Heaven's open door because of your sin. God considers sin to be a very serious offense. God sees your *every* sin and He will call every man to task for allowing his sin to bring harm to others.

2.    Man abandons God, actually turns away from God and gives God up. This may be called *spiritual abandonment*: man *spiritually abandons* God. God has given man a free will, and if a man wills to turn away from God, he can. God will not interfere with that choice. To do so would be to take away man's freedom. So God appeals to man spiritually, through mercy and love and grace, but He does not violate man's choice. To do so would be to have a coerced and mechanical universe. Man would become nothing but a robot, coerced to do this and that and to do it exactly as God wills. The result would be

---

[1]  Michael P. Green. *Illustrations for Biblical Preaching,* p.341.

tragic: man would never experience love, goodness, care, concern, or feelings. Love is not love if it is coerced. It is mechanical and meaningless. The expression of any affection or virtue is meaningless unless it is freely given. Therefore, when man turns away from God, he himself makes the choice to do so, and God *cannot* interfere. The choice is man's, and man is abandoned to do exactly as he has chosen (Hos.4:17; Eph.4:19). Therefore, God has no choice. He must...

- give man up
- let man go his own way
- spiritually abandon man
- leave man to live for that which he has chosen

> **"So I gave them up unto their own hearts' lust: and they walked in their own counsels" (Ps.81:12).**

**QUESTIONS:**
1. Continued sin forces God to give men up to their own desires. Why is this true? How can you use this strong Scripture to reach someone living in sin?
2. How far-reaching is sin's damage to the lives of other people?
3. What role does man's free will play in his abandonment of God? In God's abandonment of men?

## 2. GOD GAVE MEN UP TO UNCLEANNESS (v.24-25).

The word *uncleanness* means impurity, filthiness, immorality, defilement, pollution, contamination, infection. When men turn from God--abandon God to live unclean and immoral lives--God leaves men. He abandons them to their choice. God lets men wallow around in their filthiness. Men are judged and condemned to uncleanness.

1. The *reason* men are condemned to "uncleanness" is because of the *lusts* "in their hearts." Their hearts are filled with *lusts*, that is, passionate cravings, desires, and urges. They long after things that displease God and that dishonor their bodies. God cares deeply about the human body, and he judges any person who abuses the body.

In the Greek the lusts are said to be "*in* their own hearts." Sin takes place in the heart *before* it takes place by act.

> **"And he said, That which cometh out of the man, that defileth the man. For from within, out of the heart of men, proceed evil thoughts, adulteries, fornications, murders, thefts, covetousness, wickedness, deceit, lasciviousness, an evil eye, blasphemy, pride, foolishness: all these evil things come from within, and defile the man" (Mk.7:20-23).**

2. The result of living an unclean life is idolatry. Men "changed the truth of God into a lie and worshipped and served the creature more than the Creator." When men live in uncleanness, they begin to serve and to give their lives to one of two things.
   a. They serve themselves, giving their time and energy to their own desires, pursuits, and lusts.
   b. They serve other "gods," gods that allow them to go ahead and live as they wish. They *imagine* what god is like and they worship him either in their mind or in some graven image molded by their hands. They conceive of a *god* that is...
   - a god of some religion
   - a god of Christianity
   - a god of some part of nature
   - a god of men
   - a god of creation
   - a god of goodness

The point is this. Man abandons the only true and living God and lusts after uncleanness. He lusts and craves so much...

- that he creates a god in his own mind who allows him to satisfy his lust.
- that he rationalizes and thinks that his god understands his situation and need, and that his god will not judge him for his uncleanness and immorality.
- that he conceives of a god who will allow him to do what he wants.
- that he matches his god to fit his morals, letting his morals determine the kind of god he is going to worship.
- that he twists god to fit what he wants.
- that he allows his morals (uncleanness) to control his thoughts about God.

Man serves and gives his time and energy to the god he imagines in his mind and to the idols he creates within his imagination and thoughts. He abandons God so that he can live the unclean life he craves. Therefore, God judges man and abandons man to live in his uncleanness.

> "Love not the world, neither the things that are in the world. If any man love the world, the love of the Father is not in him. For all that is in the world, the lust of the flesh, and the lust of the eyes, and the pride of life, is not of the Father, but is of the world. And the world passeth away, and the lust thereof: but he that doeth the will of God abideth for ever" (1 Jn.2:15-17).

**QUESTIONS:**
1. Describe the meaning of "uncleanness" in your own words. What drives men to desire this kind of life?
2. Where does all sin begin? What does this tell you about your innermost thoughts, your motives, your private desires?
3. Why is idolatry a result of having an unclean life? What idols have you struggled with in the past? How did you overcome their power in your life?

## 3. GOD GAVE MEN UP TO VILE, UNNATURAL AFFECTIONS (v.26-27).

The term *vile affections* means passions, dishonor, disgrace, infamy, shame, and degradation. It means passions that cannot be controlled or governed, that run loose and wild, no matter how much a person tries to control them.

1. The reason God gives men up to vile affections is because of their unnatural passion. Men continue to lust, craving the illegitimate and unlawful. They burn in their lust one for another. And note what Scripture is talking about: *unnatural* affection, that is, homosexuality.

⇒ Women burn and lust and exchange the "natural use into that which is *against nature*." And note, it is *against nature*.
⇒ Men burn in their "lust one toward another; men with men doing that which is shameful."

Note again that the sin takes place in the heart. Men *burn within*, crave the sin before they commit the act. It is their burning, their lusting, their craving that sets them aflame to pursue the shameful act. Their hearts burn after other men, not after God. Therefore, they stand condemned, and God is forced to judge them.

2. The result of *unnatural* affection is a totally depraved nature. When men choose a life of "vile affections," God gives them up to it. It is man's choice, and since it is man's choice, God can do nothing about it. God has to give man up to what he chooses. He does not override man's will.

Note a crucial fact: Scripture says men receive "in themselves that recompence [pay back, punishment] of their error." The judgment for homosexuality is *within*, not *without* man. If a person burns after *unnatural* affection, he is given over to his burning; he is given over to burn and crave more and more. He is judged and condemned to live in his *unnatural* passion and to feel the shame of it. He is enslaved and held in bondage to it, psychologically and physically. And the judgment is "meet," that is, fit, just, exactly what it should be. If men lust and burn after *unnatural* affection, it is only fit that they be given what they so passionately crave. Therefore, God judges men by giving men up to live in their vile affections.

> **"That every one of you should know how to possess his vessel in sanctification and honour; not in the lust of concupiscence [desire, lewdness], even as the Gentiles which know not God" (1 Th.4:4-5).**
> **"Marriage is honourable in all, and the bed undefiled: but whoremongers and adulterers God will judge" (Heb.13:4).**

**QUESTIONS:**
1. What happens to the man who tries to control his vile affections?
2. Why does God give men up to vile affections? Why is this really a loving act by God?
3. Why is it so difficult for a homosexual to break free from the power of homosexuality? Is there any hope for the homosexual? If so, what is that hope?
4. Why do the excuses for practicing homosexuality not measure up to the truth from God's Word? How would you lead a homosexual into freedom from homosexuality?

## 4. GOD GAVE MEN UP TO REPROBATE, DEPRAVED MINDS (v.28-31).

The term *reprobate mind* means a mind that is rejected, disapproved, degraded, depraved; a mind that cannot stand the test of judgment.

1.  The reason God gives men up to reprobate minds is because men reject God. They know God, but they do not "like to retain God in their knowledge." They...

- do not like to approve God
- do not like to recognize God
- do not like to acknowledge God

They simply do not want God to have anything to do with their lives; therefore, they push Him out of their minds. They ignore and refuse to accept God's presence.

2.  The result is forcibly stated. God gives men over to reprobate minds, minds that are totally depraved. Men are allowed to do exactly as *they choose*; they are enslaved more and more in their depravity and unsuitable behavior. (See **A CLOSER LOOK**, Ro.1:29-31 for the meaning of the terrible sins listed.)

> **"Be not deceived; God is not mocked: for whatsoever a man soweth, that shall he also reap. For he that soweth to his flesh shall of the flesh reap corruption; but he that soweth to the Spirit shall of the Spirit reap life everlasting" (Gal.6:7-8).**

**QUESTIONS:**
1. What is an example of a reprobate mind, a depraved mind? Why do rebellious men have this kind of mind?
2. How do you think God feels when men refuse to have anything to do with Him? Is God justified when He gives men up to reprobate minds? Why or why not?
3. Sinful men arrogantly cry out for freedom. Why is this desire to be free given to them by God?

# ROMANS 1:24-32

**A CLOSER LOOK:**
(1:29-31) **Sin--Sins:** for the next several pages, a list of terrible sins is given in chart form for a clear understanding. May God use this list to turn every believer closer to God and far away from the awful choices that break the heart of God.

| Biblical Term | Definition | Application/Explanation |
|---|---|---|
| (1:29) **Unrighteousness** | injustice, wrongdoing, evil-doing, every kind of evil. | ⇒ It is the opposite of righteousness; therefore, it is... <br>• mistreating God and man, acting unjustly toward both. <br>• failing to treat God and man as a person should treat them. <br><br>Note the words "<u>all</u> unrighteousness." It is being *filled* with unjust treatment. It is focusing on oneself to the point of making oneself the center of the universe... <br>• grasping after everything, all the attention and possessions one can secure. <br>• ignoring and abusing others to get all one can. |
| (1:29) **Fornication** | a broad word including all forms and kinds of immoral and sexual acts. | ⇒ It is pre-marital sex, adultery, and abnormal sex--all kinds of sexual vice. |
| (1:29) **Wickedness** | to be depraved, to be actively evil, to do mischief, to trouble others and cause harm, to be malicious, to be dangerous and destructive. | ⇒ It is malice, hatred, and ill-will. <br>⇒ It is an active wickedness, a desire within the heart to do harm and to corrupt people. <br>⇒ It is a person who actually pursues others to seduce or to injure them. |
| (1:29) **Covetousness** | a lust for more and more, an appetite for something, a love of possessing, a cry of "give, give" (2 Pt.2:14). | ⇒ It is a grasping, a craving for possessions, pleasure, power, and fame. Covetousness lacks restraint. <br>⇒ It lacks the ability to discriminate. <br>⇒ It wants to have in order to spend in pleasure and luxury. Covetousness is an insatiable |

| Biblical Term | Definition | Application/Explanation |
|---|---|---|
| (1:29) **Covetousness** (cont.) | | lust and craving of the flesh that cannot be satisfied.<br>⇒ It is a lust and craving so deep that a person finds his happiness in things and pleasure instead of God.<br>⇒ It is idolatry (Eph.5:5).<br>⇒ It is an intense appetite for gain, a passion for the pleasure that things can bring.<br>⇒ It is an active, aggressive, grasping covetousness. |
| (1:29) **Maliciousness** | malice, viciousness, ill-will, spite, hatred. | ⇒ It means that a man has turned his heart completely over to evil. He...<br>• no longer has any good within--none whatsoever.<br>• is full of viciousness and malice.<br>• is actively pursuing evil with a vengeance. |
| (1:29) **Envy** | jealousy, covetousness, ill will, rivalry. | ⇒ It is the spirit...<br>• that wants not only the things that another person has, but begrudges the fact that the person has them.<br>• that wants not only the things to be taken away from the person, but wants him to suffer through the loss of them.<br>Every thought expresses grief that another person has something, whether honor, recognition, or position. |
| (1:29) **Murder** | to kill, to take the life of another. | ⇒ This sin is committed either by a planned murderous attack upon a person(s) or by a rash, reckless, attack. Taking a life occurs |

| Biblical Term | Definition | Application/Explanation |
|---|---|---|
| (1:29) **Murder** (cont.) | | because a person is...<br>• angry or bitter<br>• violent or uncontrolled<br>• over-passionate<br>• selfish<br>• vengeful<br>• stealing<br>• lusting<br>• coveting<br>• rebelling |
| (1:29) **Debate** | strife, discord, contention, fighting, struggling, quarreling, dissension, wrangling. | ⇒ It means that a man fights against another person in order to get something: position, promotion, property, honor, recognition. He fights in a dishonest and evil way. |
| (1:29) **Deceit** | to bait, snare, mislead, beguile; to be crafty and deceitful; to mislead or to give a false impression by word, act, or influence. | ⇒ It is a man who connives and twists the truth to get his own way. He plots and deceives, doing whatever has to be done to get what he is after. |
| (1:29) **Malignity** | evil disposition, evil in nature. | ⇒ It is a spirit full of evil, malice, and injury; a character that is as evil as it can be. It is a person who always looks for the worst in other people, who always passes on the worst about them.<br>⇒ It is the person who so often ruins other people both in reputation and body, in mind and spirit.<br>⇒ It is a person so full of evil that he is always ruining others either by word or violence. |
| (1:29) **Whisperers** | secret gossipers, secret slanderers, backbiters, murmurers. | ⇒ It is a person...<br>• who whispers behind another person's back, chewing and tearing him up.<br>• who passes on tales about others, whether true or not.<br>• who destroys the reputation of others. |

| Biblical Term | Definition | Application/Explanation |
|---|---|---|
| (1:30) **Backbiters** | slanderers, liars, censurers. | ⇒ The word differs from the quiet, secret slanderer.<br>⇒ It is a loud, open slanderer, a person who broadcasts the tale.<br>⇒ Again, whether the tale is true or not does not matter. The backbiting slanderer burns within to tell the gossip to everyone. |
| (1:30) **Haters of God** | hating God and being hateful to God. | ⇒ It is a person...<br>• who dislikes the commandments and restraints of God.<br>• who wants nothing to do with God and His restrictions and laws.<br>• who wants the license to do exactly as he wishes.<br>• who wants to be the god of his own life, doing his own thing as he wishes, determining both what he should and should not do. |
| (1:30) **Despiteful** | insolent, insulting, spiteful, and defying. | ⇒ It is a spirit of spite, of attack and assault, verbally or physically.<br>⇒ It is despising and attacking, inflicting injury either by word or act.<br>⇒ It is a man who...<br>• lives his life as he wishes, ignoring both God and men.<br>• lives as though his rights and affairs are the only rights and affairs which matter.<br>• stands toe to toe with both God and men, acting as though he needs neither.<br>• acts so independent in life that he dares God or men to get in his way.<br>• does what he wants when he wants, even |

| Biblical Term | Definition | Application/Explanation |
|---|---|---|
| (1:30) **Despiteful** (cont.) | | if it hurts or destroys others.<br>The sin of despite, of being insolent and insulting, is the spirit that hurts and harms others in order to do what one wants. |
| (1:30) **Proud** | self-exaltation, conceit, arrogance; being haughty; putting oneself above others and looking down upon others; scorn, contempt. | ⇒ It means...<br>• to show oneself<br>• to lift one's head above another<br><br>• to hold contempt for another<br>• to compare oneself with others<br>⇒ Pride can be hidden in the heart as well as openly displayed. God resists the proud (Jas.4:6; 1 Pt.5:5; Pr.3:24). |
| (1:30) **Boasters**: | braggards, pretenders, vaunters, swaggerts, boasters. | ⇒ It is a person who...<br>• boasts in what he has.<br>• boasts in what he can do.<br>• pretends to have what he does not have or pretends to have done what he has not done.<br>Bragging may involve a job, a deal, a possession, an achievement--anything that may impress others.<br>⇒ It is a person who feels the need to push himself above others even if it involves *pretension, deception, make believe,* or *lies.* |
| (1:30) **Inventors of evil things** | inventors of new sins, of more sensational forms of excitement and vice. | ⇒ It is a person who is tired of the old forms of sin and who feels the need to seek out new ways and forms of vice. |
| (1:30) **Disobedient to parents** | refusing to do what one's parents say; rebelling against one's parents; showing disrespect to parents; rejecting parental instruction; dishonoring parental example. | ⇒ A child who disobeys his parents is wide open to all forms of evil. |

| Biblical Term | Definition | Application/Explanation |
|---|---|---|
| (1:31) **Without understanding** | senseless, foolish, without conscience. | ⇒ It is a person who...<br>• ignores experience.<br>• will not learn no matter who the teacher is.<br>• refuses to heed the truth.<br>• closes his mind and eyes to the truth.<br>• rejects conscience. |
| (1:31) **Covenantbreakers** | breakers of promises or agreements, untrustworthy, faithless, treacherous, untruthful. | ⇒ It is a man who tragically does not keep his word or promise. He is simply untrustworthy and undependable. |
| (1:31) **Without natural affection** | abnormal affection and love, heartless, without human emotion or love, a lack of feeling for others, abuse of normal affection and love. | ⇒ It is a person who uses people; others become little more than pawns for the man's own use and...<br>• benefit<br>• pleasure and purposes<br>• excitement and stimulation<br>⇒ Abnormal affection, sex and perversion prevail. |
| (1:31) **Implacable** | incapable of giving in, of being appeased or pacified, inflexible. | ⇒ A person is just unwilling to make peace or come to an agreement. |
| (1:31) **Unmerciful** | without pity; unwilling to show mercy. | It is a person...<br>• craving to have and to possess others regardless of their welfare.<br>• craving to use others as one wills regardless of hurt and shame.<br>• craving to satisfy one's own pleasure even if it means the hurt or death of others.<br>It is an absence of consideration or feelings for others. What matters is one's own pleasure and rights, not the pleasure and rights of others. |

**QUESTIONS:**
1. What practical steps can you take to protect yourself from sin's strong pull?
2. Why is sin so destructive?
3. What is your greatest resource in helping other people pull out of sin's enslavement?

## 5. GOD ASSURES FINAL JUDGMENT: DEATH (v.32).

There are two reasons why men will be judged and condemned to death.

1. Men will be judged because they sin and take pleasure in others who sin by doing the same things (v.29-31). Men have appetites, desires, and lusts; and they spend their lives seeking to fulfill them. The great tragedy is that they not only *take pleasure* in their own sins, but they *take pleasure* in the sins of others. They *approve and talk about* their selfishness and exploits and that of their friends. They focus their lives upon...

- extravagant living
- stylish dress
- wealth
- power
- position
- fame
- material possessions
- sexual affairs

As a result of such selfishness, the sins listed in the Scripture tear at the world and destroy human life (v.29-31); therefore, the judgment of God is assured. Those who commit such things and *take pleasure* in the sins of others shall die, that is, be separated from God eternally.

> **"Ye have wearied the LORD with your words. Yet ye say, Wherein have we wearied him? When ye say, Every one that doeth evil is good in the sight of the LORD, and he delighteth in them; or Where is the god of judgment?" (Mal.2:17).**

2. Men will be judged because they are without excuse: they know through an inner sense that the judgment of God is coming upon the world. Men sense that some higher power (God) is going to straighten out the mess in the world: that injustices and inequities will be brought to judgment, condemned, and punished.

> **"For the wages of sin is death; but the gift of God is eternal life through Jesus Christ our Lord" (Ro.6:23).**
> **"The soul that sinneth, it shall die" (Ezk.18:4).**

**ILLUSTRATION:**
There is no mistaking God's intent in dealing with unrepentant sin. He will judge it harshly and efficiently. Some would conclude that God is being too harsh on sinners. This story illustrates why God is not too harsh.

> *"A man with an axe was attacked by a vicious dog, and in defending himself had to kill the animal. The owner was furious and asked the man how he dared kill his dog. The man replied that if he had not killed it, the dog would have torn him to pieces. 'Well,' said the owner, 'why did you hit with the blade? Why didn't you just hit it with the handle?' 'I would have,' replied the man, 'if it had tried to bite me with its tail.'"[2]*

God knows that when a sinner bares his teeth, the only thing he will respond to is God's final judgment: death!

---

[2] Spiros Zodhiates, Th.D. *Illustrations of Bible Truths.* (Chattanooga, TN: AMG Publishers, 1995), p.234.

# ROMANS 1:24-32

**QUESTIONS:**
1. God's final judgment upon sin is death. Why is this necessary?
2. There is a saying that misery loves company. What kind of sick comfort can a sinner gain by pulling others down with him?
3. Why are men without excuse?

## SUMMARY:

Yes, God is love. But God is also a God of wrath. The terrible sin of men will always evoke a response of wrath from a holy and righteous God. This Scripture is both a warning and a comfort to the believer. If you believe, truly trust in Christ, you can take comfort in the fact that you are covered and protected by the blood of Christ, that you are saved from the wrath of God. But the warning should drive every believer to pray for the unrepentant sinner. Unless the sinner repents, turns away from his sin, he will be lost forever. He will face God's terrible wrath. How does God reveal and execute His wrath upon man?

1. God gives men up to do as they will.
2. God gives men up to uncleanness.
3. God gives men up to vile, unnatural affections.
4. God gives men up to reprobate, depraved minds.
5. God assures final judgment: death.

## PERSONAL JOURNAL NOTES
### (Reflection & Response)

1. The most important thing that I learned from this lesson was:

2. The area that I need to work on the most is:

3. I can apply this lesson to my life by:

4. Closing Statement of Commitment:

**CHAPTER 2**

**C. God's Case Against the Moralist: Judgment, 2:1-16**

1. **The moralist**
   a. He judges others
   b. He is inexcusable: He condemns himself because he is guilty of the same things

2. **The judgment of God is according to truth: Perfect justice**

   a. The moralist thinks he will escape

   b. The moralist thinks God is too good to punish

   c. The moralist thinks man is basically good

   d. The moralist hardens his heart against the judgment of God
      1) Refuses to repent
      2) Result: Stores up wrath against himself

3. **The judgment of God is according to deeds: Eternal reward or punishment**
   a. The well-doer's reward

   b. The evil-doer's

Therefore thou art inexcusable, O man, whosoever thou art that judgest: for wherein thou judgest another, thou condemnest thyself; for thou that judgest doest the same things.

2 But we are sure that the judgment of God is according to truth against them which commit such things.

3 And thinkest thou this, O man, that judgest them which do such things, and doest the same, that thou shalt escape the judgment of God?

4 Or despisest thou the riches of his goodness and forbearance and longsuffering; not knowing that the goodness of God leadeth thee to repentance?

5 But after thy hardness and impenitent heart treasurest up unto thyself wrath against the day of wrath and revelation of the righteous judgment of God;

6 Who will render to every man according to his deeds:

7 To them who by patient continuance in well doing seek for glory and honour and immortality, eternal life:

8 But unto them that are contentious, and do not obey the truth, but obey unrighteousness, indignation and wrath,

9 Tribulation and anguish, upon every soul of man that doeth evil, of the Jew first, and also of the Gentile;

10 But glory, honour, and peace, to every man that worketh good, to the Jew first, and also to the Gentile:

11 For there is no respect of persons with God.

12 For as many as have sinned without law shall also perish without law: and as many as have sinned in the law shall be judged by the law;

13 (For not the hearers of the law are just before God, but the doers of the law shall be justified.

14 For when the Gentiles, which have not the law, do by nature the things contained in the law, these, having not the law, are a law unto themselves:

15 Which show the work of the law written in their hearts, their conscience also bearing witness, and their thoughts the mean while accusing or else excusing one another;)

16 In the day when God shall judge the secrets of men by Jesus Christ according to my gospel.

severe judgment

c. Every evil-doer is to be judged

d. Every well-doer is to be rewarded

4. **The judgment of God is without respect of persons: Absolute impartiality**
   a. The man who sins without law & the man who sins in the law will both be judged

   b. The doers, not the hearers, of the law will be justified

   c. The heathen have a threefold witness
      1) Their nature: An instinctive knowledge of right & wrong

      2) Their conscience: Bears witness to what is right & wrong
      3) Their thoughts: Accuse or defend their behavior

5. **The judgment of God is to be executed by Jesus Christ & His gospel**

# ROMANS 2:1-16

## Section II

## SIN AND CONDEMNATION: THE WORLD'S
## NEED TO GET RIGHT WITH GOD
### Romans 1:18-3:20

**Study 3: God's Case Against the Moralist: Judgment**

**Text:** **Romans 2:1-16**

**Aim:** To expose the hypocrisy of the moralist: being *as good as you can* is not good enough.

**Memory Verse:**
> "Brethren, if a man be overtaken in a fault, ye which are spiritual, restore such an one in the spirit of meekness; considering thyself, lest thou also be tempted. Bear ye one another's burdens, and so fulfil the law of Christ" (Gal.6:1-2).

## INTRODUCTION:
Years ago, a phrase was coined that attempted to discourage people from drug abuse: *Just Say No!* This campaign was an attempt to help people look elsewhere when they were tempted...
- to escape from reality
- to feel good
- to experiment with their minds
- to go along with the crowd
- to project an image of themselves that was not true
- to push a personal life-style agenda

Did people stop abusing narcotics just because someone on television said "*Just Say No!*"? Perhaps the campaign helped some. But history notes that drug abuse continues to be a curse on people.

Unknowing to many, there have been a lot of people who have said no to drugs. These people are good people from all outside appearances. They obey the laws. They are the ones who write letters to the editor of the local paper, taking issue with the lack of morality in the community. They have the perfect family, the perfect résumé, the perfect reputation--and yet, they are addicted to a habit-forming narcotic. What is this narcotic? It is self-righteousness--the belief that they are good enough within themselves, good enough for God to accept them; the belief that God will accept them because of their own righteousness; the belief that God would never reject them, they are just too good, never bad enough for God to reject them.

This is one of the passages that covers several subjects and can be studied from the viewpoint of any one of them. It is an excellent study on judging, criticizing others, the judgment of God, self-righteousness, the moralist, and the legalist. It also deals with the judgment of the heathen, and answers the question so often asked: "What will happen to the heathen, to the person who never hears about Jesus Christ?" (v.11-15). The present study is entitled: "God's Case Against the Moralist."

# ROMANS 2:1-16

**OUTLINE:**
1. The moralist (v.1).
2. The judgment of God is according to truth: perfect justice (v.2-5).
3. The judgment of God is according to deeds: eternal reward or punishment (v.6-10).
4. The judgment of God is without respect of persons: absolute impartiality (v.11-15).
5. The judgment of God is to be executed by Jesus Christ and His gospel (v.16).

## 1. THE MORALIST (v.1).

In the eyes of Scripture, a moralist is a person who lives a moral and clean life, but he judges others because they do not live as *he thinks* they should. He is moral, upright, just, good, decent, and honorable. The moralist has strong values, standards, and principles. He is well disciplined and able to control his life. He lives just as everyone thinks he should. He knows right from wrong and he lives it. He knows how to behave and he does it. In the eyes of society he is just what a person should be. He is a good neighbor, an excellent worker and provider, and an ideal citizen. But note three things.

1. The moralist judges others. The word *judge* means to criticize, to find fault, to condemn. This is the terrible flaw of the moralist. Note: any person becomes a moralist when he sets himself up as a judge of others. Any time we judge another person, we are declaring that we...

- are living by some rule that another person is not living by
- are more moral than someone else
- are better than someone else
- are superior to someone else
- are more righteous than someone else
- are more acceptable to God than someone else

Judging others says, "I am right, and he is not; I succeed, but he fails." Therefore...
- "Look at me, but ignore him."
- "Draw near to me, but shun him."
- "Esteem me, but put him down."
- "Approve me, but condemn him."
- "Be my friend, but withdraw from him."

Very simply, judging others raises self and lowers others, exalts self and debases others; and in the eyes of God this is wrong. It is sin. It is being full of self-righteousness, pride, and arrogance. It sets self up as a moralist, and it makes a person judgmental and critical.

> **"Judge not, that ye be not judged" (Mt.7:1).**
>
> **"Who art thou that judgest another man's servant? to his own master he standeth or falleth. Yea, he shall be holden up: for God is able to make him stand" (Ro.14:4).**

**ILLUSTRATION:**

The truth be known, there is probably a little bit of moralist in all of us. The nature of man is to put someone else down when the opportunity presents itself. The moralist is too quick to judge before finding out all the facts.

> *"Several years ago a young man dressed in overalls and workshoes entered an auto dealer's showroom in Bodo, Norway, and inquired, 'Have you got 16 cars on hand--all the same model?' The proprietor, noticing the rather unkempt look of the stranger and concluding that he was poor, said gruffly, 'I've no time*

*for jokes, Mister! Buzz off!' Turning on his heel, the man went directly across the street to a competitor in the same business. When he received considerate treatment there, he agreed to purchase an entire fleet of automobiles for $47,000! Later it was discovered that the crudely dressed individual was one of the 16-man crew from a Norwegian fishing vessel. Having caught a record quantity of herring that season, the sailors had decided to buy new cars; so they sent him as their representative to secure the largest possible discount by getting all of their vehicles from the same place. One can well imagine the dismay of the first salesman who lost the biggest order of the year because he miscalculated a potential customer on the basis of a critical first-glance appraisal."[1]*

Have you ever lost out on something--a friendship, a personal relationship, a business opportunity, a compliment--because you were too quick to judge someone else, to give someone a fair chance?

2.    The moralist is inexcusable, and he condemns himself because he does the very same things. He fails just as the man whom he judges fails. Scripture says...

**"[All] temptation is <u>common</u> to man" (1 Cor.10:13).**

In God's eyes, sin is a matter of the heart and mind, not just an act. The thought and desire makes a person just as guilty as the act itself. God knows that many would carry out their thoughts *if they had the courage or opportunity*. God knows the heart, the mind, and the thoughts. Sin, whether thoughts in the mind or acts in public, comes short of God's glory. All stand guilty before God; therefore, the moralist, the person who judges, is as guilty as the one judged. It is for this reason that we are not to judge, criticize, or find fault with others.

**"And why beholdest thou the mote that is in thy brother's eye,**
**but considerest not the beam that is in thine own eye?" (Mt.7:3).**

## APPLICATION:
This point does not mean that judicial systems of the state are wrong nor that discipline is not to be exercised within families, organizations, and the church. Scripture teaches that both justice and discipline are to be exercised by men. What Scripture means is this: we are not to go around criticizing and finding fault with each other and putting each other down when one of us fails. Instead we are to reach out, trying to redeem and help each other. Imagine what a different world this would be if all tongues were stopped! If all criticism and fault-finding ceased! If everyone actually reached out and tried to redeem and save those who failed!

**"Brethren, if a man be overtaken in a fault, ye which are spiri-**
**tual, restore such an one in the spirit of meekness; considering thy-**
**self, lest thou also be tempted. Bear ye one another's burdens, and**
**so fulfil the law of Christ" (Gal.6:1-2).**

## QUESTIONS:
1. What are some typical traits of a moralist?
2. How does spiritual pride relate to a moralist?
3. Why is God more concerned about what is inside the heart of men? Why do men tend to make judgments only on what is seen?

---

[1]    *INFOsearch Sermon Illustrations* (Arlington, TX: The Computer Assistant, 1-888-868-9029, 1986-1996).

## 2. THE JUDGMENT OF GOD IS ACCORDING TO TRUTH: PERFECT JUSTICE (v.2-5).

God's judgment will be executed in perfect justice. The word *truth* means true as opposed to false. It means what really is; what actually exists; what exactly takes place. God's judgment is *perfectly* just, exactly what it should be, nothing more and nothing less. His judgment is based upon...

- what really happens
- what the facts are
- what actually takes place
- what a person really is within his heart and what the person actually did

> **"The Lord seeth not as man seeth; for man looketh on the outward appearance, but the LORD looketh on the heart" (1 Sam. 16:7).**

God knows the truth, the whole truth and nothing but the truth; therefore, He will judge according to truth. His judgment will be perfect, conforming exactly to our deeds. It will match our deeds perfectly.

Note four points.
1. The moralist thinks he will escape. His offense is much greater, for he is like all other men--sinful and short of God's glory--yet he criticizes and judges those whose failures are discovered and exposed, and he thinks he will escape. He forgets that God sees the *inner recesses* of the human heart, and that God will judge men not only for their deeds but for their thoughts...

- for the lust of the flesh
- for the lust of the eyes
- for the pride of life (1 Jn.2:15-16)

> **"Ye serpents, ye generation of vipers, how can ye escape the damnation of hell?" (Mt.23:33).**
> **"How shall we escape, if we neglect so great salvation; which at the first began to be spoken by the Lord, and was confirmed unto us by them that heard him" (Heb.2:3).**

2. The moralist thinks God is too good to punish. When he thinks of God, he thinks of the riches of...

- God's goodness: His kindness and grace and love
- God's forbearance: His refraining, holding back, abstaining and controlling His justice
- God's longsuffering: His suffering a long time, being patient and slow in judging sin

God, of course, is all this and much more. But what the moralist fails to see is that God's goodness...

- is not a blank check for sin
- does not give license to sin
- does not condone sin
- does not indulge sin
- does not overlook sin

God's goodness is to lead men to repentance, not to sin. The fact that God *will* forgive sin should stir men to seek forgiveness and to please God. If a man goes out and sins, thinking that God will just overlook and forgive his sin, he is despising God's goodness. He is taking God's goodness and making it a sham, a mockery, a joke, a thing of indulgence. The man who *despises* God's goodness--who sins thinking God will just overlook and forgive his sin--is wrong. He is mistaken. God does not just overlook and forgive his sin; He does not condone, indulge, nor give license to his sin. God will judge him and the judgment will be according to the truth.

> **"Know ye not that the unrighteous shall not inherit the kingdom of God? Be not deceived: neither fornicators, nor idolaters, nor adulterers, nor effeminate, nor abusers of themselves with mankind, nor thieves, nor covetous, nor drunkards, nor revilers, nor extortioners, shall inherit the kingdom of God. And such were some of you: but ye are washed, but ye are sanctified, but ye are justified in the name of the Lord Jesus, and by the Spirit of our God" (1 Cor. 6:9-11).**

3.    The moralist thinks man is basically good. He thinks that man can be good enough for God to accept. He thinks God looks for the good in man and that within each man is *enough good* for God to accept. The moralist thinks that God's goodness accepts man's...

- good works
- good thoughts
- good behavior
- good feelings
- good nature
- good tendencies

God, of course, is pleased with whatever good is in man. But what the moralist fails to see is that *God's goodness is perfect*. It cannot accept...

- any imperfect work
- any foul thoughts
- any evil behavior
- any ugly feelings
- any corruptible nature
- any sinful urges

God can only accept perfection. No man is perfect: not in nature, thought, or behavior. Therefore, all men are unacceptable to God. No man is good enough to be acceptable to God, no matter how good he is. The goodness of God is to lead men to repentance: to turn men to God for righteousness, *not to declare man's self-righteousness*. The fact that God allows men to repent should stir men...

- to confess their imperfection and self-righteousness
- to seek God's righteousness which is in Christ Jesus the Lord

### APPLICATION:

Most people think that God will accept them, that in the final analysis they are good enough for God to accept them. They never dream that God will reject them, not when everything is said and done. What they fail to see is that God's judgment is based upon truth--the truth of what a person's thoughts and motives are, of what is really within a person's mind and heart. God's judgment is based upon the truth of a person's *imperfect nature and behavior*.

> **"When they knew God, they glorified him not as God, neither were thankful; but became vain in their imaginations, and their foolish heart was darkened. Professing themselves to be wise, they became fools" (Ro.1:21-22).**

4.    The moralist hardens his heart against the judgment of God. He refuses to repent. He just cannot accept the fact...
- that he is not good enough for God to accept
- that God's goodness and love would ever condemn him

But note the term *righteous judgment*, which means just, fair, impartial, correct, exact. God's judgment is a judgment that should be, that should and will take place. In fact, God must judge, for God is love. As love, He must straighten out all the injustices on earth. He must right the wrongs and correct all the injustices of men. He must judge men with a perfect and "righteous judgment."

Note also the term *treasurest up*, which means to store up, to heap up, to lay up. The man who hardens his heart and refuses to repent stores up more and more wrath against himself in the day of judgment. The fact is clearly seen. Just think how terrible it is for a man to rebel against God's goodness. He has the glorious privilege of knowing God's goodness, of hearing His goodness proclaimed day by day, week by week, month by month, and year by year. Yet he despises God's goodness, refusing to repent and rejecting God's goodness time and time again. His rejection is bound to store up wrath against himself. His judgment is bound to be greater than the judgment upon a person who has *never* had the privilege of hearing about the goodness of God.

> **"He that believeth on the Son hath everlasting life: and he that believeth not the Son shall not see life; but the wrath of God abideth on him" (Jn.3:36).**

**QUESTIONS:**
1. Only God knows the absolute truth about the innermost thoughts and desires of your heart. God's judgment is always perfectly just: Are you satisfied that your heart is as pure and righteous as it can be?
2. The moralist says that man is basically good. Why is this a false concept?
3. Why is just being *as good as you can be* not the basis for eternal life? How good do you have to be in order to go to heaven on your own merit?

## 3. THE JUDGMENT OF GOD IS ACCORDING TO DEEDS: ETERNAL REWARD OR PUNISHMENT (v.6-10).

Everyone will either be eternally rewarded or eternally punished. No one shall be exempt; no one will escape.

Now note: judgment is to be based upon a man's *deeds* or works. This does not mean that *faith* is not necessary. Contrariwise, there is no such thing as...
- faith without works
- righteous and acceptable works without faith

God's works--the works that are truly of and for God, that truly please God--are the result of faith. Men believe in and serve and work for many different things in the world. Some believe and work...

- for religion
- for service organizations
- for social clubs
- for humanity

What God demands is that men first believe and work for Him, reaching out to a world lost and gripped in desperate need. When a man truly believes God, he works for God. God is going to either reward or punish every man according to his works, according to what he has done *with and for God.*

# ROMANS 2:1-16

**"Even so faith, if it hath not works, is dead, being alone. Yea, a man may say, Thou hast faith, and I have works: show me thy faith without thy works, and I will show thee my faith by my works. Thou believest that there is one God; thou doest well: the devils also believe, and tremble. But wilt thou know, O vain man, that faith without works is dead?" (Jas.2:17-20).**

1. There shall be the well-doer's wonderful reward. Note three things about the well-doer.
   a. Note what he seeks for: glory, honor, and immortality (see **A CLOSER LOOK**: on each subject--Ro.2:7).
   b. Note how the well-doer seeks: *by patient continuance*. The word means to be stedfast and constant; to endure, persevere, stick to, and continue. The well-doer is faithful in doing good works.
      ⇒ He does not just start, he finishes.
      ⇒ He does not live an inconsistent, up and down life. He continues and keeps on doing good deeds.
      ⇒ He does not give in to hardships, difficulties, or opposition. He endures and perseveres, always doing good.

   **"And let us not be weary in well doing: for in due season we shall reap, if we faint not" (Gal.6:9).**

   c. Note the wonderful reward of the well-doer: eternal life. Eternal life is said to be the inheritance of a world of glory, honor, and peace (v.10; cp. Ro.4:13).
2. There shall be the evil-doer's terrible and severe judgment. The evil-doer is to be judged for three reasons.
   a. He is contentious against God (see **A CLOSER LOOK**--Ro.2:8). The evil-doer does not like what God says; therefore, he strives against it. He wrangles and wrestles, struggles and fights against God. He refuses to buckle under and surrender to God's will. When dealing with God, the evil-doer is contentious.
   b. He does not obey the truth. He sees and hears and knows the truth. He even knows the truth is to be done, but he refuses to do it. He refuses to be persuaded and refuses to believe. He rejects both Christ, the Living Truth, and the Word of God, the written truth. He simply goes about his own life, running and controlling it as he wills. He rejects and refuses to believe and to do the truth.
   c. He does unrighteousness (see **A CLOSER LOOK**--Ro.2:8 for discussion).
3. Every evil-doer is to be judged, both Jew and Gentile. No evil-doer shall escape. "Every soul of man that doeth evil" shall suffer, and the judgment will be severe and terrible. His judgment will involve indignation and wrath, tribulation and anguish (see **A CLOSER LOOK**--Ro.2:8; **A CLOSER LOOK**--Ro.2:9 for discussion).

   **"And these shall go away into everlasting punishment: but the righteous into life eternal" (Mt.25:46).**

4. Every well-doer is to be rewarded, both Jew and Gentile. No well-doer shall be exempt or overlooked. "Every man that worketh good" shall receive...
   - immortality (v.7)
   - eternal life (v.7)
   - glory (v.7, 10)
   - honor (v.7, 10)
   - peace (v.10)

# ROMANS 2:1-16

**QUESTIONS:**
1. What can you do to guarantee an eternal reward for yourself?
2. God demands that men believe and then work for Him. What diversions distract men from working for God?
3. What causes God to judge the evil-doer? Are there areas of your life that need improvement?
4. What has God promised to do for the well-doer?

**A CLOSER LOOK:**
(2:7) **Reward-Rewards**: the following terms describe the blessings that God has promise to those who are well-doers.

| Biblical Term | Definition | Scriptural Application |
|---|---|---|
| (2:7) **Glory** | It means to possess and to be full of perfect light; to dwell in perfect light, brilliance, splendor, brightness, luster, and magnificence with God. | "Then shall the righteous shine forth as the sun in the kingdom of their Father. Who hath ears to hear, let him hear" (Mt.13:43). <br><br>"And if children, then heirs; heirs of God, and joint heirs with Christ; if so be that we suffer with him, that we may be also glorified together" (Ro. 8:17). |
| (2:7) **Honor** | ⇒ It means to be acknowledged, recognized, approved, accepted, esteemed, and exalted by God. <br> ⇒ It means to be privileged and exalted to a position of responsibility and service for God. | "And he said unto him, Well, thou good servant: because thou hast been faithful in a very little, have thou authority over ten cities" (Lk.19:17). <br><br>"If any man serve me, let him follow me; and where I am, there shall also my servant be: if any man serve me, him will my Father honour" (Jn.12:26). |
| (2:7) **Immortality** | ⇒ It means living forever with God; to be incorruptible, perfected, and made permanent and eternal. <br> ⇒ It means to be free from pain and tears, from being tired and weary, from trials and sin, from defilement, weakness, frailty, sickness, suffering, and death. | "For we know that, if our earthly house of this tabernacle were dissolved, we have a building of God, a house not made with hands, eternal in the heavens" (2 Cor.5:1). <br><br>"And God shall wipe away all tears from their eyes; and there shall be no more death, neither sorrow, nor crying, neither |

| (2:7) **Immortality** (cont.) | It means to be free from an imperfect world and to be placed into a perfect world with God—a world that lasts forever and ever. | shall there be any more pain: for the former things are passed away" (Rev.21:4). |

---

**A CLOSER LOOK:**
(2:8) **Judgment; Punishment**: the following terms describe the rebellious traits of the evil doer.

| Biblical Term | Definition | Scriptural Application |
|---|---|---|
| (2:8) **Stubborn—Contentious** | It means to strive, struggle, fight, quarrel, wrangle, argue, debate; to be divisive, factious, contentious, argumentative, and belligerent. | "And might not be as their fathers, a stubborn and rebellious generation; a generation that set not their heart aright, and whose spirit was not stedfast with God" (Ps.78:8). "If ye will not hear, and if ye will not lay it to heart, to give glory unto my name, saith the LORD of hosts, I will even send a curse upon you, and I will curse your blessings: yea, I have cursed them already, because ye do not lay it to heart" (Mal.2:2). |
| (2:8) **Unrighteousness** | It means wickedness, iniquity, injustice, wrong-doing, sin, evil, lawlessness, a violation of law. | "Be ye not unequally yoked together with unbelievers: for what fellowship hath righteousness with unrighteousness? and what communion hath light with darkness?" (2 Cor.6:14). "That they all might be damned who believed not the truth, but had pleasure in unrighteousness" (2 Thes.2:12). "If we confess our sins, he is faithful and just to forgive us *our* sins, and to cleanse us from all unrighteousness" (1 Jn.1:9). |

**A CLOSER LOOK:**
(2:8-9) **Judgment; Punishment**: the following terms describe the awful judgment that Go
promises to pour out on the evil-doer.

| Biblical Term | Definition | Scriptural Application |
|---|---|---|
| (2:8) **Indignation** | It means anger, fury, rage, wrath. It is God's anger against sin. | "Behold, the name of the LORD cometh from far, burning *with* his anger, and the burden *thereof is* heavy: his lips are full of indignation, and his tongue as a devouring fire" (Is.30:27). |
| (2:8) **Wrath** | It means fury, indignation, vengeance. It is God's wrath against sin. *Thumos* is an anger that is felt more deeply than the *orge* anger of God; therefore, it arises more quickly. *Thumos* anger is the anger that arises out of deep hurt; therefore, it bursts forth with terrifying judgment. | "Let no man deceive you with vain words: for because of these things cometh the wrath of God upon the children of disobedience" (Eph.5:6). |
| (2:9) **Tribulation** | It means distress, oppression, suffering, affliction, pressure; it means being pressed, put in some strait. | "And I will bring distress upon men, that they shall walk like blind men, because they have sinned against the LORD: and their blood shall be poured out as dust, and their flesh as the dung" (Zeph.1:17). |
| (2:9) **Anguish** | It means to be put into a narrow place; to be compressed together; to experience extreme pain, sorrow, distress, affliction, and calamity. | "Why criest thou for thine affliction? thy sorrow *is* incurable for the multitude of thine iniquity: *because* thy sins were increased, I have done these things unto thee" (Jer.30:15). |

**QUESTIONS:**
1. What things prevent you from glorifying God?
2. Think about all the people you know: Who most honors God with his or her service? What traits does he possess that would improve your testimony as a believer?
3. Why do certain men constantly strive against God? What can they possibly gain from opposing God's sovereign will?
4. God's judgment is severe for those who stand against Him. What has God promised to do to these people?

#### 4. THE JUDGMENT OF GOD IS WITHOUT RESPECT OF PERSONS: ABSOLUTE IMPARTIALITY (v.11-15).

God's judgment will be executed with absolute impartiality, showing no favoritism whatsoever. God does not favor the...

- moralist
- religionist
- educated
- wealthy
- benevolent
- famous
- outstanding
- honorable

All men stand on an equal footing before God's judgment. *God loves and cares for all.* Therefore, in the great day of judgment, all will be judged by the same rule and by the same principle.

1. The man who sins without the law and the man who sins in the law will both be judged. Again, sin is the basis of judgment. Men will be judged *for sin*.

    a. The man who sins *without law* will also perish without law. The word for law is a general word. It refers to the law of God in both the Scriptures and nature. Therefore, the man who does not have the law of Scripture *does have* the law of nature to guide him. If he sins against the law of nature, he will still be judged and perish. He had the opportunity to know through nature itself (see outline and notes--Ro.1:19; 1:20 for more discussion).

    b. The man who sins *in the law* will be judged by the law. His judgment, of course, will be greater, for he had every privilege and opportunity imaginable.

> **"For there is no difference between the Jew and the Greek: for the same Lord over all is rich unto all that call upon him" (Ro.10:12).**

2. The doers and not the hearers of the law will be justified. It is not enough just to have the law or the Word of God; it is not enough...

- to hear and see it
- to understand and know it
- to possess and profess it
- to proclaim and teach it

A person must be a doer of the law; he must obey and live the law. The law was not given just to sit on a bookshelf or on a table, not given just to be heard and to secure verbal agreement. The law was given to be obeyed and lived out, to govern and control life so that life could be lived to the fullest. Therefore, those who only hear the law will not be justified before God, but the doers of the law will be justified.

> **"Not every one that saith unto me, Lord, Lord, shall enter into the kingdom of heaven; but he that doeth the will of my Father which is in heaven" (Mt.7:21).**

3. The heathen have a threefold witness, a witness that is strong enough to lead them to God.

    a. Men have their nature--the nature of man that speaks loudly and clearly--that points toward God. Note exactly what the verse says.

    ⇒ Men may not have the law (the Scriptures)...
    ⇒ But they can do the law *by nature*.
    ⇒ They can become "a law unto themselves."

There is that within man, within his nature, that can stir him to do the law. Man has within him an instinctive knowledge of right and wrong. His very nature gives him the opportunity to do what is right.

Something else is meant here as well. Man can look at nature (creation) and see that he is part of it. He can instinctively see by nature the great eternal power and deity of God. (See note--Ro.1:20 for a list of the things nature reveals about God.)

> **"For the invisible things of him from the creation of the world are clearly seen, being understood by the things that are made, even his eternal power and Godhead; so that they are without excuse" (Ro.1:20).**

b. Men have their consciences that bear witness to what is right and wrong. When they do right, they sense approval; when they do wrong, they sense reproach. Man's conscience gives him the opportunity to live righteously and to do good.

> **"How much more shall the blood of Christ, who through the eternal Spirit offered himself without spot to God, purge your conscience from dead works to serve the living God?" (Heb.9:14).**

c. Men have their thoughts, their reasoning ability which can approve or disapprove, excuse or accuse them and others. Men's thoughts bear witness to how they should and should not live, whether their behavior is excused (acceptable) or accused (condemned). Now note two critical points.

First, men can learn a great deal about God and about right and wrong through their nature, conscience, and thoughts. Men can look at themselves and creation and learn that they are to live...

- by order and law and rules
- in obedience and respect and peace
- giving recognition and honor and esteem
- being clean and pure and moral
- showing care and concern and love
- without stealing and lying and cheating

Second, men cannot be saved apart from Jesus Christ. No matter how morally they may live--whether they live by law or by nature--they do not live a sinless and perfect life. They sin and come short of God's glory. Therefore, no matter how morally men live, they have to be *perfected* by the "righteousness of God" which is in Christ Jesus Himself.

> **"Jesus saith unto him, I am the way, the truth, and the life: no man cometh unto the Father, but by me" (Jn.14:6).**

**QUESTIONS:**
1. God does not play favorites when He pours out His judgment. Why do some people feel God will judge them using a different set of rules?
2. What is the basis of God's judgment?
3. Do you think a man who has never heard the law is accountable for his sin? Why or why not?
4. What kinds of things has God put in the heart of the heathen that can lead them to God? Why do some of them reject these things? Whose fault is it--the heathen's or God's? Why?

**5. THE JUDGMENT OF GOD IS TO BE EXECUTED BY JESUS CHRIST AND HIS GOSPEL (v.16).**

Note these facts.

1.    A specific day of judgment is coming. It is fixed.

> **"When the son of man shall come in his glory, and all the holy angels with him, then shall he sit upon the throne of his glory: and before him shall be gathered all nations: and he shall separate them one from another, as a shepherd divideth his sheep from the goats"** (Mt.25:31-32).
>
> **"And as it is appointed unto men once to die, but after this the judgment"** (Heb.9:27).

2.    In that day "the secrets of men" will be judged. All secrets will be exposed, the secret thoughts and deeds done...

- in the dark
- behind closed doors
- off to the side
- silently
- alone
- quietly

> **"Therefore judge nothing before the time, until the Lord come, who both will bring to light the hidden things of darkness, and will make manifest the counsels of the hearts: and then shall every man have praise of God"** (1 Cor.4:5).

3.    Jesus Christ is the One who will do the judging. He is the One who...

- has earned the right to judge by obeying God perfectly. He is the One who has lived a sinless life and died for men.
- has experienced life on earth in the flesh and can understand and sympathize with men in their infirmities (Heb.2:15-18; 4:15-16).

> **"For the Father judgeth no man, but hath committed all judgment unto the Son"** (Jn.5:22).

4.    The standard or rule by which men shall be judged is the gospel.

> **"He that loveth me not keepeth not my sayings: and the word which ye hear is not mine, but the Father's which sent me"** (Jn.14:24).

**ILLUSTRATION:**

You can count on it: Jesus Christ--the One who came as a Lamb--is going to judge the world like the Lion of Judah. He is going to judge the rich and the poor, the educated and the uneducated, the good and the bad. The challenge for you is clear: Resist the temptation to substitute good works for a personal relationship with Christ.

> *"Ben Putnitoff was a member of the Lord's church. Morally, he was a good man. He did not lie, curse, drink, beat his wife, or smoke. He paid his income tax, came to Bible class and worship services, paid his bills and gave a 'few bucks' to the Lord. He was never opposed to anything that was good.*
>
> *"One day old Ben Putnitoff died and stood before the Righteous Judge. The Judge said, 'Ben, you are charged with trying to close the church. Are you guilty or not guilty?'*
>
> *"'Not guilty,' pleaded Ben Putnitoff. 'I didn't do a thing!'*

*"'Guilty as charged,' the Judge ruled. And then He continued, 'Ben, you have confessed to the most effective way ever devised of closing the church. You "did not do a thing." You did not visit the sick. You did not encourage the weak. You did not feed the hungry. You did not reach out to the lost with the gospel.'*

*"'But, Judge,' Ben pleaded, 'I intended to do all of those things, but I was too busy making a living and enjoying myself. I have just been putting it off.'"*[2]

There is one thing that you should not put off: taking care of your place in eternity. The day of judgment *is* coming. What will be your fate before the Righteous Judge?

## QUESTIONS:

1. The day of judgment is coming. It is fixed. Knowing this, how should this make you pray for the lost?
2. What will be like to see your secrets exposed, secrets that you thought no one would ever know about?
3. The basis for judgment is the gospel. Are you doing all you can to be obedient to the gospel?

## SUMMARY:

Being *as good as you can* is not good enough, not if you want to spend eternity with God. A moralist specializes in being good, but to no avail. The truth of this passage is striking and clear: God will judge the moralist just like He will judge the man who has lived the most evil life imaginable. God has a case against the moralist:

1.   The moralist.
    a.  Judges others
    b.  Is inexcusable: he condemns himself because he is guilty of the same things
2.   The judgment of God is according to truth: perfect justice.
3.   The judgment of God is according to deeds: eternal reward or punishment.
4.   The judgment of God is without respect of persons: absolute impartiality.
5.   The judgment of God is to be executed by Jesus Christ and His gospel.

## PERSONAL JOURNAL NOTES
### (Reflection & Response)

1. The most important thing that I learned from this lesson was:


2. The area that I need to work on the most is:


3. I can apply this lesson to my life by:


4. Closing Statement of Commitment:

---

[2]   Ted Kyle & John Todd. *A Treasury of Bible Illustrations*, p.223.

**D. God's Case Against the Religionist (Jew), 2:17-29**

**1. The religionist professes religion**
a. Rests in the Word
b. Professes God

c. Knows God's will
d. Approves better things
e. Is taught God's law

f. Is sure he is a guide of the blind
g. Is sure he is a light to those in darkness
h. Is sure he is an instructor of the foolish
i. Is sure he is a teacher of the immature
j. Has the law, the embodiment of truth

**2. The religionist fails to live what he professes**
a. The fact: His life does not match what he says

17 Behold, thou art called a Jew, and restest in the law, and makest thy boast of God,
18 And knowest his will, and approvest the things that are more excellent, being instructed out of the law;
19 And art confident that thou thyself art a guide of the blind, a light of them which are in darkness,
20 An instructor of the foolish, a teacher of babes, which hast the form of knowledge and of the truth in the law.
21 Thou therefore which teachest another, teachest thou not thyself? thou that preachest a man should not steal, dost thou steal?
22 Thou that sayest a man should not commit adultery, dost thou commit adultery? thou that abhorrest idols, dost thou commit sacrilege?
23 Thou that makest thy boast of the law, through breaking the law dishonourest thou God?
24 For the name of God is blasphemed among the Gentiles through you, as it is written.
25 For circumcision verily profiteth, if thou keep the law: but if thou be a breaker of the law, thy circumcision is made uncircumcision.
26 Therefore if the uncircumcision keep the righteousness of the law, shall not his uncircumcision be counted for circumcision?
27 And shall not uncircumcision which is by nature, if it fulfil the law, judge thee, who by the letter and circumcision dost transgress the law?
28 For he is not a Jew, which is one outwardly; neither is that circumcision, which is outward in the flesh:
29 But he is a Jew, which is one inwardly; and circumcision is that of the heart, in the spirit, and not in the letter; whose praise is not of men, but of God.

b. Result: His hypocrisy causes others to abuse God's name

**3. The religionist believes that a ritual (circumcision) is the way to secure God's approval**
a. But circ. counts only if a man keeps the law
b. The uncircumcised man who keeps the law is counted as circumcised (ritually accepted)

c. The uncircumcised man who keeps the law shall judge the religionist who breaks the law

**4. The religionist misses the point: A true religionist is a man who is righteous inwardly**
a. Not an outward thing
b. An inward thing—of the heart, in the spirit
c. Its praise is not of men (not physical, of the flesh) but of God

---

**Section II**

**SIN AND CONDEMNATION: THE WORLD'S NEED TO GET RIGHT WITH GOD**
**Romans 1:18-3:20**

**Study 4: God's Case Against the Religionist (Jew)**

**Text: Romans 2:17-29**

# ROMANS 2:17-29

**Aim:** To recognize and avoid the shallow faith of a religionist.

**Memory Verse:**
> "But he *is* a Jew, which is one inwardly; and circumcision *is that* of the heart, in the spirit, *and* not in the letter; whose praise *is* not of men, but of God" (Ro.2:29).

## INTRODUCTION:
How *genuine* is your faith? It has become very fashionable in some circles to appear spiritual. But modern man is looking for significance in all the wrong places, probing and then adopting a false religion, a false spirituality. In an effort to fool others, himself, and even God, this man has embraced a cheap imitation of the real thing.

> "For many centuries genuine pearls commanded a high price because of their scarcity. Great quantities of oysters had to be examined before a few could be found that contained the coveted treasures. Then suddenly the market became flooded with them. After some investigation the mystery of the abundant supply was revealed. Enterprising individuals had discovered that if a foreign object is lodged in its tender flesh, the oyster will form a glistening pearl around the source of discomfort. Deciding to help nature along, these men artificially induced the process by inserting irritants such as tiny beads and buckshot into the shells. When the pearls had formed, they were carefully harvested. Wealthy patrons became suspicious, however, and insisted that the lustrous jewels be subjected to special tests. Though outwardly they seemed perfect, the x-ray showed their impurity, for they had 'false hearts' of lead or glass."[1]

This is the condition of the religionist:
- ⇒ He is impure.
- ⇒ false heart.
- ⇒ He does not have a genuine faith in God.

This passage is an excellent study of the Christian religionist or church member as well as of the Jew. God's case against the Christian religionist includes four points.

## OUTLINE:
1. The religionist professes religion (v.17-20).
2. The religionist fails to live what he professes (v.21-24).
3. The religionist believes that a ritual (circumcision) is the way to secure God's approval (v.25-27).
4. The religionist misses the whole point: a true religionist is a man who is righteous inwardly (v.28-29).

---

### A CLOSER LOOK:

(2:17-29) **Religionists**: a religionist is a person who is interested in religion and professes religion. It was because of the Jews' extreme interest in religion that they were looked upon as the epitome of religionists. However, most people are considered religious and profess some religion regardless of nationality. Therefore, most people can be called religionists. There are two classes of religionists.

---

[1] *INFOsearch Sermon Illustrations* (Arlington, TX: The Computer Assistant, 1-888-868-9029, 1986-1996).

1. There are those who feel they are *good enough* for God as they are, that they are doing enough good for God to accept them. They cannot believe that God would reject them when they stand face to face with Him. True, they do wrong; but not that much wrong, they feel, not enough for God to reject and condemn them for eternity. These persons go about living as they wish, worshipping God only enough to satisfy their consciences. The vast, vast majority of people are in this class of self-righteousness. Few men believe they will be rejected by God and refused entrance into heaven. They feel they have *enough goodness* to make them acceptable to God.

> **"Not by works of righteousness which we have done, but according to his mercy he saved us, by the washing of regeneration, and renewing of the Holy Ghost" (Tit.3:5).**

2. There are those who have a sensitive conscience and feel the need to give themselves to *good works* as much as is humanly possible. They work and do good in order to secure the favor of God. They believe that good works is what it takes to make them righteous and to build them up in the eyes of God. Therefore, they labor all their lives trying to build up virtue and merit before God. They try their best to make themselves acceptable to God.

> **"Therefore by the deeds of the law there shall no flesh be justified in his sight: for by the law is the knowledge of sin" (Ro.3:20).**
> **"For by grace are ye saved through faith; and that not of yourselves: it is the gift of God: not of works, lest any man should boast" (Eph.2:8-9).**

Note that a genuine believer is not being classified as a religionist. The reason is pointed: the true believer does not follow a religion; he follows Jesus Christ. Jesus Christ is alive; He is living in another world--the spiritual world, the spiritual dimension of being. The believer is in touch with Him daily, communicating through the Holy Spirit and prayer. What the believer does is follow Christ; he lives the life of Jesus Christ, not the rules of a religion. Therefore, the genuine believer is a disciple of Christ, not of religion.

> **"I am crucified with Christ: nevertheless I live; yet not I, but Christ liveth in me: and the life which I now live in the flesh I live by the faith of the Son of God, who loved me, and gave himself for me" (Gal.2:20).**

<u>**QUESTIONS:**</u>
1. Using the simplest of words, how would you define what a religionist does?
2. Why is spiritual pride such a snare to the religionist?
3. How would you describe the major difference between a true believer and a religionist?

## 1. THE RELIGIONIST PROFESSES RELIGION (v.17-20).

The religionist accepts the name of his religion whatever it may be, whether Jew, Moslem, or Buddhist; and he shows enough interest in his religion to give him security. Jewish and Christian religionists make ten mistakes.

1. The religionist "rests in the law," that is, in the Word of God (v.17). He possesses the Scriptures (Bible); he...

- has it in his home
- carries it with him to church
- sometimes reads it
- honors it as the Word of God

Because of this, he feels that he pleases God. He rests upon the fact that he possesses God's Word. By having God's Word, he feels he has God's approval and acceptance. But this is the very mistake of the religionist: God does not accept a person because he happens to have God's Word in his possession. God approves and accepts the person who *does* the Word of God, who lives and obeys the law of God.

> **"What advantage then hath the Jew [Christian]? or what profit is there of circumcision [baptism]? Much every way: chiefly, because that unto them were committed the oracles of God" (Ro.3:1-2).**

2. The religionist professes God. To *profess* means to boast, to glory, to feel proud about one's profession of God and religion. The idea is that one *openly* professes that he believes in God. He is not ashamed of his belief and religious affiliation. He believes in God and he feels safe and secure in his belief. He confesses God and he feels that God accepts him because of his profession.

However, this is *the mistake* of the religionist. God is not interested in a man's profession but in a man's life. God wants a man living for Him, not just professing and talking about Him.

> **"For I bear them record that they have a zeal of God, but not according to knowledge. For they being ignorant of God's righteousness, and going about to establish their own righteousness, have not submitted themselves unto the righteousness of God. For Christ is the end of the law for righteousness to every one that believeth" (Ro.10:2-4).**

3. The religionist knows God's will (v.18). He is familiar with the law and the commandments of God. He knows what God wants done; he knows right from wrong. Therefore, he feels he has God's approval.

However, the religionist fails to see something: knowing God's will is not enough--a man must do God's will.

> **"And they come unto thee as the people cometh, and they sit before thee as my people, and they hear thy words, but they will not do them: for with their mouth they show much love, but their heart goeth after their covetousness. And, lo, thou art unto them as a very lovely song of one that hath a pleasant voice, and can play well on an instrument: for they hear thy words, but they do them not" (Ezk.33:31-32).**

4. The religionist approves the excellent or better things in life (v.18). He not only knows God's will, right from wrong; but he...
- is able to discern the more excellent, the better things to do.
- approves, expresses, and proclaims pleasure in the right things.

Because he supports and pushes and approves the better things in life, the religionist feels he pleases God. But this is his mistake. God is not interested in man's approval of the better things in life. Most men do approve and talk about the better things of life. God wants man living out the better things, living on the level of the more excellent.

> **"My little children, let us not love in word, neither in tongue; but in deed and in truth" (1 Jn.3:18).**

5.    The religionist is taught God's law and Word (v.18). He is instructed by family, teacher, preacher, friend. The religionist learns God's Word from someone, and because he knows God's Word, he feels he has a right relationship with God. But again, God's concern is not in what a person knows, but in what a person does. God expects a person to take what he has learned and put it into practice. God expects a person to live as he has been taught.

> **"But ye have not so learned Christ; if so be that ye have heard
> him, and have been taught by him, as the truth is in Jesus: that ye
> put off concerning the former conversation [behavior] the old man,
> which is corrupt according to the deceitful lusts" (Eph.4:20-22).**

6.    The religionist is sure he is a guide to the blind (v.19). The word *confident* means persuaded and sure. The religionist is convinced that religion is true, that religion is the way men should live. He believes that a man who does not believe in God and live a religious life is blind and needs to be guided to the truth. By living a religious life, he feels...
- he is an example to men
- he is a guide to help men find God
- he can cure men of their blindness to God and religion

However, being "confident" that one is a guide of the blind does not mean that one is a true guide. A person must be sure that he himself is following the truth, Jesus Christ (Jn.14:6). There are many guides in the world who are leading people down the wrong road. They are blind guides, the blind leading the blind (Mt.15:14).

> **"And he spake this parable unto certain which trusted in them-
> selves that they were righteous, and despised others" (Lk.18:9).**

7.    The religionist is sure he is an instructor of the foolish (v.20). The word *foolish* means thoughtless, senseless, undirected. It refers to people who walk through life giving no thought to life's purpose, as to...
- where they have come from
- why they are here
- where they are going

The religionist is persuaded that religion answers all these questions, the basic questions of life. Therefore, he feels he can help the foolish discover meaning and purpose and significance in life. The critical point for the instructor or the religionist is to make sure that his instruction is true. What he instructs must be the truth or else it is all for nothing.

> **"He that trusteth in his own heart is a fool: but whoso walketh
> wisely, he shall be delivered" (Pr.28:26).**

8.    The religionist is sure he is a light to those in darkness (v.20), to those who stumble about searching for the light but are unable to find it. The religionist feels he has found the light; therefore, he is a light to those who are searching for it. However, the religionist makes a serious mistake. Religion is not the light of the world--Jesus Christ is.

> **"Jesus said unto them, If ye were <u>blind</u>, ye should have no sin:
> but now ye say, We see; therefore your sin remaineth" (Jn.9:41).**

9.    The religionist is sure he is a teacher of the immature (v.20). The word *babes* means the infant, the immature, the novice, the proselyte, the new church member. The

point is the same: a religionist is not mature in God just because he...
- has been baptized and has been a church member for a long time
- thinks he is mature
- serves as a teacher

What makes a person mature and capable of teaching the immature of the world is experience with Christ, having walked and served with Christ for a long time.

> **"Wherefore the Lord said, Forasmuch as this people draw near me with their mouth, and with their lips do honor me, but have removed their heart far from me, and their fear toward me is taught by the precept of men" (Is.29:13).**

10. The religionist has the law of God, the embodiment of knowledge and truth (v.20). The religionist has the Scriptures, the Word of God, at his disposal. He has every opportunity in the world to know the truth. But again, having and knowing and thinking that one can instruct and teach another is not enough. God accepts and uses only those who live the Word, who keep the laws and commandments of God. This is the mistake of the religionist, of the person who professes and does not live.

> **"Having a form of godliness, but denying the power thereof: from such turn away" (2 Tim.3:5).**

**QUESTIONS:**
1. Being totally honest, how often does your Bible sit on a table without being read? Is there any real security in just possessing a Bible?
2. A lot of people profess to know God and to know right from wrong. They even profess to know God's will. But what essential step separates the religionist from the true believer? How can you be sure your profession is the real thing?
3. A religionist will lead someone else down the wrong road. How do people who are following your example know where you are going--your friends, fellow employees, family?
4. What does it take to make a person a mature believer? Are these principles at work in your own life? What do you need to do to become more spiritually mature?

## 2. THE RELIGIONIST FAILS TO LIVE WHAT HE PROFESSES (v.21-24).

This is seen in five pointed questions.
1. "You who teach others, do you not teach yourself?" The question is not only for teachers, but for everyone, because we all teach others. Throughout life we all claim to know some truths about morality and about how people should live and behave. We often share those truths with our children, friends, fellow workers, and others. When we share and teach, do we not listen to the truth? Do we not teach ourselves? What right do we have to tell others how to live if we do not live that way? This is the sin of hypocrisy, a sin committed by so many religionists.

> **"And why call ye me, Lord, Lord, and do not the things which I say?" (Lk.6:46).**

2. "You who say that a person should not steal, do you steal?" Do you take from others; do you...
- steal money?
- steal from your neighbor?
- steal while shopping?
- steal from your job?
- steal from your family?
- steal or cheat while taking tests in school?

If you steal, what right do you have to say that others should not steal--that everyone else should not have the right to take what they want from whom they want? If enough people began to take what they wanted when they wanted, then the world would exist in utter chaos. If you say that men should not steal, why do you steal? This is the sin of too many religionists.

Stealing is a sin that leads to utter chaos. Because of its devastating effect, it is one of the ten commandments, and note: it is so important a commandment, it is repeated time and again.

> **"Thou shalt not steal" (Ex.20:15; Lev.19:11; Dt.5:19; Mt.19:18; Ro.13:9).**
> **"Let him that stole steal no more: but rather let him labour, working with his hands the thing which is good, that he may have to give to him that needeth" (Eph.4:28).**

3. "You who say that a person should not commit adultery, do you commit adultery?" You who want pure *brides* and spouses, husbands and wives, sons and *daughters*, do you live purely? What are you looking at and watching, reading and hearing? Do you...

- look a second time?
- read pornographic books, magazines, or novels?
- have lustful thoughts?
- harbor sexual thoughts?
- dress in a manner exposing your body?
- watch and support television films that have or suggest scenes of immorality?

Regardless of man's denial, we do what we think; and our thoughts come from what we see and watch, read and hear. Therefore, if we look and watch, read and listen to sexual suggestions, our thoughts center upon fleshly desires. This is the reason for the breakdown of morals in society. If you say a man should not commit adultery, do you commit adultery? Do you commit it in your mind? This is a major sin among some religionists. Christ knew this; therefore, He said...

> **"Ye have heard that it was said by them of old time, Thou shalt not commit adultery: but I say unto you, That whosoever looketh on a woman to lust after her hath committed adultery with her already in his heart" (Mt.5:27-28).**

4. "You who abhor idols, do you commit sacrilege?" The word *sacrilege* means to violate one's commitment to God and to rob from God. It means to consider something more important than God, something so important that it *requires*...

- the commitment that you owe God.
- the tithes and offerings that you owe God.

You say that you worship God and abhor idols; yet you take what belongs to God--your commitment, your time, your energy, your tithes--and you give it to something else. You make something else more important than God; you make it an idol. This is one of the major sins of the religionists.

> **"Take heed to yourselves, that your heart be not deceived, and ye turn aside, and serve other gods, and worship them" (Dt.11:16).**

5.   "You who boast and take pride in the law [the Bible], through breaking the law do you not dishonor God?" The answer is clear.

⇒  We do dishonor God when we talk about His Word yet break His commandments.

⇒  We do dishonor God before men, causing His name to be blasphemed.

When we boast in God's Word yet break His commandments, we give great occasion for the world and its people to take the name of God and...

- blaspheme
- curse
- reproach
- ridicule
- mock
- deny
- insult
- profane

Many a person is doomed because of the hypocrisy of religionists. This is one of the terrible sins of religionists.

> **"They profess that they know God; but in works they deny him, being abominable, and disobedient, and unto every good work reprobate" (Tit.1:16).**

## QUESTIONS:

1. "Practice what you preach." This cliché is overused, but it rings true of what each believer must do: live a life that is consistent with the truth. What are some hard areas for you to practice what you preach? How can you become more consistent in this area?
2. How would those who know you best grade your "hypocrisy score"? Using this scale, how would you fare:
    ⇒  5 points means you are a first-class hypocrite.
    ⇒  4 points means you are one step away from being a full-fledged hypocrite--but on occasions a shred of honesty shows up.
    ⇒  3 points means you could go either way: a hypocrite in some things and an honest person in others.
    ⇒  2 points means you are not perfect, you still slip, but you do at least make an attempt to be consistent and honest.
    ⇒  1 point means you have gotten a good handle on letting people see who you really are--inside and out.
    ⇒  0 points means you are perfect--and your friends are not being honest with you!

## 3. THE RELIGIONIST BELIEVES THAT A RITUAL (CIRCUMCISION) IS THE WAY TO SECURE GOD'S APPROVAL (v.25-27).

Just take the word circumcision and substitute whatever ritual a church says is essential for salvation and the meaning of the passage becomes clear. For example, take the ritual of *church membership*.

"Church membership profits a man if he keeps the law: but if he breaks the law, his church membership is made or counted as *unchurch* membership."

If a religionist does not keep (practice) God's law and Word, then his ritual does not count. The man becomes...

- unbaptized
- unchurched
- uncircumcised
- unwhatever

The point is obedience, not ritual. A person is acceptable to God because he lives for God and obeys Him, not because he has undergone some ritual. The next two verses make this pointedly clear (v.26-27).

⇒ "The uncircumcised man who <u>keeps</u> the righteousness of the law is counted as circumcised [that is, acceptable to God]" (v.26). A man is not acceptable to God because he has been baptized or joined some church. He becomes acceptable to God because he obeys God, and God's basic commandment is clear, unquestionably so:

> **"And this is his commandment, That we should believe on the name of his Son Jesus Christ, and love one another, as he gave us commandment" (1 Jn.3:23).**

⇒ The uncircumcised man who keeps the law actually judges the man who has been circumcised and breaks the law (v.27). The basis of judgment is not to be a ritual, whether circumcision or baptism or church membership; it is to be obedience. No ritual will ever save a man if he transgresses the law, and no ritual will ever cause a man to be lost if he keeps the law.

> **"But be ye doers of the word, and not hearers only, deceiving your own selves" (Jas.1:22).**

## APPLICATION:

Do you have the difference between a ritual and a Scriptural command settled in your mind? To simplify this, remember that only what is found in the Bible is a Scriptural command. Anything else is nothing more than a man-made ritual. Rituals in and of themselves are not right or wrong. But most important to remember is that rituals do not make you acceptable to God. Rituals do not and cannot save you. Some examples of man-made rituals are...

- a narrow acceptance of different types of music, clothing, or hairstyles
- dietary choices based on legalism
- praying, fasting, or giving money for show
- the length or order of events during a worship service
- the wearing of choir robes
- the pastor or choir marching in procession to begin the service
- only observing church in a 'church building'

With a little bit of imagination and from your own observations, you could probably add to this list. How tragic it is when men replace the reality of God's Word with the vain traditions of fallen man.

> **"But he answered and said unto them, Why do ye also transgress the commandment of God by your tradition?" (Mt.15:3).**

## ILLUSTRATIONS:

What keeps a ritual in place? Tradition.

> *"William Poteet wrote in <u>The Pentecostal Minister</u> how in 1903 the Russian czar noticed a sentry posted for no apparent reason on the Kremlin grounds. Upon inquiry, he discovered that in 1776 Catherine the Great found there the first flower of spring. 'Post a sentry here,' she commanded, 'so that no one tramples that flower underfoot!'*
> *"Some traditions die hard."*[2]

---

[2] Craig B. Larson. *Illustrations for Preaching and Teaching*. (Grand Rapids, MI: Baker Book House, 1994), p.264.

Do not allow useless or foolish traditions to waste your time. Remember, your time belongs to God!

**QUESTIONS:**
1. What rituals do you keep that have nothing to do with obedience to God's Word? Are they honoring to God or do they only glorify man?
2. Why are some men motivated to replace obedience to God with a ritual that is man-made?
3. Rituals are a religionist's best friend. Bound to a life of rules and regulations, carefully crafted ritual can change the religionist's focus from God to worldly things. What rituals take the focus away from the Lord?

## 4. THE RELIGIONIST MISSES THE WHOLE POINT: A TRUE RELIGIONIST IS A MAN WHO IS RIGHTEOUS INWARDLY (v.28-29).

This fact is so critical that everyone needs to give heed and do something about it. The point is that every man breaks or transgresses the law. Paul has just said:

> **"If thou be a breaker of the law, thy circumcision or baptism is made uncircumcision or unbaptism."**

Paul will say very shortly:

> **"There is none righteous, no, not one" (Ro.3:10).**
> **"All have sinned, and come short of the glory of God" (Ro.3:23).**

No law and no ritual, whether circumcision or baptism (or any other ritual), is able to make man acceptable to God. Being acceptable to God is not an outward thing. It is...
- not the keeping of any ritual or law (Ro.2:21-27).
- not nationality or heritage.
- not being born of any particular race or family, whether Jewish or Christian (Ro.3:1-20; 9:6-13).

True religion--being acceptable to God--is inward. It is of the heart, of the spirit. It is of God. It is being born again of God's Spirit (Jn.3:3-8). It is not of man; therefore, God is to be praised, not man (Ro.2:28-29).

> **"A new heart also will I give you, and a new spirit will I put within you: and I will take away the stony heart out of your flesh, and I will give you a heart of flesh" (Ezk.36:26).**

God's true people are the people who have been circumcised spiritually--in the heart. The real Jews, God's true people, are those who have had the skin of disease (sin) cut out of their hearts. They are the people who have been spiritually converted.

> **"In whom also ye are circumcised with the circumcision made without hands, in putting off the body of the sins of the flesh by the circumcision [operation, cutting] of Christ" (Col.2:11).**

Moses confessed that he was a man of "uncircumcised lips" (Ex.6:12, 30). Man's "uncircumcised heart" must be humbled if he wishes God to remember His covenant and give man the promised land of heaven (Lev.26:41-42).

**ILLUSTRATION:**
What the world calls religion is nothing more than an empty shell, void of any life or meaning.

> *"The story is told of two brothers who grew up on a farm. One went away to college, earned a law degree, and became a partner in a prominent law firm in the state capital. The other brother stayed on the family farm. One day the lawyer came and visited his brother, the farmer. He asked, 'Why don't you go out and make a name for yourself and hold your head up high in the world like me?' The brother pointed and said, 'See that field of wheat over there? Look closely. Only the empty heads stand up. Those that are well filled always bow low.'*
> *"Said differently, 'The branch that bears the most fruit is bent the lowest to the ground.'"[3]*

Is your religion one of the heart or one of appearance only?

**QUESTIONS:**
1. List all the things you can do to make yourself acceptable to God.
2. True religion is an inward experience. Why do so many people concentrate on the outside? How can you keep your focus where it should be?

## SUMMARY:

The religionist does not grasp the need for a personal relationship with Jesus Christ. Bound to a man-made system of rules and regulations, the religionist will fail every time he takes a step in the name of religion. Why is the religionist doomed to failure? Because...

1. The religionist only professes religion.
2. The religionist fails to live what he professes.
3. The religionist believes that a ritual is the way to secure God's approval.
4. The religionist misses the whole point: a true religionist is a man who is righteous inwardly.

## PERSONAL JOURNAL NOTES
### (Reflection & Response)

1. The most important thing that I learned from this lesson was:

2. The area that I need to work on the most is:

3. I can apply this lesson to my life by:

4. Closing Statement of Commitment:

---

[3]  Michael P. Green. *Illustrations for Biblical Preaching*, p.197-198.

# ROMANS 3:1-8

| | CHAPTER 3 | justified in thy sayings, and mightest overcome when thou art judged.<br>5 But if our unrighteousness commend the righteous of God, what shall we say? Is God unrighteous who taketh vengeance? (I speak as a man)<br>6 God forbid: for then how shall God judge the world?<br>7 For if the truth of God hath more abounded through my lie unto his glory; why yet am I also judged as a sinner?<br>8 And not rather, (as we be slanderously reported, and as some affirm that we say,) Let us do evil, that good may come? whose damnation is just. | His Word<br>d. God will overcome those who judge Him & His Word<br>3. **Is God unjust if He takes vengeance?**<br><br>a. Perish the idea<br>b. God is moral: He must judge the world<br>c. The contradiction of such an argument<br><br><br>d. The damnation of persons who argue such is just |
|---|---|---|---|
| | **E. The Arguments of the Religionist (Jew) Against a Heart Religion, 3:1-8**<br>(Cp. Ro.2:23-29) | | |
| **1. What profit is there in being a Jew, a religionist—in being circumcised or baptized?**<br>a. He is privileged<br>b. He is entrusted with the Word of God<br>**2. Does unbelief void God's promises—make God a liar?**<br><br>a. Perish the idea<br>b. God's Word stands even if every man is a liar<br>c. God will prove | **W**hat advantage then hath the Jew? or what profit is there of circumcision?<br>2 Much every way: chiefly, because that unto them were committed the oracles of God.<br>3 For what if some did not believe? shall their unbelief make the faith of God without effect?<br>4 God forbid: yea, let God be true, but every man a liar; as it is written, That thou mightest be | | |

## Section II

### SIN AND CONDEMNATION: THE WORLD'S NEED TO GET RIGHT WITH GOD
### Romans 1:18-3:20

**Study 5: The Arguments of the Religionist (Jew) Against a Heart Religion**

**Text:** Romans 3:1-8

**Aim:** To make absolutely sure that your religion is a heart religion--a religion that is living, eternal, and true.

**Memory Verse:**
**"For what if some did not believe? shall their unbelief make the faith of God without effect?" (Romans 3:3).**

## INTRODUCTION:
The pages of history are littered with men who have challenged God every step of the way. Casting away the desire to know God better, some men would rather debate God and His ways than simply obey Him and believe Him.

So it is with the person who is convinced he can set his own agenda for reaching heaven, hoping to change the mind of Almighty God by...

- joining the right church
- living a good and moral life
- learning the appropriate religious clichés

99

The religionist *hopes* God will accept him on his own terms, thus avoiding the cross. The religionist, the superficial church member, debates God in hopes that he can be proven right--that eternal life does not come by faith in Christ. What he fails to realize is that God will not change. God will not make an exception for anyone. No matter what the religionist says, his feeble efforts to change God's mind will never succeed.

Paul has said there is no difference between Jew and Gentile, between a religionist and other men (chapters 1-3). All men stand before God guilty of sin and condemned. Now at this point Paul imagines the religionist seeing exactly what he is saying. The religionist also sees the tremendous weight of Paul's argument; therefore, he strains to counter Paul with three arguments, arguments often made by Christian religionists and church members who profess Christ and attend church only enough to salve their consciences. (See **A CLOSER LOOK, Religionists**--Ro.2:17-29; 2:17-20 for a discussion of who the religionist is.)

**OUTLINE:**
1. What profit is there in being a religionist--in being circumcised or baptized (v.1-2)?
2. Does unbelief void God's promises--make God a liar (v.3-4)?
3. Is God unjust if He takes vengeance (v.5-8)?

## 1. WHAT PROFIT IS THERE IN BEING A JEW OR A RELIGIONIST--IN BEING CIRCUMCISED OR BAPTIZED OR A CHURCH MEMBER (v.1-2)?

The promise of God to Abraham was that his seed (the Jewish nation) would be the children of God (see Jn.4:22; cp. Gen.12:1-4). If a man is born a Jew (born into a Jewish family) and he professes to be a Jew, a follower of God, is he not acceptable to God? If not, then what profit is there in being a professing Jew, a follower of God? Is there no advantage in being a Jew or a child of Abraham?

The application of this passage concerns every man. If a man is born a Jew or a Christian (that is, the right nationality), or if a man is born into a Jewish or Christian family (that is, the right heritage), or if a man claims to be a Jew or a Christian religionist, and he is *still* not acceptable to God, what profit is there in being a religionist?

Paul's answer is simple: the advantages are great. The Jew and Christian are highly privileged, especially in that God has committed His Word to them (Ro.3:2; 9:4-5). They have the privilege...

- of possessing God's Word
- of reading, hearing, seeing, obeying, and living God's Word
- of living within a society that has been affected by God's Word

These are enormous privileges. A man born within a nation and a family that has God's Word has every advantage in coming to God and in living for God. In fact, such a man could have no greater privilege. His privileges are so great that he is left without excuse if he fails to live for God.

> "Verily, verily, I say unto you, He that heareth **my word**, and believeth on him that sent me, hath everlasting life, and shall not come into condemnation; but is passed from death unto life" (Jn.5:24).

# ROMANS 3:1-8

**ILLUSTRATION:**
God has done so much for us. The gift of His Son, the Lord Jesus Christ, should compel every believer to live only for Him. Unfortunately, this is not always true. Different things come our way that distract us from living for God. Author Bill Hybels shares one such story.

"*In 1981 Dr. Jim Judge entered into practice with twelve other physicians. He quickly developed a new plan. He would spend three years in private practice and then return overseas as a missionary doctor. Even though he loved his job, he didn't always see it as <u>real</u> ministry. In 1983 the Judges had the opportunity to return to Africa--this time to fill a short-term need for doctors at a medical center in Kenya. With their four-year-old and two-year-old daughters and Cindy [Jim's wife] six-months pregnant, they went to Kijabe for the first time and stayed about three months. They loved the ministry.*

"*When he returned home, Jim expected to hear from God at any moment about the direction of his life. A divine plan. But there was dead silence. In looking back, Jim is not sure what he wanted. A note on the refrigerator? A vision in the night? What he got was angry. During the next year, Jim's relationship with God began to erode in the acid of disappointment.*

"*For a few years, the Judges were involved in important ministries. Jim taught at his church, soon become one of its leaders. But over time both Jim and Cindy found their Christianity--once vital and filled with passion--dissolving into a lifestyle. The church they were attending, although strong in teaching and biblical wisdom, often seemed inwardly focused. The spiritual fire of evangelism, the very thing that had connected the two of them in the first place, was missing.*

"*The Judges, disconnected, began a slow, almost unnoticeable slide into materialism and busyness, the twin plagues of suburbia. There was almost this kind of subconscious reasoning: If God was going to ask them to have a ministry in the suburbs, then they would need to fit in. Or: A bigger house is an investment; we <u>need</u> to buy one if we are to be good stewards. They even resorted to reasoning framed by their tax bracket.*

"*The Judges bought a big old house, certainly not elaborate by their community's standards, but quite comfortable. Or so they thought. Soon Cindy found herself struggling with exhaustion--the house seemed to be sucking her energy. And for Jim there was the pool....Like some kind of Edgar Allan Poe nightmare, THE POOL began to make demands: feed me chlorine; get that leaf out of here; change my chemistry. There were, in fact, entire months when the family did not feel free to travel because of THE POOL. This was getting ridiculous. 'When I reached seventy [said Dr. Judge] would I best be remembered for how clean I kept my pool?'*"[1]

What are you doing with the privileges God has given you? Using them for Him or using them as excuses to fit in with the world?

**QUESTIONS:**
1. What advantages does a person have if he is raised in a Christian home? What would be some possible disadvantages?
2. We live in a time when the gospel can be heard almost everywhere: on radio, television, in a football stadium, or in a tent. If you live in a community where this is a reality, have you taken advantage of the opportunity?
3. Why do so many people place their trust in having their names on a church roll?

---

[1]    Bill Hybels & Rob Wilkins. *Descending Into Greatness*. (Grand Rapids, MI: Zondervan Publishing House, 1993), p.81-83.

## 2. DOES UNBELIEF VOID GOD'S PROMISES--MAKE GOD A LIAR (v.3-4)?

Or to say it another way, "What if some disbelieve and reject God's Word; will their unbelief cause God to void His Word and promises? God promised the Jews a special place and special privileges through Abraham and his seed (see Jn.4:22). If some Jews do not believe God's promises and God condemns them, isn't He breaking His promise to Abraham and his seed? Isn't He voiding His Word and Covenant and making Himself a liar? God's Word could not be based on heart religion and on moral character alone. There has be to something else, something outward--a rite (circumcision, baptism, church membership)--that shows we are religious (Jews). If we go through the rite or ritual, then God is bound to accept us. He has promised to accept us. He is not going to break His Word."

The application of this question concerns every religionist. The thinking religionist poses the same objection and question: "If you say some religionists do not believe and are condemned, doesn't that void God's Word and make God a liar? God's Word promises the religious person special privileges and the hope of eternal life. His Word tells us to believe Christ and to possess His Word, be baptized and join the fellowship of the church. If we do that and God still condemns us, is He not voiding His Word and becoming a liar?"

⇒ God forbid.

⇒ God will be faithful. His Word and promise of salvation will stand even if *every* man lies about believing and lies about giving his heart to serve Jesus.

⇒ God will prove His Word: He will be justified and proven faithful in what He has said. He will still save *any person* who gives his heart to Jesus and obeys Jesus.

⇒ In fact, God will overcome; He will prove His Word another way. He will judge all who make a false profession and who judge Him and His Word, who accuse Him of being unfaithful and voiding His Word. David himself said that God would judge the unfaithful or disobedient man (Ps.51:4). David had sinned greatly, not keeping the commandments of God, so God judged David and charged him with sin. David did the right thing: he confessed his sin and repented, beginning to live righteously. But David did something else: he declared that God's charge and judgment against him were *just*, that God was perfectly justified. And God was, for God is always just, and He is always justified in what He says and does.

The point is twofold.

1. God is not unfaithful. God never breaks or voids His Word when He rejects the religionist. The religionist who possesses God's Word and belongs to a church but does not obey God's Word is not acceptable to God. It is righteousness God is after, not religion. God is not after an outward religion, but an *inward righteousness*. God wants a heart that will not only possess the Bible, but will keep His commandments. God is after a spiritual rebirth, a new creation, a man who has been truly born again. God wants a heart and life that are focused upon Christ and that keep the commandments of Christ. The only man who is acceptable to God is the man who has given his heart and life to Christ and who lives righteously, trusting God to accept His faith in Christ. (Cp. Ro.2:28-29.)

2. God never voids His Word or promises; He never has and never will be a liar. God has promised salvation and eternal life to men. Even if there should never be a single person who believed God's promise, His promise would still stand. He would still save any person who did what He said.

The problem is in doing what God says, in coming to God as He dictates. God demands that men give their hearts and lives to His Son, Jesus Christ. God demands that men live for Christ, worship and obey Him. But this is too hard for men. They want an *easier* salvation. They want to be able to do something, get it over with, and then be free to live as they wish, giving God some attention here and there. Therefore, men prefer to be saved by being religious: being baptized, joining a church, buying a Bible, and then being free to go about their own lives. But this is *not enough* for God; it is *not doing everything* that God says; it is not giving one's heart and life to live for Jesus Christ by obeying, worshipping, and serving Him. Therfore, God...

- charges the religionist with sin
- judges and condemns the religionist

Now note another fact. God fulfills His Word by judging the religionists. God has told men how to live and what would happen if they failed. Therefore, He is "justified in His sayings" by following through and by judging the religionists.

⇒ God will not void and break His Word. He will fulfill it all.
⇒ God is justified in fulfilling His Word by doing exactly what He said, that is, in accepting men *only* as He said and in judging men if they do not come to Him as He commands.

**QUESTIONS:**
1. God is *NEVER* wrong. What is the real root of the problem that causes people to blame God when things go wrong?
2. What are some examples from your own life when God proved His Word to you?
3. What keeps God from being a liar? Why is trust such a difficult thing if we know that God will never lie?

---

**A CLOSER LOOK:**

(3:3) **Unbelief--Man, Errors**: this is one of two common but gross deceptions of men-- that unbelief in something makes the thing ineffective and voids it. A man argues: "If I deny something, ignore it, refuse to accept it, push it out of my mind, it will not be, nor will it come to pass." Some even think of God's Word in this way. They think they can deny and reject some part of it and it will not be so. They accept the Scriptures that stress the love of God and allow them to live as they wish, but they reject the Scriptures that stress the supernatural and miraculous power of God and the desperate need of man to be saved from sin, death, and an eternal hell. They reject the Scriptures that demand that man live responsibly.

> **"For verily I say unto you, Till heaven and earth pass, one jot or one tittle shall in no wise pass from the law, till all be fulfilled"** (**Mt.5:18**).
> **"Heaven and earth shall pass away: but my words shall not pass away"** (**Lk.21:33**).

---

**QUESTIONS:**
1. Does an unbeliever's denial of the Bible invalidate the truth of the Scriptures?
2. Do you ever *pick and choose* selected promises from God's Word while ignoring those promises that are more challenging, that demand a deeper commitment from you? Why is it important for you to apply the whole counsel of God to your life?

---

**A CLOSER LOOK:**

(3:4) **Judging--Judgment**: men judge God. They judge Him to be true or false. They judge whether He exists or does not exist. They judge His Word. But in the final hour, God will end up judging men. He will overcome all those who judged Him to be less than He is and less than what He said.

> "But we are sure that the judgment of God is according to truth against them which commit such things" (Ro.2:2).
> "For I am the LORD: I will speak, and the word that I shall speak shall come to pass; it shall be no more prolonged: for in your days, O rebellious house, will I say the word, and will perform it, saith the Lord GOD" (Ezk.12:25).

---

**QUESTIONS:**
1. In what ways do you judge God? Do you ever wonder, "Does He really mean what He says? Will He really send people to hell? Can He really help us and heal us when needed? Can He really save me for all eternity?"
2. God is God. There is no one like Almighty God. What is the most profound thing you have come to know about God in the past year? How has this knowledge impacted your life?

## 3. IS GOD UNJUST IF HE TAKES VENGENANCE (v.5-8)?

"If my unbelief and sin give God a chance to overcome (v.4) and to show His justice, then my sin brings greater glory to Him. It gives Him a chance to fulfill His Word. How can He punish me for that? Is He not unjust in inflicting punishment?" The answer is fourfold.

1.    Perish the idea. God forbid such a thought!
2.    God is moral; therefore, He must judge the world. He would not be moral and just if He did not judge the world.
3.    Such an argument is contradictory. Think about it. "If my sin and disobedience give God a chance to demonstrate His righteousness, why then am I called a sinner for that? My sin is really a good thing. It gives God a chance to show how good He is. I may sin, yes, but only good has come out of it. When God accepts me as I am, a sinner, God has a chance to show how gloriously merciful He is. You can't condemn me for giving God a chance to show His mercy."
4.    The damnation of persons who argue this point is *just*; it is not unjust. Such arguments are common among every generation of men, but the arguments are gross deceptions. A man exclaims: "A God of love cannot take vengeance. He is too good and loving. He will be denying His very nature of love if He judges me."

What this argument fails to see is that *genuine love is just*. Love expressed unjustly is not love; it is license and indulgence. God's love is perfect, absolutely unbiased and impartial. It is shed upon all of us (Jn.3:16; 1 Jn.2:2). In no respect can it be unjust by failing to judge. Neither can God be accused of being unloving when He executes justice (Ro.2:2-16). God's justice is the demonstration of perfect love. The cross was where God imposed His perfect justice upon His Son, and it is the perfect example of the glorious truth.

# ROMANS 3:1-8

⇒ The cross is the perfect demonstration of both the love and the justice of God.

> **"For God so loved the world, that he gave his only begotten Son, that whosoever believeth in him should not perish, but have everlasting life" (Jn.3:16).**

⇒ Men shall be judged and condemned if they have rejected the love and salvation of God provided in His Son, Jesus Christ.

> **"For we must all appear before the judgment seat of Christ; that every one may receive the things done in his body, according to that he hath done, whether it be good or bad" (2 Cor.5:10).**

## APPLICATION:
The typical testimony of most children who have grown into adulthood is this: "My parents became smarter the older I got." The wisdom of a parent is best seen when that child grows up and has his own children. Then, the "wiser" child comes to realize what he has to do in order to give his own children who disobey the very best:
⇒ He must give the best discipline
⇒ He must give the best training
⇒ He must give the best mentoring
⇒ He must give the best experiences
⇒ He must give the best love

In order to give the very best, he must be willing to do those things that might be perceived as "unfair" by his children. The parent who really loves his children will be willing to dispense justice--no matter the cost.

> **"Train up a child in the way he should go: and when he is old, he will not depart from it" (Pr.22:6).**

## ILLUSTRATION:
The cross of Jesus Christ is the place where God has provided for lost man to find his way out of condemnation. The cross is real. It is:
⇒ a real place
⇒ provided by a real God
⇒ for real sinners
⇒ the only place to receive a real salvation

> *"The geographical heart of London is Charing Cross. All distances are measured from it. This spot is referred to simply as 'the cross.' A lost child was one day picked up by a London 'bobby' [policeman]. The child was unable to tell where he lived. Finally, in response to the repeated questions of the bobby, and amid his sobs and tears, the little fellow said, 'If you will take me to the cross I think I can find my way from there.*
> *"The Cross is the point where men become reconciled to God. If we find our way to God and home we must first come to the Cross."*

We should be eternally thankful that God chose to be merciful as well as execute justice--or else we would all be doomed to eternal damnation!

---

[2] Walter B. Knight. *Knight's Treasury of 2,000 Illustrations*. (Grand Rapids, MI: Eerdmans Publishing Company), 1963, p.97-98.

**QUESTIONS:**
1. Why do some people struggle with the goodness of God when He judges the un-repentant sinner?
2. Do you truly believe that God's vengeance is a demonstration of God's love? How can you explain it to an unbeliever?
3. You can really appreciate the extent of God's vengeance when you look at the cross of Christ. How can you show your appreciation for God's supreme act of love?

**SUMMARY:**

A person can have a list of questions for God that stretches on for miles. But the greatest question that must be resolved is this: Are you sure, absolutely sure, that you are saved and will live eternally with God? Always remember: No person has ever won a debate with God--no person, not even the people who ask God these kinds of questions:

1. What profit is there in being a Jew or religionist--in being circumcised or bap-tized?
2. Does unbelief void God's promises--make God a liar?
3. Is God unjust if He takes vengeance?

**PERSONAL JOURNAL NOTES**
**(Reflection & Response)**

1. The most important thing that I learned from this lesson was:

2. The area that I need to work on the most is:

3. I can apply this lesson to my life by:

4. Closing Statement of Commitment:

| | **F. God's Case A-gainst All Men, 3:9-20** | their lips: | |
|---|---|---|---|
| | | 14 Whose mouth is full of cursing and bitterness: | c. Piercing & poison-ous |
| | | | d. Cursing & bitter |
| **1. The charge: All men are under the power of sin** | 9 What then? are we better than they? No, in no wise: for we have before proved both Jews and Gen-tiles, that they are all under sin; | 15 Their feet are swift to shed blood: | **4. The case of sinful acts** |
| | | 16 Destruction and misery are in their ways: | a. Murderous |
| | | | b. Oppressive, caus-ing misery |
| | | 17 And the way of peace have they not known: | c. Restless, disturbed, warring |
| **2. The case of a sinful nature** | 10 As it is written, There is none right-eous, no, not one: | 18 There is no fear of God before their eyes. | d. Godless, irreverent, disrespectful |
| a. Unrighteous | | | |
| b. Ignorant | 11 There is none that understandeth, there is none that seeketh after God. | 19 Now we know that what things soever the law saith, it saith to them who are under the law: that every mouth may be stopped, and all the world may become guilty before God. | **5. The case of the law** |
| c. Indifferent—selfish | | | a. It speaks to all who have the law |
| d. Crooked | 12 They are all gone out of the way, they are together become unprofitable; there is none that doeth good, no, not one. | | b. It stops all boasting |
| | | | c. It makes all the world guilty |
| e. Useless | | | |
| f. Evil | | | |
| **3. The case of a sinful tongue** | 13 Their throat is an open sepulchre; with their tongues they have used deceit; the poison of asps is under | 20 Therefore by the deeds of the law there shall no flesh be justi-fied in his sight: for by the law is the knowl-edge of sin. | d. It justifies no flesh |
| a. Foul & corrupt | | | e. It shows man that he is sinful |
| b. Deceitful | | | |

## Section II

## SIN AND CONDEMNATION: THE WORLD'S NEED TO GET RIGHT WITH GOD
### Romans 1:18-3:20

**Study 6: God's Case Against All Men**

**Text:**   Romans 3:9-20

**Aim:**   To acknowledge your sinfulness; to accept the hope of salvation in Jesus Christ.

**Memory Verse:**
>   "As it is written, There is none righteous, no, not one" (Romans 3:10).

**INTRODUCTION:**
   Guilt is a strong force. You know you have done wrong. You know you are going to be punished. Guilt will not let you forget what you have done. Guilt comes:
   ⇒ when you have done something wrong and you are caught.
   ⇒ when you get pulled over by a policeman for driving too fast.

⇒ when you exceeded the lawful limit while hunting or fishing and the fish and game officer is there to confront you.

⇒ when you turn down a social invitation because you are 'under the weather' only to run into the host somewhere else that very day.

⇒ when you speak before you have a chance to pull back the ugly words.

⇒ when you get caught spreading rumors and gossip.

Let these statements sink in for a moment: *Man is sinful. Man is lost.* No matter what you do, the lethal pull of sin is stronger. What hope do you have? There is great hope if you are willing to allow Christ to redeem you, to set you free from sin's control. You are guilty, but Christ came to redeem sinful men. Jesus Christ came to save men...

- who cannot save themselves
- who cannot overcome sin
- who cannot be perfect

In looking at such passages as this, a person must keep in mind the whole point of the passage. The point is not to charge man with sin, nor to berate man; it is not to look upon man with cynical contempt. The point is not to call man to hopelessness and despair, leaving him with a hanged head and low self-esteem. The point is to give man hope: to challenge man to seek a right relationship with God through the Lord Jesus Christ. Man must *never minimize* his sin, lest he ignore or neglect the right way to God. But neither must he minimize the redeeming power of Jesus Christ, lest he hang his head in hopelessness, or wallow in self-pity, or roam the world in despair.

**OUTLINE:**
1. The charge: all men are under the power of sin (v.9).
2. The case of a sinful nature (v.10-12).
3. The case of a sinful tongue (v.13-14).
4. The case of sinful acts (v.15-18).
5. The case of the law (v.19-20).

## 1. THE CHARGE: ALL MEN ARE UNDER THE POWER SIN (v.9).

The words *under sin* mean to be subject to the power of or under the authority of. A man outside of Jesus Christ is under the power of sin and he is helpless to escape from it (cp. Gal.3:10, 25; 4:2, 21; 5:18; 1 Tim.6:1).

The religionist (Jew) is "under sin" just as much as other men are "under sin." The Scripture has just declared that being religious does not make men acceptable to God (cp. Ro.2:17-28). Religionists are shocked: "What then! Are we not better--do we not have any advantage over other men? Are we not better if we...

- have the Bible?"
- profess God?"
- know God's will?"
- approve the best things?"
- study the Word of God?"
- guide and teach others?"
- know the truth?"

The answer is a strong exclamation: "No! Not at all! Not in any way are you better than other people. Both Jews and Gentiles, both religionists and non-religionists--you are all under sin."

Now note. This has been the point of all that has been said in Romans...

- God has a case against all ungodliness and unrighteousness of men (Ro.1:18-32).
- God has a case against the moralist (Ro.2:1-16).
- God has a case against the religionist (Jew) (Ro.2:17-3:8).

Scripture shows that God has a case against all men. All men are "under sin." And the fact is clearly seen by any person who will honestly look at man and his world.

> **"For all have sinned, and come short of the glory of God" (Ro.3:23).**
>
> **"Wherefore, as by one man sin entered into the world, and death by sin; and so death passed upon all men, for that all have sinned" (Ro.5:12).**
>
> **"If we say that we have no sin, we deceive ourselves, and the truth is not in us" (1 Jn.1:8).**
>
> **"All we like sheep have gone astray; we have turned every one to his own way; and the LORD hath laid on him the iniquity of us all" (Is.53:6).**

**QUESTIONS:**
1. Being under the power of sin is a lot like being caught in a bed of quicksand. Why is it impossible for men to save themselves from sin?
2. Have you ever felt acceptable to God because of your heritage, your education, your nationality, your church membership? Why does God reject someone who is simply religious? What is the answer to becoming acceptable to God?
3. Does this verse apply to the 'really good people' in society? Why or why not?

## 2. THE CASE OF A SINFUL NATURE (v.10-12).

1. *A sinful nature is unrighteous* (v.10; cp. Ps.14:1): "There is none righteous, no, not one." Not a single person is righteous, that is, perfect and sinless--not by nature nor by act. No man has ever lived a perfect life, not perfect...
- in every thought
- in every word
- in every act

"There is none righteous [perfect, sinless] no, not one." By nature, man is sinful.

> **"The world cannot hate you; but me it hateth, because I testify of it, that the works thereof are evil" (Jn.7:7).**

2. *A sinful nature is ignorant* (v.11; cp. Ps.14:2): "There is none that understands." Not a single person grasps, comprehends, or perceives. The word literally means *to put things together*. It means to look at things and to intelligently discern and comprehend the truth. No man looks at the world and thinks and puts the truth of things together--not perfectly--not about...
- God
- man
- the world
- the origin of all
- the purpose of all
- the destiny of all

No one looks at the world and intelligently discerns the truth of things, not in grasping the truth...
- of where they have come from
- of why they are here
- of where they are going

"There is none that understands."

**"For the heart of this people is waxed gross, and their ears are dull of hearing, and their eyes have they closed; lest they should see with their eyes, and hear with their ears, and understand with their heart, and should be converted, and I should heal them" (Acts 28:27).**

3. *A sinful nature is indifferent and selfish* (v.11; cp. Ps.14:2): "There is none that seeks after God." The word *seek after* means to seek out and search for. The idea is that of a diligent, careful, determined seeking and searching. No one searches and seeks after God, not after the only living and true God, not with so careful and determined a spirit. Why? Because men are indifferent and selfish. Men want gods that allow them to do their own thing.
  ⇒ Some want gods that allow them to glory in self by demonstrating their extreme self-discipline and sacrifice.
  ⇒ Others want gods that demand less and who allow them to live as they wish, in the pleasures and greed and possessions of this world.

Men do not want a God who is true and living. If He is true and living, it means He is Supreme, the only One who is to be glorified, honored, and obeyed. Therefore, in dealing with the only living and true God, men are indifferent and selfish. "There is none that seeketh after God." By nature men are sinful, indifferent, and selfish.

**"Knowing this, that the law is not made for a righteous man, but for the lawless and disobedient, for the ungodly and for sinners, for unholy and profane, for murderers of fathers and murderers of mothers, for manslayers, for whoremongers, for them that defile themselves with mankind, for menstealers, for liars, for perjured persons, and if there be any other thing that is contrary to sound doctrine" (1 Tim.1:9-10).**

4. *A sinful nature is crooked* (v.12; cp. Ps.14:3): "They are all gone out of the way." The Greek means that men lean out, turn away, and turn aside...
  • from God
  • from the way that leads to God
  • to another way

Men are crooked; they are not straight with God. They do not follow God nor pursue the right way to God. They take another path, another road, another way.

**"For ye were as sheep going astray; but are now returned unto the Shepherd and Bishop of your souls" (1 Pt.2:25).**

5. *A sinful nature is useless* (v.12; cp. Ps.14:3): "They are together become un-profitable". The word means to become worthless, useless, sour, bad. (Cp. sour milk.) All men without Christ are worthless, useless, sour, bad.

**"Ye are the salt of the earth: but if the salt have lost his savour, wherewith shall it be salted? it is thenceforth good for nothing, but to be cast out, and to be trodden under foot of men" (Mt.5:13).**

6.   *A sinful nature is evil* (v.12; cp. Ps.14:3): "There is none that doeth good, no, not one." The word *good* means moral goodness, kindness, graciousness, gentleness, justice. All men fail in being good toward God and their neighbors, in being...

- kind
- gracious
- gentle
- just

Men come short--too often, too much. "There is none that doeth good [not always, not perfectly], no, not one."

> **"Woe unto you, scribes and Pharisees, hypocrites! for ye are like unto whited sepulchres, which indeed appear beautiful outward, but are within full of dead men's bones, and of <u>all uncleanness</u>" (Mt.23:27).**

### ILLUSTRATION:
Men who are living in habitual sin have gained a pride and an arrogance that keeps them from seeing the evil of their ways.  Sin is nothing to be proud of!

> *"A certain man used to come home dead drunk each night.  He was always so inebriated [drunk] that he would fall into bed fully clothed, pass out, and then snore loudly all night long.  His wife was losing so much sleep because of his snoring that she went to a doctor and said, 'Doctor, I can't stand it any longer.  If you will tell me how to keep him from snoring, I will pay you anything!' The doctor told her that whenever her husband passed out and started snoring, she was to take a ribbon and tie it around his nose, and his snoring would stop.*
> *"That night, her husband came in as usual, fell across the bed fully dressed, passed out, and started snoring.  The wife got up, pulled a blue ribbon from her dresser, and tied it around his nose.  Sure enough, the snoring stopped.  The next morning, the wife woke up refreshed from a solid night's sleep.  She asked her husband as he was awakening, 'Where were you last night?' The husband, still fully clothed, looked in the mirror and seeing the blue ribbon around his nose, replied, 'I don't know, but wherever I was, I won first prize!'"[1]*

### QUESTIONS:
1. Are there sins in your life you are immune to?  Proud of?  Happy to get away with?  What kind of change do you need to make in your attitude?
2. Think of a day when you were on your best behavior.  Were you perfect?  Were you beyond temptation?  Why do you still need God no matter how good you are, no matter how religious you are, no matter how old you are?

## 3. THE CASE OF A SINFUL TONGUE (v.13-14).

1.   A sinful tongue is foul and corrupt (v.13; cp. Ps.5:9): "Their throat is an open sepulchre [grave]." An open grave is foul, and it is a symbol of corruption. So is a man with a sinful mouth. His mouth is...

- foul
- dirty
- obscene
- polluted
- filthy
- detestable
- profane
- dishonorable
- offensive

---

[1]   Michael P. Green. *Illustrations for Biblical Preaching*, p.346-347.

The obscene mouth may range from off-colored humor to dirty jokes, from immoral suggestions to outright propositions. But no matter, a man with a foul mouth stinks just like an open grave; his filthiness causes corruption, the decay of character. The filth from his mouth eats and eats away at his character and at the character of his listeners so much that he becomes as offensive as that of a decayed corpse. The foul, filthy mouth kills character, its attractiveness, trust, faithfulness, morality, honor, and godliness.

## APPLICATION:

Bad breath, 'morning breath,' halitosis--these are so offensive that most people would not even consider going off to work, school, or on a date without brushing their teeth first. And yet the foul odor of bad breath is not nearly as offensive as the foul words men allow to come out of their mouths without a second thought. We should all be as wise to clean our language, our thoughts, and our hearts as we are to clean our teeth and breath!

> **"And the tongue is a fire, a world of iniquity: so is the tongue among our members, that it defileth the whole body, and setteth on fire the course of nature; and it is set on fire of hell" (Jas.3:6).**

2. A sinful tongue is deceitful (v.13; cp. Ps.5:9): "They have used deceit." The Greek says, "They <u>make</u> smooth their tongue." A deceitful person has...

| | | |
|---|---|---|
| • a false tongue | • a misleading tongue | • a deluding tongue |
| • a lying tongue | • a treacherous tongue | • a flattering tongue |
| • a cheating tongue | • a beguiling tongue | • a smooth talking tongue |

The word *deceit* is continuous action: "They kept on deceiving." Man is not only guilty of deceiving but of constantly deceiving. He is *constantly* hiding and camouflaging his true thoughts, feelings, and behavior, seeking to protect himself or to get whatever he is after.

> **"His mouth is full of cursing and deceit and fraud: under his tongue is mischief and vanity" (Ps.10:7).**
> **"The heart is deceitful above all things, and desperately wicked: who can know it?" (Jer.17:9).**

3. A sinful tongue is piercing and poisonous (v.13; cp. Ps.140:3): "The poison of asps is under their lips." The asp is the cobra, a deadly snake. God charges men with having tongues that are just as piercing and poisonous as the tongue of the deadly cobra. The idea is that the tongues of some people have a diabolical nature; they are filled with so much malice that they set out to inflict punishment. A poisonous tongue...

| | |
|---|---|
| • talks about and gossips | • desires to cause suffering |
| • strikes out against | • lies in wait to strike |
| • inserts and spreads venom | • seeks to hurt and destroy |
| • poisons character and reputation | |

> **"They have sharpened their tongues like a serpent; adders' poison is under their lips" (Ps.140:3).**

4. A sinful tongue is full of cursing and bitterness (v.14; cp. Ps.10:7): "Whose mouth is full of cursing and bitterness." Cursing is sin; a cursing tongue is a sinful tongue. (See Mt.5:33-37 and 23:16-22.) Jesus Christ says:

> "Swear not at all....but let your communication be, Yea, yea; Nay, nay: for whatsoever is more than these cometh of evil" (Mt.5:34, 37).

a. Men use profanity; in fact, their mouth is full of cursing and swearing. They curse both God and men. Their cursing may range from what society considers to be a mild word of slang to using God's name in vain. No matter how mild or how acceptable to society, it is sin. God's case against man is that his mouth is full of cursing (cp. Jas.3:8-10).

> "But I say unto you, Swear not at all; neither by heaven; for it is God's throne" (Mt.5:34).

Note a man's cursing shall fall upon him.

> "As he loved cursing, so let it come unto him: as he delighted not in blessing, so let it be far from him. As he clothed himself with cursing like as with his garment, so let it come into his bowels like water, and like oil into his bones" (Ps.109:17-18.)

b. Man's mouth is also full of bitterness. His tongue is often...

| | | | |
|---|---|---|---|
| • sharp | • cold | • intense | • distasteful |
| • resentful | • harsh | • relentless | • unpleasant |
| • cynical | • stressful | | |

Any expression involving any of these is sin to God. God desires men to be filled with love, joy, and peace and to express such. Anything less than the expression of these is sin. This is God's case against men: a tongue full of cursing and bitterness.

> "Let all bitterness, and wrath, and anger, and clamour, and evil speaking, be put away from you, with all malice" (Eph.4:31).

**QUESTIONS:**
1. Think back over the past week: Have all of the things you said been kind, true, necessary? Is it really possible to control every word and every motive behind every word? How?
2. Why does a filthy mouth cause such damage to its owner?
3. What can you do when you are around someone who is using language that is off-colored, foul, mean-spirited, or untrue?

## 4. THE CASE OF SINFUL ACTS (v.15-18).

1. Sinful acts are murderous acts (v.15; cp. Is.59:7): "Their feet are swift to shed blood." Note the word *swift*. Men jump to kill; they are ready to spill and pour out blood...
- out of hurt and shame
- out to have their own way
- out to get what they want

Men are cruel; they have natures that are prideful, selfish, and greedy. They continually seek to possess, even if it means turning against others...

- inflicting pain and suffering
- killing and slaughtering
- causing grief and injury
- mutilating and mangling
- teasing and tormenting

God's case against man is that he is a murderer. His feet are "swift to shed blood."

> **"Thou shalt not kill" (Ex.20:13).**
> **"Whosoever hateth his brother is a murderer: and ye know that no murderer hath eternal life abiding in him" (1 Jn.3:15).**

2. Sinful acts are oppressive acts that destroy and cause misery (v.16; cp. Is.59:7): "Destruction and misery are in their ways." Man is oppressive; he destroys and causes misery wherever he goes. Because of his pride, selfishness, and greed, man destroys...

- the land (pollution)
- the country
- the shops
- the cities
- the government
- the houses
- the nations
- the people
- the property

He destroys and causes misery wherever he goes, even within his own family, neighborhood, and city. Whether by simple argument within his own family or by war, he is so destructive and full of misery that he brings destruction and misery wherever he goes.

3. Sinful acts are restless, disturbing, and warring acts (v.17; cp. Is.59:8): "And the way of peace have they not known." The idea is that men do not experience peace. They do not possess peace within themselves nor among others. They do not know peaceful ways, do not know...

- how to secure peace
- how to keep peace

Men are not peaceful within; they are restless. Their own souls are in a civil war that experiences constant conflict. Therefore, men fail to secure peace not only within themselves but among others. Wherever men are, they disturb and bring conflict and war to others. This is God's case against men.

> **"In the morning thou shalt say, Would God it were even! and at even thou shalt say, Would God it were morning! for the fear of thine heart wherewith thou shalt fear, and for the sight of thine eyes which thou shalt see" (Dt.28:67).**
> **"The way of peace they know not; and there is no judgment in their goings: they have made them crooked paths; whosoever goeth therein shall not know peace" (Is.59:8).**

4. Sinful acts are godless, irreverent, disrespectful acts (v.18; cp. Ps.36:1): "There is no fear of God before their eyes." Their eyes and their attention are focused upon other things. They ignore and neglect God, living as though there is no God. They sense little if any responsibility toward God. They do not fear God; they do not fear His anger or wrath or judgment against them. They sense little desire or need to worship God or to study His Word and will. They seldom if ever praise and honor Him or do as He commands. The fear of God is not before their eyes; therefore, this is God's case against men.

> **"And even as they did not like to retain God in their knowledge, God gave them over to a reprobate mind, to do those things which are not convenient" (Ro.1:28).**
> **"They would none of my counsel: they despised all my reproof" (Pr.1:30).**

# ROMANS 3:9-20

**ILLUSTRATION:**
One of society's greatest tragedies has been the loss of the fear of God. What is being dumped on our culture is shocking:
⇒ Brazen crimes are being committed in broad daylight.
⇒ Pornography on television and in books and movies is graphic, destructively graphic.
⇒ God's name is constantly being used as a derogatory slang word.
⇒ Morality is being mocked as "old-fashioned."
⇒ Violent and militant hate groups are springing up all over the world.

It is this kind of arrogance that has leveled every safeguard put in place by God-fearing people. Now, even the houses of worship are under attack!

*It was a dark summer night, 1996, small town, USA. The final step of an evil plan that was even darker than the night was getting ready to be carried out. Two men whose eyes were red with hate stepped close to the window of the country church. Peering inside the empty building, they saw the rows of pews that usually held the devoted flock of believers. Looking across the room was the pulpit that resounded with triumph every Sunday. The choir loft, empty now, seemed to ring with the yielded voices of praise. Weddings that brought believers together were a part of this building. Funerals that told believers good-bye until a later day were the glue that helped the flock keep the faith. Yes, there were a lot a memories in this meeting place.*

*The memories. That was all that was left of the old country church the next morning. The arsonist's fire had completely destroyed the building. Standing outside the smoldering ruins that day, a little girl held her daddy's hand and said, "Daddy, why? Aren't people afraid of God anymore?"*

The little girl asked a good question: *Aren't people afraid of God anymore?* This scene could have been in any church, any town, any country, any time of the day. No person, no place, no organization has a monopoly on sinful acts. Day by day the world grows a little more arrogant and bold in its misdeeds. Where do you fit in? Do *you* fear the Lord? Will *you* take a stand?

**QUESTIONS:**
1. Sinful men are intoxicated with the feeling and power of sin. How can you guard yourself from being overcome by the desires and power of sin?
2. Hopefully you would never harm much less murder a person. But have you ever held hate in your heart for someone? Have you ever wished someone ill-will? How do these kinds of emotions enter your heart? What is the best way to deal with these emotions?
3. The depraved nature of man destroys and causes misery. What has man destroyed that has affected you personally?
4. In today's society, the fear of God has been forgotten by many--even by some believers. What causes this spiritual tragedy? In what ways can you reinforce your fear of God?

## 5. THE CASE OF THE LAW (v.19-20).
Note five points.

1. *The law or Scripture speaks to all.* Note the words "we know." Paul means that this is an obvious truth, a clear truth that cannot be missed. All that has just been said has been quoted from Scripture (v.9-18), and Scripture speaks and is intended for everyone. Therefore, all are guilty before God, both Jew and Gentile. Scripture charges everyone

with sin, declaring that "all are under sin"--all are subject to its power and authority. No one escapes the charge of God's law. The case of God's law is against everyone, both religionist and heathen.

2. *The law or Scripture stops all boasting*, every mouth that acts self-sufficient and declares the goodness of men. In light of man's sinful nature and tongue and behavior, who can boast? Who can declare man's goodness and righteousness and capabilities? Who can say anything against God's case against men? Scripture declares that no man is good, leaving only One who could be good, and that is God. God alone is good; God alone deserves praise and honor and glory. Man can boast in God and in God alone. Man is silenced; he has no reason and no right to boast in himself. The law, God's case against man, stops his mouth.

> **"For they being ignorant of God's righteousness, and going about to establish their own righteousness, have not submitted themselves unto the righteousness of God" (Ro.10:3).**
> **"[The law] was added because of transgressions" (Gal.3:19).**

3. *The law or Scripture makes all the world guilty before God*. God's law declares:

> **"For as many as are of the works of the law are under the curse: for it is written, Cursed is every one that continueth not in all things which are written in the book of the law to do them" (Gal.3:10).**

No one escapes. All the world stands face to face before God--stands imperfect, stands short of His glory, stands guilty of sin.

4. *The law justifies no flesh*. Note carefully what is being said.
   ⇒ No law and no deed of the law will ever justify a man (make him acceptable to God).
   ⇒ Man cannot be justified by keeping any law or work.
   ⇒ Man cannot be justified by any righteousness or good deed of his own.
   ⇒ No flesh, no man, will be justified in God's sight, not by the law.

> **"Knowing this, that the law is not made for a righteous man, but for the lawless and disobedient, for the ungodly and for sinners, for unholy and profane, for murderers of fathers and murderers of mothers, for manslayers, for whoremongers, for them that defile themselves with mankind, for menstealers, for liars, for perjured persons, and if there be any other thing that is contrary to sound doctrine" (1 Tim.1:9-10).**

5. *The law shows man that he is sinful*. The purpose of the law is not to justify, but to point out sin, to tell a man that he is a sinner. The law was given to make a man aware of his sin. Why? So that man would know he is sinful and that he needs to seek God for forgiveness and salvation.

> **"But now the righteousness of God without the law is manifested, being witnessed by the law and the prophets; even the righteousness of God which is by faith of Jesus Christ unto all and upon all them that believe: for there is no difference: for all have sinned, and come short of the glory of God; being justified freely by his grace through the redemption that is in Christ Jesus" (Ro.3:21-24).**

## QUESTIONS:
1. What is the ultimate purpose of the law? Do you allow the law to do its work-- what it is supposed to do--in your heart and life?
2. What does the law do to the pride of any man?
3. Without the law, how would you have come to see your need for Christ?

## SUMMARY:

Remember: every man is sinful. Every man is lost. Your only hope of escaping condemnation is in Jesus Christ. For thousands of years, people all over the world have come to their end without hope. But Jesus Christ came to earth and died for our sins. The believer now has hope, even though God has a solid case against mankind.

1. The charge: all men are under the power of sin.
2. The case of a sinful nature.
3. The case of a sinful tongue.
4. The case of sinful acts.
5. The case of the law.

## PERSONAL JOURNAL NOTES
### (Reflection & Response)

1. The most important thing that I learned from this lesson was:

2. The area that I need to work on the most is:

3. I can apply this lesson to my life by:

4. Closing Statement of Commitment:

| | Scripture | Outline |
|---|---|---|
| **III. FAITH AND JUSTIFICATION: THE WAY FOR THE WORLD TO BE RIGHT WITH GOD, 3:21-5:21** | difference:<br>23 For all have sinned, and come short of the glory of God; | 1) All have sinned<br>2) All come short of God's glory |
| **A. Righteousness: The Way to Be Right with God, 3:21-26** | 24 Being justified freely by his grace through the redemption that is in Christ Jesus: | 3. Rgt. is only possible through justification<br>a. Is free—by grace<br>b. Is through redemption |
| **1. Righteousness is now revealed**<br>a. The rgt. without law<br>b. The rgt. foretold | 25 Whom God hath set forth to be a propitiation through faith in his blood, to declare his righteousness for the remission of sins that are past, through the forbearance of God; | 4. Rgt. is by an act of God alone: By propitiation (sacrifice)<br>5. Rgt. has one great purpose: To proclaim God's personal righteousness |
| **21** But now the righteousness of God without the law is manifested, being witnessed by the law and the prophets; | | a. That He forgives sin<br>b. That He is forbearing |
| c. The rgt. by Christ<br>**2. Rgt. is for everyone**<br>a. All who believe<br>b. All who need: "There is no difference" | 22 Even the righteousness of God which is by faith of Jesus Christ unto all and upon all them that believe: for there is no | 26 To declare, I say, at this time his righteousness: that he might be just, and the justifier of him which believeth in Jesus. | c. That He is just<br>d. That He is the justifier of believers |

## Section III

## FAITH AND JUSTIFICATION: THE WAY FOR THE WORLD TO BE RIGHT WITH GOD
### Romans 3:21-5:21

**Study 1: Righteousness: The Way to be Right With God**

**Text:** **Romans 3:21-26**

**Aim:** To accept the gift of God's righteousness; to get right with God.

**Memory Verse:**
"For all have sinned, and come short of the glory of God" (Romans 3:23).

**INTRODUCTION:**
You might have heard about the man who wanted to get right with God. *Assuming* that God loved chocolate cake, this man determined in his heart to make a cake for God every day. This ritual went on for years. All the time, this man thought he was doing something that pleased God. One day while a friend was visiting, the friend remarked, "Why are you making all these cakes?" The man was quick to respond with a hint of pride, "I'm making these cakes for God." "But why?" asked the friend. "Don't you know that God loves ANGEL FOOD CAKE!"

In every generation, men have assumed to know what God liked. They assumed:
⇒ that God could be known by the wisdom of men
⇒ that the way to gain God's favor was by good behavior
⇒ that despite sin, man could still become acceptable to God by doing a good deed here and there
⇒ that the way to get right with God was by acting religious

None of these assumptions are valid. Too often, men put more trust in assumptions than they do in God's Word. God has a lot to say about what He requires from men who want to get right with Him.

The "righteousness of God" is used in three ways in Scripture.
1. Righteousness refers to God's character. It means the righteousness, justice, and perfection which God Himself possesses and shows.
2. Righteousness reveals man's lack of godly character. It reveals the sinful, depraved, unrighteous, unjust, and imperfect nature and behavior of man.
3. Righteousness means the perfection which God provides for man in Christ Jesus. When a man allows the Lord Jesus Christ to take his sins, he is given the righteousness of God. Christ robes the man in the righteousness of God Himself--by faith (2 Cor.5:21; Ph.3:9).

The context is usually clear as to which meaning is meant. (See Mt.5:6)

**OUTLINE:**
1. Righteousness is now revealed (v.21-22).
2. Righteousness is for everyone (v.22-23).
3. Righteousness is only possible through justification (v.24).
4. Righteousness is by an act of God alone: by propitiation (sacrifice) (v.25).
5. Righteousness has one purpose: to proclaim God's personal righteousness (v.25-26).

## 1. RIGHTEOUSNESS IS NOW REVEALED (v.21-22).

God has "now" revealed *how* man is to get right with Him. The word "now" is a significant turning point in the message of Romans. It indicates a pivotal point in human history. It is saying two things.
⇒ Before, back then, hundreds and hundreds of years ago, God had patience in that He put up with man's attempts at self-righteousness through the law. *But now* the period of God's righteousness has come--the righteousness that is found in God's very own Son.
⇒ Before, back then, man sinned and sinned, learning the impossibility of putting away his own sin. Man's period of time under law showed him the impossibility of securing righteousness on his own. *But now* the period of God's righteousness has come--the righteousness that is found in God's very own Son.

1. God's righteousness for man is "without law." Righteousness has to be without law, for the law fails in two critical areas.
   a. The law does not allow disobedience; it requires obedience. Anyone who disobeys the law becomes a lawbreaker, a transgressor. He is guilty and to be condemned. And everyone is disobedient at some time and is, therefore, guilty.
   b. The law does not have the power to make a person obedient. It does not have the power to prevent a person from disobeying. It only shows a person's disobedience and inadequate strength to be obedient. It only reveals a person's inability to secure any righteousness whatsoever by self-effort. Therefore, if God was to have men living in His presence, He had to provide a righteousness "without law." There had to be a righteousness that had nothing to do with law.
2. God's righteousness for man was foretold by the Old Testament (prophets and law). This is clearly seen in the next chapter in the lives of Abraham and David (Ro.4:1f). (Cp. Jn.5:39, 46; 1 Pt.1:10-11.)

3. God's righteousness is revealed in Jesus Christ. When Jesus Christ came to earth, He came to *reveal* the perfect righteousness of God. Jesus Christ came to live...

- the sinless life
- the perfect life
- the Ideal life
- the representative life
- the pattern life

Jesus Christ is the perfect embodiment of God's righteousness. In fact, Jesus Christ is God's righteousness; or to say it another way, the righteousness of God is Jesus Christ. God's righteousness is now revealed in and through Jesus Christ Himself.

> **"[That I may] be found in him, not having mine own righteousness, which is of the law, but that which is through the faith of <u>Christ, the righteousness which is of God</u> by faith" (Ph.3:9).**

### ILLUSTRATION:
Having the righteousness of God in your life makes all the difference in the world. This story reminds us how futile the righteousness of men is.

> *There was a young man who really liked to play baseball. He was a novice; he couldn't hit very well, but he really liked to play during those Saturday afternoon games at the park. Seeking to improve his skills, he made a trip to the local sporting goods store and bought a brand-name bat--just like the one his favorite professional player used. Thinking to himself, the young man said, "If that guy can hit the ball a mile with this bat, then so can I!"*
> *And so he bought the bat and used it every Saturday that summer. But nothing changed. The man swung the bat just like he always had and the only thing he hit was the ground as he threw down his prized bat.*

This man came to learn a very important lesson that summer: the secret is not in the bat, but in the one who is swinging the bat. The same principle can be applied to righteousness. Our righteousness does not come from how hard *we* try, but from the One who is the very embodiment of righteousness Himself.

### QUESTIONS:
1. Think about it. If you could only achieve righteousness through obedience to the law, would you ever achieve it? How did God use the law to bring you to Christ?
2. Why is the law powerless to make you obedient?
3. God's righteousness is revealed in Jesus Christ. Why is this so much better than God demanding that you keep the law?

## 2. RIGHTEOUSNESS IS FOR EVERYONE (v.22-23).

Scripture is clear in its declaration.

1. Righteousness is for all who believe. Note that righteousness is both *given to* the believer and *laid upon* the believer.

    a. Righteousness is given *to* the believer as a *possession*.

> **"Whereby are given unto us exceeding great promises: that by these ye might be partakers of the <u>divine nature</u> [righteousness], having escaped the corruption that is in the world through lust" (2 Pt.1:4).**

b. Righteousness is laid _upon_ the believer as a *covering* or clothing.

> **"For he hath made him to be sin for us, who knew no sin; that we might be made the righteousness of God in him" (2 Cor.5:21).**

2. Righteousness is needed by all. There is no difference and no distinction between men. There are two reasons.

    a. All men are sinners. The word *sinned* here is a once-for-all happening. It looks back to the historical entrance of sin into the world. This means that all men...

- inherited the nature of their sinful fathers and mothers
- have sinned and are sinners
- cannot keep from sinning and will sin

> **"For all have sinned, and come short of the glory of God" (Ro.3:23).**
> **"But the scripture hath concluded all under sin, that the promise by faith of Jesus Christ might be given to them that believe" (Gal.3:22).**

    b. All men "come short of God's glory." The tense is present: all men are *coming short*, that is, *continually coming short* of God's glory. Men are in a state or condition of being short of God's glory (see **A CLOSER LOOK, Glory--** Ro.3:23 for discussion).

**QUESTIONS:**
1. Righteousness has been given to every believer as a personal possession. What did you do to deserve this gift?
2. The Bible says our righteousness is like filthy rags (Is.64:6). What makes God's righteousness better than ours? Which one are you more prone to wear? Your own righteousness or God's righteousness? Why?
3. Are you aware of the need for God's righteousness in your life? How can you become more conscious of the need?

---

**A CLOSER LOOK:**

(3:23) **Glory--God, Glory of**: the "glory of God" is God's standard for man. It means His *moral glory*. It means His excellence, splendor, brilliance, brightness, magnificence, preeminence, dignity, majesty, and grace. It means the absolute perfection of God, the perfection of His person. It is this "glory of God" which demands that man correspond perfectly with God--if man wishes to be at peace with God and to live in His presence.

    1. Glory is *light*, perfect light. It is the very highest degree of light: the perfection of splendor, brightness, brilliance, resplendence. This is seen in many passages.

    ⇒ John saw how bright the glory of God is when he had the vision of the new Jerusalem. (The new Jerusalem will be the center or capital of world government in the new heavens and earth.)

> **"The holy Jerusalem...having the glory of God: and her light was like unto a stone, most precious, even like a jasper stone, clear as crystal" (Rev.21:10-11).**
> **"And the city had no need of the sun, neither of the moon, to shine in it: for the glory of God did lighten it, and the Lamb is the light thereof" (Rev.21:23).**

⇒ Jesus experienced the light of God's glory.

> **"And [Jesus] was transfigured before them: and His face did shine as the sun, and His raiment was white as the light" (Mt.17:2).**

⇒ Paul experienced the light of God's glory.

> **"There shone a great light round about me. And I fell unto the ground....And when I could not see for the glory of that light, being led by the hand of them that were with me, I came into Damascus" (Acts 22:6, 11; cp. 9:3-9).**

⇒ Moses experienced the light of God's glory.

> **"Moses wist [knew] not that the skin of his face shone while he [God] talked with him...the skin of his face shone; and they [the people] were afraid to come nigh him" (Ex.34:29-30; cp. 29-35).**

2. Glory is *purity*, perfect purity. It is the very highest degree of virtue and goodness, of quality and morality. It is the highest excellence of character and the perfection of being.

> **"God is light, and in Him is no darkness at all" (1 Jn.1:5).**
> **"There is none good but One, that is, God" (Mt.19:17).**
> **"Your Father which is in heaven is perfect" (Mt.5:48).**
> **"Thou only art holy" (Rev.15:4).**

3. Glory is *majesty*, perfect majesty. It is the very highest degree of preeminence and magnificence, of dignity and honor, of meriting worship and praise.

> **"I saw also the Lord sitting upon a throne, high and lifted up....And one cried unto another, and said, "Holy, holy, holy is the Lord of hosts: the whole earth is full of His glory" (Is.6:1, 3).**

4. Glory is *being*, perfect being. It is the very highest degree of worth, quality and merit, preciousness and value. (See Jn.17:2-3.)

> **"Thou art worthy, O Lord, to receive glory and honour and power: for thou hast created all things, and for thy pleasure they are and were created" (Rev.4:11).**

**QUESTIONS:**
1. Do you think it is possible for mortal man to experience the light of God's glory? Why or why not?
2. God has called men to live in His presence. How often do you take advantage of His gracious offer? What do you need to rearrange in your schedule so you can spend more time in God's presence?

## 3. RIGHTEOUSNESS IS ONLY POSSIBLE THROUGH JUSTIFICATION (v.24).

Remember: When a person believes the gospel--really believes that Christ saves him--God takes that person's faith and *counts it* for righteousness. The person is not righteous; he is still imperfect, still corruptible, and still short of God's glory as a sinful human being. But he does believe that Jesus Christ saves him. Such belief honors God's Son, and because of that, God accepts and counts that person's faith as righteousness. Therefore, he becomes acceptable to God. This is *justification*; this is what is meant by being justified before God.

Note two significant facts.

1. Justification is a free gift of God. Man in no way earns it. Man is justified by God's grace and by God's grace alone. (See Ro.4:16; Tit.2:15.)

2. Justification is only through the redemption that is in Christ Jesus (see **A CLOSER LOOK, Redemption**--Ro.3:24 for discussion).

### QUESTIONS:

1. Righteousness and justification have a major factor in common. What is that factor?
2. Why is justification such an important element in the believer's life? Do you live like it is important to you?
3. Are you faithful to tell others what justification means and why it is important? How can you become more comfortable and competent in talking about justification?

---

### A CLOSER LOOK:

(3:24) **Redemption**: to redeem, to deliver by paying a price. The word is used three ways in the New Testament.

1. It means to redeem: to deliver; to set free from the slave market of sin, death, and hell.

> **"For ye are bought [redeemed] with a price: therefore glorify God in your body, and in your spirit, which are God's" (1 Cor. 6:20).**

2. It means to redeem *out of*: to deliver *out of* the enslavement to sin, death, and hell. It means to be delivered *out of* and never returned.

> **"Christ hath redeemed us from the curse of the law, being made a curse for us: for it is written, Cursed is every one that hangeth on a tree" (Gal.3:13).**

3. It means to redeem: to deliver by paying a price, to buy.

> **"Who gave himself for us, that he might redeem us from all iniquity, and purify unto himself a peculiar people, zealous of good works" (Tit.2:14).**

Redemption is "in Christ Jesus," brought about through His death and sufferings. Of this there can be no doubt; the fact is critical to a person's destiny. Redemption is *not* brought about...

- by the life of Christ
- by the power of Christ
- by the example of Christ

---

Scripture is abundantly clear about this. His cross and His sacrifice in death are what brought about redemption. Redemption is...

- accomplished
- brought about
- produced

- effected
- fulfilled
- a fact

- a reality
- a truth

...because of the shed blood of Jesus Christ, God's very own Son.

> "For the life of the flesh is in the blood: and I have given it to you upon the altar to make an atonement for your souls: for it is the blood that maketh an atonement for the soul" (Lev.17:11).
>
> "Even as the Son of man came not to be ministered unto, but to minister, and to give his life a ransom for many" (Mt.20:28).

**QUESTIONS:**
1. What has Jesus Christ redeemed you *out of*? Do you live each day in a spirit of gratitude for what He has done? Or do you tend to forget and take your redemption for granted?
2. Why is the shed blood of Christ such a critical truth for the believer to understand?

## 4. RIGHTEOUSNESS IS BY AN ACT OF GOD ALONE: BY PROPITIATION (SACRIFICE) (v.25).

Propitiation means to be a sacrifice, a covering, a satisfaction, a payment, an appeasement for sin. Note two very significant points.
1. God is the One who *set forth* Christ to be the propitiation for man's sins.
    ⇒ God set Christ *before Himself*, purposed that He be the propitiation or the sacrifice for man's sin.
    ⇒ God set Christ publicly *before the world*, showing that He is definitely the propitiation for the world's sins.

2. It is Christ Himself who is the propitiation for man's sins. But note: it is not His teachings, power, example, or life that make Christ the propitiation. It is His blood--His sacrifice, His death, His sufferings, His cross--that causes God to accept Jesus as the propitiation. It is the blood of Christ that God accepts as...
- the *sacrifice* for our sins
- the *covering* for our sins
- the *satisfaction* for our sins
- the *payment* for the penalty of our sins
- the *appeasement* of His wrath against sin

What does the Bible mean by "the blood of Christ"? It means *the willingness* of Christ to die (shed His blood) for man. It means *the supreme sacrifice* Christ paid for man's sins. It means *the terrible sufferings* Christ underwent for man's sins. (See Mt.20:19.) It means *the voluntary laying down of His life* for man's sins (Jn.10:17-18).

> "Wherefore in all things it behooved him to be made like unto his brethren, that he might be a merciful and faithful high priest in things pertaining to God, to make reconciliation [propitiation] for the sins of the people" (Heb.2:17).

## APPLICATION:

Have you ever made a sacrifice for someone? Covered a payment for someone? Concealed someone else's mistake? Tried to smooth things over for someone? In each of these cases, you were doing something for someone...

- not because you wanted to abandon the person but because you loved or cared for the person
- not because you had to but because you chose to
- not because the person asked you to help but because the person could not help himself
- not because the person necessarily deserved your help but because he needed your help

This is what Christ did for you. This is what propitiation means. Christ died for you because...

- He loves you
- He chose to die for you
- you could not help yourself
- you needed His help

## QUESTIONS:

1. If Christ had not been your propitiation, your sacrifice, how could you become acceptable to God?
2. Do you fully appreciate what Christ did in sacrificing His life for you? How can you show your appreciation?

## 5. RIGHTEOUSNESS HAS ONE GREAT PURPOSE: TO PROCLAIM GOD'S PERSONAL RIGHTEOUSNESS (v.25-26).

God is righteous and just; therefore, He always does what is right, and He always acts justly toward all persons. This is the reason He has provided a perfect righteousness for man. It was the thing to do: the right thing and the just thing. He is righteous by nature; therefore, he provided righteousness for man. God's righteousness is seen in four glorious facts.

1. *God's righteousness is seen in that He forgives sin.* Christ died for our sins, and God accepts His death as the propitiation or the sacrifice for our sins. Now note: God did not betray Christ or man; He did not reject Christ's death. He did not act unjustly and unrighteously. On the contrary, God did what was right. He acted righteously and justly. He accepted the death of Christ as the sacrifice for our sins; therefore, His forgiveness of sins declares that He is righteous.

**"For this is my blood of the new testament, which is shed for many for the remission of sins" (Mt.26:28).**

2. *God's righteousness is seen in His forbearance, that is, in His patience and long-suffering with man's sin.* Note a most glorious fact: God did not punish man for His sin by destroying all flesh from off the earth; God waited until Christ came before condemning sin *in the flesh.* Remember God is perfect righteousness; therefore, He has to provide a perfect righteousness for man "in the flesh."

⇒ There was no man who could embody perfect righteousness.
⇒ Only God's Son could and did embody perfect righteousness.

The fact that God waited until Christ came, that God was forbearing in holding back the punishment of sin, shows that God is righteous. God's righteousness and His justice are declared by His forbearance.

> **"For what the law could not do, in that it was weak through the flesh, God sending his own Son in the likeness of sinful flesh, and for sin, condemned sin in the flesh" (Ro.8:3).**

3.   *God's righteousness is seen in His justice.* God accepted the death of Christ as the substitute for our sins; He imposed the punishment for sin upon Christ. He did the right and just thing. His righteousness is declared by His justice.

> **"Surely he hath borne our griefs, and carried our sorrows: yet we did esteem him stricken, <u>smitten of God</u>, and afflicted. But he was wounded for our transgressions, he was bruised for our iniquities: the chastisement of our peace was upon him; and with his stripes we are healed. All we like sheep have gone astray; we have turned every one to his own way; and the LORD hath laid on him the iniquity of us all" (Is.53:4-6).**

4.   *God's righteousness is seen in His being the justifier of all who believe.* God takes our faith and counts it as righteousness. He takes our faith and judges us acceptable to Him. Now every thinking man knows he is not righteous: not pure, not holy, not sinless. The fact that God accepts the death of Christ as the sacrifice for our sins and justifies us shows a marvelous truth: it shows that God is righteous and just. The fact that God is our Justifier declares His righteousness.

> **"Wherefore the law was our schoolmaster to bring us unto Christ, that we might be justified by faith" (Gal.3:24).**

### APPLICATION:
A good parent will show his true colors when his child does wrong.   He should...
* be forgiving
* be patient
* punish fairly
* restore the relationship with the child

This is what God does with each of His children--only perfectly so.. What an example for us to follow!

### ILLUSTRATION:
God has given every believer the great gift of faith.   In turn, He takes the faith He has given and counts it as righteousness.   This story illustrates the point.

> *"You've probably heard it said, 'It doesn't matter what you believe; it's how you live that counts.*
> *"A. J. Gordon encountered this philosophy one time as he talked with a fellow passenger on a train.   The man believed he could get to heaven by his good works.   Pointing to the conductor who was making his way through the coach, Gordon asked his new friend, 'Did you ever notice how carefully he always examines the ticket but takes no pains whatever to inspect the passenger?'...*
> *"'You see,' continued Gordon, 'the passenger and the ticket are accepted together.   If he doesn't have one, or has the wrong one, he will be asked to get off*

*the train--no matter how honest he might appear to be. Just as the ticket stands for the man, faith stands for you.'"*[1]

Christ has already paid for your ticket. He has already offered you a trip for all eternity into God's presence. The question is, have you accepted His offer? Are you on your way? Or are you still trying to achieve God's righteousness on your own?

## QUESTIONS:
1. God is *ALWAYS* right. Why do people still question God's timing or ways?
2. Have you ever felt that God could never forgive something you did before you became a believer? What assurance does God give you in this passage?

## SUMMARY:

*Are you right with God?* This is one of the most important questions you will ever be asked. It is a question that will chart your present and your future. The way to be right with God is to receive His righteousness and let it clothe your life. How does God's righteousness have a bearing on your life?

1. Righteousness is now revealed in Jesus Christ.
2. Righteousness is for everyone.
3. Righteousness is only possible through justification, through redemption in Jesus Christ.
4. Righteousness is by an act of God alone: by propitiation, through the sacrifice of Jesus Christ.
5. Righteousness has one purpose: to proclaim God's personal righteousness.

## PERSONAL JOURNAL NOTES
### (Reflection & Response)

1. The most important thing that I learned from this lesson was:



2. The area that I need to work on the most is:



3. I can apply this lesson to my life by:



4. Closing Statement of Commitment:

---

[1]  Michael P. Green. *Illustrations for Biblical Preaching*, p.142.

| | B. Faith: The Way that Puts an End to Human Boasting & Pride, to Self-Righteousness & Works, 3:27-31 | law.<br>29 Is he the God of the Jews only? is he not also of the Gentiles? Yes, of the Gentiles also: | 3. Faith reveals only one God who deals with all equally<br>a. He created all: He is the God of all |
|---|---|---|---|
| 1. Faith excludes boasting<br>  a. Works cause boasting in oneself<br>  b. Faith causes boasting in God<br>2. Faith justifies a man without the works of the law | 27 Where is boasting then? It is excluded. By what law? of works? Nay: but by the law of faith.<br>28 Therefore we conclude that a man is justified by faith without the deeds of the | 30 Seeing it is one God, which shall justify the circumcision by faith, and uncircumcision through faith.<br>31 Do we then make void the law through faith? God forbid: yea, we establish the law. | b. He is the only God: All are justified in the same way—by faith<br><br>4. Faith upholds & establishes the law |

## Section III

### FAITH AND JUSTIFICATION: THE WAY FOR THE WORLD TO BE RIGHT WITH GOD
### Romans 3:21-5:21

**Study 2: Faith: The Way that Puts an End to Human Boasting and Pride, to Self-Righteousness and Works**

**Text:** Romans 3:27-31

**Aim:** To discover the great value of true faith, the faith that is truly placed in God.

**Memory Verse:**
> "Therefore we conclude that a man is justified by faith without the deeds of the law" (Romans 3:28).

### INTRODUCTION:
As you go through an average day, what things do you place your faith in? Think about it for a moment. Is your faith in...
- the stability of the economy?
- the goodness of mankind?
- your own abilities and strength?

Faith in God should be the greatest tool in the believer's life. But as great as faith is, it is often misguided. Faith becomes misguided when the object of your faith is not in God. Whenever faith is removed from God and placed in anything else, the results are predictable.

*You have probably heard about the man who amazed the crowd as he walked on a tight-rope across Niagara Falls. The man who performed this death-defying act received the nervous applause of the people. Scanning the crowd, he asked a certain boy this question: "Do you think I can carry a man on my shoulders on this tight-rope to the other side?" The boy nodded yes. Then the high-wire specialist asked the boy another question: "Do you think I can carry YOU across these falls?" The boy answered with his feet as he quickly ran back into the crowd!*

As the story vividly points out, *claiming* to have faith and *having* faith are two entirely different things! This passage discusses the power of true faith, revealing four things that faith does.

**OUTLINE:**
1. Faith excludes boasting (v.27).
2. Faith justifies a man without the works of the law (v.28).
3. Faith reveals only one God, who deals with all equally (v.29-30).
4. Faith upholds and establishes the law (v.31).

## 1. FAITH EXCLUDES BOASTING (v.27).

Boasting is now excluded and eliminated, banished and made impossible. No man can boast in himself before God. No man can boast in his own righteousness, goodness, merit, or virtue.

What is it that keeps man from boasting and glorying in himself? This is puzzling. Think about it, all the advancements of man...
- the scientific and technological advancements
- the medical and health advancements
- the commercial and farming advancements
- the comfort and recreational advancements

When man is considered, the power of his mind and all that he is able to produce, it is very difficult for some to understand why man cannot boast in himself. What is it, then, that forbids man to boast in himself? What kind of law would prohibit man from glorying in his ability and achievements?

1. It is not the *law of works*. The law of works does not exclude boasting; it promotes boasting. When a man looks at what he has done, at the works of his hands, he is led to boast and to glory in himself. A law of works does not discourage boasting, it encourages it. A law of works encourages a man to be selfish, self-centered, prideful, and self-righteous. It causes a man to stand before God and other men and declare that he...
- is more acceptable than others
- is more deserving than others
- has achieved more than others
- is more sufficient than others
- is more adequate than others
- has no need beyond himself and this world

A law of works causes men to be focused upon self. It causes men to center the world around themselves: to look upon themselves as the power that creates and sustains the world, as the power that gives purpose, meaning, and significance to life. A law of works encourages boasting; it does not exclude it.

> **"Mind not high things, but condescend to men of low estate. Be not wise in your own conceits" (Ro.12:16).**

### ILLUSTRATION:
A person who has bound his life to the law of works is bound to be full of pride. There can be no other result, no other conclusion. The law of works enthrones self as the most important person in the universe.

*Andy was a key employee in a small local business. Working with a team of other well-trained employees, it did not take long for the business to make great gains. And as the business began its rapid rise, Andy rose with it. After being promoted to assistant manager, Andy's personality began to change. As the praise began to flow down from upper management, Andy was quick to take all the credit. "After all," he told himself, "I'm the driving force behind the business."*

*Forgetting the fact that the strength of the business was in how the whole team worked together, Andy began to place his picture on all the advertisements. The more his ego was stroked, the more attention he sought. As the result of an ambitious marketing campaign, Andy's picture was all across town. It amused him to drive down main street and see his picture on a billboard. "If I keep up the good work, the sky is the limit!"*

*One day Andy's fame was converted to shame. Not satisfied with his current income, he wanted more. He was able to rationalize his decision to cheat the company and steal from his customers because 'he deserved to make a little more.' It did not take long for this twisted decision to give Andy the kind of publicity he did not want. This key employee quickly became a disgraced ex-employee--a man whose picture reminded his former customers just what kind of person Andy really was: an egotistical, self-centered crook.*

There is a real temptation to over-emphasize our own importance. This temptation will quickly become sin if we are bound to a law of works, of always having to *prove* our value to others. How prone are you to use other people as your stepping stones to success?

2.    It is the *law of faith*. The law of faith excludes boasting. Man has to boast in God when man believes what Scripture has just declared (Ro.1:18-3:26)...
- that *God is* (does exist),
- that God is the Creator of the universe and can be known by man,
- that man is short of God's glory and righteousness,
- that God has provided righteousness for man *through faith*.

It is God who has created and given man his ability, who has provided righteousness for man. God has provided the way for man to be saved from sin, death, and hell. Therefore, man has to boast in God and not in self, for God is the One who has given man all that he has, both his natural ability and his eternal salvation. It is the law of faith, not the law of works that eliminates boasting.

> **"But let him that glorieth glory in this, that he understandeth and knoweth me, that I am the LORD which exercise lovingkindness, judgment, and righteousness, in the earth: for in these things I delight, saith the LORD" (Jer.9:24).**

## QUESTIONS:
1. What have you done personally that you *could* boast or brag about? How can you overcome the temptation to boast?
2. Why is it so important to boast in Christ and not in yourself? What harm can you cause by boasting in yourself? Why *should* you overcome the temptation to boast?

## 2. FAITH JUSTIFIES A MAN WITHOUT THE WORKS OF THE LAW (v.28).

This is of extreme importance. A man is justified by faith and not by the deeds of the law. Boasting shows this. Who is to be praised and set up as the subject of glory? Is man the one in whom to boast? Is man the one who is to be glorified? If man created himself and saved himself from sin and death by his own works and deeds, then he would be the one to be glorified. But what man can do these things? Man did not make himself nor can man save himself. When we consider that man is corruptible, and that man can do nothing beyond this life, then boasting is excluded. Therefore man is not justified before God by the deeds of the law; he is justified by faith--by believing in God and His righteousness.

## APPLICATION:

Despite the great ability and all the marvelous achievements of man, man is still unable to control things morally, unable to live in love, joy, and peace with others. He is unable to control the shame and devastation of selfishness and greed, disease and accident, sin and death. Man's only hope is to come before God...

- not boasting and glorying in self, but bowing in all humility
- believing in the law of faith: that God saves and justifies man by believing in the righteousness of Jesus Christ

"And he [Abraham] believed in the LORD; and he counted it to him for righteousness" (Gen.15:6).

## QUESTIONS:

1. Do you know any person who can save himself? Who has the power to make himself live eternally, the power to keep from dying? Why do men ignore God and try to save themselves?
2. Why is it so difficult to believe that works have nothing to do with salvation?
3. In the simplest terms, what is man's only hope? How did you come to receive this hope?

## 3. FAITH REVEALS ONLY ONE GOD WHO DEALS WITH ALL EQUALLY (v.29-30).

1. God created everyone; therefore, He is the God of all. There is not one God of the Jew (religionist) and another God of the Gentile. There are not different gods of the races and nations of the world, not a different god of Africa and a different god of India, and a different god for Arabs, and a different god for Americans and on and on. Imagine the foolishness of such an idea! Yet how common the idea is! There is only one God who created the universe and only one God who is the God of all mankind.

   a. There is only one God who created all things: "One God, the Father of whom are all things and we in Him"(1 Cor.8:6).
   b. There is only one God who has made all men alike: "Who made of one blood every nation of men" (Acts 17:26).
   c. There is only one God "in whom we live and move and have our being" (Acts 17:28).

   "And call no man your father [god] upon the earth: for one is your Father, which is in heaven" (Mt.23:9).

2. God is the *only* God; therefore, all are justified--made acceptable to God--in the *same* way: by faith. God does not play favorites or show partiality. God does not make it more difficult for some to be saved. God is God; that is, He is perfectly just and equitable in all His dealings.

   a. There "is [only] one God, who shall justify the circumcision by faith and the uncircumcision through faith" (Ro.3:30).
   b. "There is [only] one God, and one Mediator between God and man, the man Christ Jesus" (1 Tim.2:5).

**"Then Peter opened his mouth, and said, Of a truth I perceive that God is no respecter of persons" (Acts 10:34).**

1. In a world that claims to have millions of gods, how can you explain the existence of only one true and living God to an unbeliever?
2. Why is it so important to believe in the only true and living God, the Creator of all things? What difference does it make who or what you believe in?

## 4. FAITH UPHOLDS AND ESTABLISHES THE LAW (v.31).

This means at least three things.

1.   Jesus Christ established the law. Jesus was everything that God said a man should be. He was the ideal of all that God wants man to be. Therefore, Jesus fulfilled the law perfectly.

But there is something more. Jesus not only fulfilled the statutes of the law, He fulfilled the penalty of the law. He took the penalty and the punishment of man upon Himself and died for man. Man is thereby absolved from the penalty and punishment commanded by the law. Therefore, Jesus established the law by fulfilling both the statutes and penalty demanded by the law.

**"Think not that I am come to destroy the law, or the prophets: I am not come to destroy, but to fulfil" (Mt.5:17).**

2.   The believer establishes the law when he admits he is a law-breaker or a sinner. In so doing, he admits that the law is good. The law is good because it points out his sin (Ro.3:19-20; 5:20; 7:7; Gal.3:19). It makes him guilty and it leads him to confess his need for help outside of himself. But the law is also good because it points man to Christ. It makes man cast himself upon Christ *for righteousness*. It forces him to believe in God and to honor God. Therefore, the believer's faith establishes the law.

**"But the scripture hath concluded all under sin, that the promise by faith of Jesus Christ might be given to them that believe....Wherefore the law was our schoolmaster to bring us unto Christ, that we might be justified by faith" (Gal.3:22, 24).**

3.   The believer establishes the law (much more than a legalist) because in seeing what Christ has done for him, he is driven to please God. The believer sees Christ bearing the guilt and punishment for his crimes (sins), then bows in love and adoration, then arises to work in appreciation for such amazing love. The believer tries to be good, not to earn or to win righteousness, but to serve God. He does not try to put God in debt for salvation, but he thanks God for righteousness, seeing that he owes God whatever service he can do. The genuine believer has come to know above all others that love is a much stronger force than fear.

**"For the love of Christ constraineth us; because we thus judge, that if one died for all, then were all dead: and that he died for all, that they which live should not henceforth live unto themselves, but unto him which died for them, and rose again" (2 Cor.5:14-15).**
**"I am crucified with Christ: nevertheless I live; yet not I, but Christ liveth in me: and the life which I now live in the flesh I live by the faith of the Son of God, who loved me, and gave himself for me" (Gal.2:20).**

## ILLUSTRATION:

The only way a believer can effectively serve God is by walking as Jesus Christ walked, in obedience. Too often, people settle for a life lived in the shadows of sin instead of a life that allows the Light of the world to shine through.

> *"A little boy attended a church that had beautiful stained-glass windows. He was told that the windows contained pictures of Saint Matthew, Saint Mark, Saint Luke, Saint John, Saint Paul, and other saints.*
> *"One day he was asked, 'What is a saint?' He replied, 'A saint is a person whom the light shines through.'"*[1]

The more you choose to walk in the light, the more His light will shine through you.

## QUESTIONS:

1. Since Jesus Christ is greater than the law, why is it even necessary for us to worry about obeying the law?
2. When did you first realize that you were a law-breaker (a sinner)? How did you come to this knowledge?
3. What motivates you to please God: your fear of punishment for breaking the law or your devotion to Him?

## SUMMARY:

How active is your faith? Faith in God is one of the greatest forces in all the world. The charge to each believer is to use faith and not abuse it through neglect. Why is faith in God so important? Because...

1. Faith excludes boasting.
2. Faith justifies a man without the works of the law.
3. Faith reveals only one God, who deals with all equally.
4. Faith upholds and establishes the law.

## PERSONAL JOURNAL NOTES
### (Reflection & Response)

1. The most important thing that I learned from this lesson was:


2. The area that I need to work on the most is:


3. I can apply this lesson to my life by:


4. Closing Statement of Commitment:

---

[1] Michael P. Green. *Illustrations for Biblical Preaching*, p.310.

| | **CHAPTER 4** | worketh is the reward not reckoned of grace but of debt. | **worker or laborer** a. Works necessitate debt |
|---|---|---|---|
| | **C. Logic: The Evidence that Faith Alone Justifies a Man, 4:1-8** | 5 But to him that worketh not, but believeth on him that justifieth the ungodly, his faith is counted for righteousness. | b. Believing in God results in righteousness |
| **1. The logic of Abraham's justification** | **W**hat shall we say then that Abraham our father, as pertaining to the flesh, hath found? | 6 Even as David also describeth the blessedness of the man, unto whom God imputeth righteousness | **3. The logic of David's example: A blessed man** |
| a. He was not justified by works (works cannot qualify one to glory before God) | 2 For if Abraham were justified by works, he hath whereof to glory; but not before God. | without works, 7 Saying, Blessed are they whose iniquities are forgiven, and | a. The blessed man is the man who is counted righteous without works |
| b. He was justified by believing God | 3 For what saith the scripture? Abraham believed God, and it was counted unto him for righteousness. | whose sins are covered. 8 Blessed is the man to whom the Lord will | b. The blessed man is the man whose sins are forgiven & covered |
| **2. The logic of the** | 4 Now to him that | not impute sin. | c. The blessed man is the man whose sins are not counted |

## Section III

## FAITH AND JUSTIFICATION: THE WAY FOR THE WORLD TO BE RIGHT WITH GOD
### Romans 3:21-5:21

**Study 3: Logic: The Evidence that Faith Alone Justifies a Man**

**Text:** Romans 4:1-8

**Aim:** To logically prove one clear fact: faith alone--not works--justifies a man.

**Memory Verse:**
> "For what saith the scripture? Abraham believed God, and it was counted unto him for righteousness" (Romans 4:3).

## INTRODUCTION:

Many people are familiar with a piece of equipment called a treadmill. They can be found in all exercise gyms and in a good number of homes. Their styles and prices range from the moderate to the extravagant, but most treadmills at least have a speed adjustment so the user can control how fast or slow he wants to walk or run.

This same piece of equipment is also found in many hospitals to measure the amount of stress upon the heart. The man who takes the treadmill test there is unable to control the speed according to his own comfort level. There it is the doctor who controls the rate of speed. When a man with a bad heart takes the treadmill test in the hospital, although he does the best he can, he is not good enough to pass the test. The test reveals a clear fact: he needs the immediate care of the doctor.

Likewise, if men are left on their own to set their own standards and pace in life, they might feel they are doing just fine. But when put to the test by the Great Physician, the

Lord Jesus Christ, they fail every time. It is then and only then that they recognize they need help beyond themselves, help that only God can provide.

This is the importance of understanding that it is your faith in Christ alone that makes you acceptable to God, not just doing the best you can. Most people actually believe they secure God's approval by being reasonably good: by being a respectable and upright citizen and by occasionally helping others who are less fortunate. But note a startling fact: a man is not justified by works but by faith. Logic proves the fact.

**OUTLINE:**
1. The logic of Abraham's justification (v.1-3).
2. The logic of the worker or laborer (v.4-5).
3. The logic of David's example: a blessed man (v.6-8).

---

**A CLOSER LOOK:**

(4:1-25) **Abraham--Jews, the Seed--Justification--Righteousness--New Creation**: Abraham held a unique position in the Jewish nation, for he was the founder of the nation. He was the man whom God had challenged to be a witness to the other nations of the world--a witness to the only living and true God. God had appeared to Abraham and challenged him to leave his home, his friends, his employment, and his country. God made two great promises if Abraham would follow God unquestionably: Abraham would become the father of a new nation, and all nations of the earth would be blessed by his seed (Gen.12:1-5; 13:14-17; 15:1-7; 17:1-8, 15-19; 22:15-18; 26:2-5, 24; 28:13-15; 35:9-12; Jn.4:22).

Scripture says Abraham did as God requested. He went out not knowing where he went (Heb.11:8). He completely and unquestionably trusted God and took God at His word.

Now note: it was not Abraham's keeping of the law that pleased God. In fact, the law had not yet been given (Gal.3:17). What pleased God and what caused God to justify Abraham was Abraham doing as God had said. Abraham simply *believed* the promise of God that God would give him a new life--in a new nation--with a new people. (See Gal.3:8, 16; Heb.11:8-10; 11:13-16; 11:17-19.)

Note several things.
1. Abraham and his "seed" were the only ones to whom God gave the promises. This is emphatically stated (Ro.4:13-25; Gal.3:6-16, 26, 29).
2. Only a promise was given to Abraham (Ro.4:13-21; Gal.3:14, 18-21, 29). No other information whatsoever was given. God did not identify the country nor tell Abraham where he was to go. Neither did God tell Abraham when his wife (Sarah) would bear the seed (the male child) from whom the promised nation would be born. God made a simple promise, and all Abraham had to go on was that simple promise, that is, the sheer Word of God.
3. Only one condition was attached to the promise. Abraham had to believe God. No works whatsoever were involved.
4. Abraham did believe God (Gen.12:4-5; Ro.4:3, 11-22; Gal.3:6; Heb.11:8f).
5. Abraham was *counted righteous* because he believed God (Ro.4:3-5, 9-13, 19-22; Gal.3:6; cp. Gen.15:6). God did not count him righteous because of who he was or what he had done. He simply believed God. Therefore, God took his faith and *counted* his faith as righteousness.
6. The proof that Abraham really believed God was that he did what God had said. His faith *preceded* his obedience. He believed God and then he obeyed God. If he had not believed God, he would not have left his home or his employment. He would not have left

his familiar surroundings and meaningful relationships and personal attachments. The fact that he did as God asked was evidence that he believed the promise of God.

7. The man who believes God is the man who receives the promises of God (Ro.4:5-12, 16-17, 23-25; Gal.3:7-9, 14, 22, 26, 29). Paul argues that neither heritage nor nationality, neither merit nor works, neither the law nor the rules of the law have anything to do with the promises of God (Gal.3:6-7). The true children of Abraham are those who believe God--any person of any nation. In fact, God's promise that a nation would be born to Abraham and "his seed" was the promise of an eternal nation. This eternal nation is to be of another world, of another dimension of being: the spiritual dimension, a dimension just as real as the physical dimension. But it is to have one distinction: every citizen is to be a believer--one who has believed God and His Word. This is exactly what this passage is saying: "They who believe are the children of Abraham, the children of God's promise. They are to be blessed along with faithful Abraham. They are to be the citizens of God's Kingdom, of 'the new heavens and the new earth.'" (Cp. Heb.11:8-18; 2 Pt.3:10-14.)

## QUESTIONS:

1. What promises did God make to Abraham? How can you benefit from what God promised Abraham?
2. What specifically did Abraham do that pleased God? How often do you please God in the way that Abraham did?
   _____When I'm in a good mood.
   _____When things are going my way.
   _____When it is convenient for me.
   _____When it makes me look good to God and to others.
   Whenever He tells me to.
3. Have there been times when you failed to believe what God promised you? What did you lose from those experiences? What would you do differently if you had another chance?
4. In the believer's spiritual journey, the promises of God are the only things to hang on to. Why does God choose to have you trust Him for the things that you cannot see?
5. What is the ultimate proof that you are trusting in God?

## 1. THE LOGIC OF ABRAHAM'S JUSTIFICATION (v.1-3).

A person can look at Abraham's life and logically see that a man is not justified by works but by faith.

1. Abraham was not justified by works, for works *cannot qualify* a person to glory before God. Now note this: if Abraham had been justified by works...
   * he *would be* qualified to glory or boast before men
   * but he *would not be* qualified to glory or boast before God

Think about it--the logic, the clarity of the matter. No man is ever qualified to glory or boast before God. No act or work or combination of acts and works could ever elevate man to such a height that he could glory or become qualified before God.

2. Abraham was justified by believing God. What happened was this. Abraham believed God, and God took Abraham's belief and counted his belief as righteousness. It was not Abraham's works, but his faith that God took and counted as righteousness. It was all an act of God; therefore, all glory belonged to God not to Abraham. Man is saved by faith; that is, God takes a man's faith and counts that man's faith as righteousness. Such has to be the case.

⇒ God is perfect; He is perfectly righteous. No man can achieve perfection; therefore, no man can live in the presence of God.

⇒ However, God is also love. So what God does is take a person's faith (any person's faith who is truly sincere) and counts that faith as righteousness, as perfection. Therefore, a man is able to live in God's presence by faith or justification.

**"Many will say to me in that day, Lord, Lord, have we not prophesied in thy name? and in thy name have cast out devils? and in thy name done many wonderful works? And then will I profess unto them, I never knew you: depart from me, ye that work iniquity" (Mt.7:22-23).**

## APPLICATION:

Why does God justify a man through faith? There are at least two reasons.

First, God loves man with a perfect love. God wants everyone to live with Him in a *perfect state of being* throughout all eternity. God is perfect; therefore, He alone can provide the only perfect way for man to live in His presence. Because God is love, He has reached out for man by providing that perfect way through Jesus Christ, His Son.

**"Verily, verily, I say unto you, He that heareth my word, and believeth on him that sent me, hath everlasting life, and shall not come into condemnation; but is passed from death unto life" (Jn.5:24).**

Second, God loves His Son with a perfect love. Any person who honors God's Son by believing in Him is accepted by God. That is, God takes that person's belief and counts it as righteousness. The person receives the right to live in God's presence in a *perfect state of being*.

**"In whom also we have obtained an inheritance, being predestinated according to the purpose of him who worketh all things after the counsel of his own will: That we should be to the praise of his glory, who first trusted in Christ" (Eph. 1:11-12).**
**"For the Father himself loveth you, because ye have loved me, and have believed that I came out from God" (Jn.16:27).**

## ILLUSTRATION:

Take a moment and think about what God has done for you in Jesus Christ. Through the Father's perfect love for His Son, He also allows you to love Christ-- even though...

- your love is not perfect
- your life is not perfect
- your choices are not perfect

It is God and God alone who makes you righteous, who makes you perfect in His eyes.

*The students in the sculptor's studio had come for their last day of lessons. For several months, each student had tried to apply what he had learned from his teacher. The assignment for all was to create a statue that symbolized the per-*

*fection of man. Each student stood behind his finished work, waiting for his teacher's evaluation.*

*The first student's statue looked pretty good to the untrained eye: The impressive image appeared to be without any flaws. The skilled teacher took one look and remarked, "No, this one will not do. You have his eyes looking down."*

*The teacher went on to the next student. This statue looked even better than the first. Once again, the teacher noticed a flaw in this statue. "No, this one does not pass. You have his eyes closed."*

*The third student's statue did not have the same graceful curves as the other two statues. The features of the face were not sharp and striking. While he was working on his statue, a large crack had occurred--right in the middle of the stone. Try as he did, the crack was impossible to hide. The student hung his head down, expecting to hear the same judgment upon his work as the others. "Yes! This is what I am looking for. Look at the eyes...they are looking up."*

*Taken aback, the third student asked his teacher, "Master, I do not fully understand. My work is marred with an obvious defect and my craftsmanship is awful when compared to the other statues. What is so important about the eyes?"*

*The sculptor looked at all his students and said, "The first two statues were made with the hopes of being judged perfect. But the man who looks away from God will never be made perfect. However, the man who looks up toward God will be made perfect by Him--despite his many flaws."*

How are you planning to be perfect: Are you looking at yourself, or are you looking up to God?

## QUESTIONS:

1. Chances are that someone is looking at your life, seeking an example of what a Christian is like. How evident is it in your life that your salvation, your acceptance by God, has been accomplished by faith?
2. Why is it impossible for your good works to make you acceptable before God?
3. Is anyone ever qualified to stand before the Lord based upon the good things he does? Why?
4. What role does your love for Christ play in God's making you righteous?

## 2. THE LOGIC OF THE WORKER OR LABORER (v.4-5).

A person can look at the day-to-day laborer and logically see that a man is not justified by works but by faith.

1.     Works necessitates *debt*. When a man works, someone owes him something. If a man could work for righteousness, that is, work so that God would owe him righteousness, then God would owe man. But God, being God, is completely self-sufficient; therefore, He cannot be put in debt to any man. He cannot *be made or forced* to do anything.

2.     Believing in God results in righteousness. It is the "ungodly" persons who believe who are counted righteous (cp. Ro.5:6). This is because the man who admits he is ungodly is the man who rejects self, sensing his need for *godly help* in spiritual matters. He is ready to give himself up and honor and glorify God alone. Therefore, he centers and wraps his whole life around God, depending solely upon God for righteousness.

## APPLICATION:

God can never turn away from a person who senses and confesses his ungodliness, who wishes to recognize and glorify God. God is love, and God's love is bound to be moved by so humble an act and faith.

# ROMANS 4:1-8

**"Therefore being justified by faith, we have peace with God through our Lord Jesus Christ" (Ro.5:1).**

The converse teaching of Scripture needs to be remembered: the man who does not admit he is ungodly, who does not reject self and sense the need for godly help is the man declared to be self-sufficient and self-righteous. Therefore, he is pronounced unjustified, not so much because God rejects him as the fact that he has already rejected God.

**"He that believeth on him is not condemned: but he that believeth not is condemned already, because he hath not believed in the name of the only begotten Son of God" (Jn.3:18).**

**QUESTIONS:**
1. Take a moment and think back over your life. What have you done that has put God in your debt? Can anyone do enough to put God in his debt?
2. How can you use verses 4 and 5 to show an unbeliever the logic of works vs. faith? Why are these verses such an encouragement to the believer?

## 3. THE LOGIC OF DAVID'S BLESSED MAN (v.6-8).

A person can look at prophecy, at the man described by David, and see clearly that justification is not by works but by faith (cp. Ps.32:1-2). Note who the blessed man is.

1. The blessed man is the man who is *counted* righteous without works. Note the word *impute*. It means to reckon, to count, to put to one's account, to credit, to deposit. Just think for a moment. If God credits and counts a man righteous "without works," then we know something: *Man is not justified by works but by faith.*

Pure logic tells us this. Therefore, the blessed man is the man who has righteousness *imputed, credited, counted* to him...
- not because of his works,
- but because he believes God, and God loves him so much that He takes the man's belief and counts it as righteousness.

2. The blessed man is the man whose sins are forgiven and covered. Think for a moment. Lawlessness (sin) exists despite all the works and efforts of men to eliminate it. No matter how hard men try, lawlessness still exists. If lawlessness is to be handled, it has to be handled by God and God alone. He simply has to forgive man's lawlessness (sin).

Now note: logic tells us that if God loves that much, loves enough to simply forgive men for sin, then justification is not by law but by faith.

3. The blessed man is the man whose sins are not imputed or counted against him. Note: it is not the acts of men but the act of God that justifies men and does not count sin against them. A man cannot justify himself before God. No man can free himself from sin and force God to accept him--not by his own hand. Justification--complete deliverance from sin and condemnation--comes from God and God alone, not from some act of man. Therefore, logic tells us that it is not works that justifies a man but faith.

**"Let the wicked forsake his way, and the unrighteous man his thoughts: and let him return unto the Lord, and he will have mercy upon him; and to our God, for he will abundantly pardon" (Is.55:7).**

**"If we confess our sins, he is faithful and just to forgive us our sins, and to cleanse us from all unrighteousness" (1 Jn.1:9).**

# ROMANS 4:1-8

**ILLUSTRATION:**

Have you ever stopped to realize that every sin you have *yet to commit* has already been forgiven and covered by Jesus Christ?

> *"A wealthy English merchant who lived on the European continent was satisfied with nothing but the best.  This attitude extended even as far as the cars he owned.  His pride and joy was a Rolls-Royce coupe that he had owned for years and that he had given great service all that time.  One day, while driving down a bumpy road, his car hit a deep pothole, resulting in a broken rear axle.*
> *"The owner had the car shipped back to the Rolls plant in England and was surprised by the quick repair that was performed.  He received no bill for the work and, knowing his warranty had run out, he had expected one.  He waited for months and still no bill came.  So he finally communicated with the company about the bill for his car repairs.  Again the response from the factory was immediate.  The reply said, 'We have thoroughly searched our files and find no record of a Rolls-Royce axle ever breaking.'*
> *"This is a case where the integrity and excellence of that company would not permit a flaw in workmanship or materials to be made known.  The excellence of Christ does not permit our flaws to be made known to the Father.  He accomplishes* [carries out, finishes] *our forgiveness."*[1]

> **"He hath not dealt with us after our sins; nor rewarded us according to our iniquities.  For as the heaven is high above the earth, *so* great is his mercy toward them that fear him.  As far as the east is from the west, *so* far hath he removed our transgressions from us"** (Ps.103:10-12).

What a glorious truth: there is no record of your forgiven sin in heaven!

**QUESTIONS:**
1. The word "impute" is a very rich term.  What does it mean to you as a believer?
2. When Jesus Christ died on the cross for your sins, He died for *every one of them*.  Have you ever felt that the sins you committed were too great to cover, that you did not deserve forgiveness?  How can you trust God with all your sins?
3. What proof do you have that God is not keeping score with your sins (keeping count of your sins against you)?

**SUMMARY:**

"Doing the best you can" will never be good enough to make you acceptable to God.  God requires your *faith* not your *works*.  True, your faith will produce obedience, will produce good works--but it is your faith that justifies you not your works.  This was proven by:

1.  The logic of Abraham's justification.
2.  The logic of the worker or laborer.
3.  The logic of David's example: a blessed man.

---

[1]  Michael P. Green. *Illustrations for Biblical Preaching*, p.154.

# ROMANS 4:1-8

## PERSONAL JOURNAL NOTES
### (Reflection & Response)

1. The most important thing that I learned from this lesson was:

2. The area that I need to work on the most is:

3. I can apply this lesson to my life by:

4. Closing Statement of Commitment:

| | **D. Rituals, Rules, & Ordinances: The Wrong Way for a Man to Seek Justification, 4:9-12** | the sign of circumcision, a seal of the righteousness of the faith which he had yet being uncircumcised: that he might be the father of | **circumcision as a sign or symbol only** |
|---|---|---|---|
| **1. Who receives the blessing of forgiveness?** | 9 Cometh this blessedness then upon the circumcision only, or upon the uncircumcision also? for we say that faith was reckoned to Abraham for righteousness. | all them that believe, though they be not circumcised; that righteousness might be imputed unto them also: | **5. Abraham was chosen by God for a twofold purpose** |
| a. The religious only? | | | a. To be the "father" of all believers: Regardless of ritual & ordinance |
| b. The non-religious also? | | | |
| **2. Abraham was counted righteous when he believed** | | | |
| **3. Abraham was counted righteous before the ritual, that is, before circumcision** | 10 How was it then reckoned? when he was in circumcision, or in uncircumcision? Not in circumcision, but in uncircumcision. | 12 And the father of circumcision to them who are not of the circumcision only, but who also walk in the steps of that faith of our father Abraham, which he had being yet uncircumcised. | b. To be the "father" of the circumcised, the religious: Those who follow "in the steps of his faith" |
| **4. Abraham received** | 11 And he received | | |

## Section III

## FAITH AND JUSTIFICATION: THE WAY FOR THE WORLD TO BE RIGHT WITH GOD
### Romans 3:21-5:21

**Study 4: Rituals, Rules, and Ordinances: The Wrong Way for a Man to Seek Justification**

**Text:** **Romans 4:9-12**

**Aim:** To give faith its proper emphasis; to understand the relationship between rituals, faith, and salvation.

**Memory Verse:**
> **"Are ye so foolish? having begun in the Spirit, are ye now made perfect by the flesh?" (Gal. 3:3).**

## INTRODUCTION:

It is one thing to live by the rules that God has given. It is a different story altogether when men make up the rules for others to live by and do so in the name of God. Throughout history, mankind has come up with a number of erroneous rules:
⇒ The only way to God is to keep the traditions of the church.
⇒ The only way to God is to pray in a certain posture.
⇒ The only way to God is to be a part of a certain denomination.
⇒ The only way to God is to be a member of a certain church.

For many believers, traditionalism (doing that which is not Scriptural) has replaced a vital and growing relationship with Jesus Christ. Far too often, mindless habits of ritual form the essence of a man's religion--habits which have absolutely nothing to do with being a Christian. Author Leith Anderson reminds us of this very thing:

> "The outsider watched with fascination as the Danish village people filed into the Lutheran church building for worship. Each one walked up the center aisle to the place where there was a break between the pews and a plain white wall. Every worshiper paused, turned, and [knelt]... with bowed head and knee facing the blank wall, and then went to sit in their usual pews.
>
> "Since the observer couldn't figure out the meaning of this ritual, he asked both the clergy and the laity for an explanation, but no one knew. 'We've always done it that way' was the sincere but uninformed answer. Further research revealed that there was an elaborate painting of the Virgin Mary behind the white paint on the blank wall. The painting dated back hundreds of years, before the Protestant Reformation when the church was Roman Catholic.
>
> "The village people had bowed to the Virgin for generations as Catholics. When the church became Protestant and the Virgin was painted over, the worshipers just kept on bowing. Generations later the bows continued, even though the reason had long since been forgotten. It was tradition."[1]

Most people are religious in the sense that they keep some religious ordinances, rituals, and rules. This is both good and bad: good in the sense that rituals cause a person to think about some higher being, and bad in the sense that rituals are usually thought to be the way a person becomes acceptable to God. The present passage is as clear as can be: ritual is the wrong way for a man to seek acceptance and justification with God.

**OUTLINE:**
1. Who receives the blessing of forgiveness (v.9)?
2. Abraham was counted righteous when he believed (v.9).
3. Abraham was counted righteous before circumcision, that is, before the ritual (v.10).
4. Abraham received circumcision as a sign or symbol only (v.11).
5. Abraham was chosen by God for a twofold purpose (v.11-12).

## 1. WHO RECEIVES THE BLESSING OF FORGIVENESS (v.9)?

The word "blessedness" or "blessing" refers back to the *blessed man* just discussed (Ro.4:6-8). The blessed man is the man who is justified by faith...
- who is counted righteous without works
- whose sins are forgiven and covered
- whose sins are not counted against him

Such a man is greatly blessed, blessed beyond imagination. But note a critical question. Is the blessing of forgiveness intended...
- for the circumcised only, or for the uncircumcised also?
- for the Jew only, or for the non-Jew (Gentile) also?
- for the religious only, or for the non-religious also?
- for the baptized only, or for the unbaptized also?
- for the saved only, or for the unsaved also?
- for the church member only, or for the unchurched also?
- for the interested only, or for the disinterested also?

---

[1] Leith Anderson. *A Church for the 21st Century.* (Minneapolis, MN: Bethany House Publishers, 1992), Page 145.

Is the blessing of forgiveness--of being justified by faith alone--for only a few people or for all people everywhere? Abraham's experience illustrates the truth for us.

## ILLUSTRATION:

God is not just the God of the Americans, Europeans, Africans or Asians. He is the God of all men who need the Father's love and forgiveness.

> *"A small boy was consistently late coming home from school. His parents warned him that he must be home on time that afternoon, but nevertheless he arrived later than ever. His mother met him at the door and said nothing. His father met him in the living room and said nothing.*
>
> *"At dinner that night, the boy looked at his plate. There was a slice of bread and a glass of water. He looked at his father's full plate and then at his father, but his father remained silent. The boy was crushed.*
>
> *"The father waited for the full impact to sink in, then quietly took the boy's plate and placed it in front of himself. He took his own plate of meat and potatoes, put it in front of the boy, and smiled at his son.*
>
> *"When that boy grew to be a man, he said, 'All my life I've known what God is like by what my father did that night.'"*[2]

God loved you enough to send Christ to die in your place--He did not give you what you deserved; He gave you what you *did not* deserve.

## QUESTIONS:

1. What is it that makes the "blessed man" blessed? How does this apply to your life?
2. When you think of who God intends forgiveness for, how should it impact your witnessing to others?
3. Why would some Christians be hesitant to offer God's forgiveness to people who are different from themselves (i.e. different church, different race, different nationality, different economic status)?

## 2. ABRAHAM WAS COUNTED RIGHTEOUS WHEN HE BELIEVED (v.9).

His *faith* was "reckoned" for righteousness. The word *reckoned* means to credit, to count, to deposit, to put to one's account, to impute. Abraham's faith was *counted* for righteousness or *credited* as righteousness.

Note that Abraham was justified or counted righteous *by faith*; he was not justified...

- by being religious
- by performing good deeds
- by doing some good work
- by being good and virtuous
- by submitting to a ritual
- by joining some body of believers

> **"But after that the kindness and love of God our Saviour toward man appeared, not by works of righteousness which we have done, but according to his mercy he saved us, by the washing of regeneration, and renewing of the Holy Ghost" (Tit.3:4-5).**

---

[2] Craig B. Larson. *Illustrations for Preaching and Teaching*, p.26.

# ROMANS 4:9-12

**QUESTIONS:**
1. Before God can credit you with righteousness, exactly what must you do? How would you compare what you must do with what God did? Is it worth it?
2. Why do so many men fail to see the simplicity of what God requires for salvation?
3. What are some ways men wrongly attempt to receive justification with God?


**3. ABRAHAM WAS COUNTED RIGHTEOUS BEFORE THE RITUAL, THAT IS, BEFORE CIRCUMCISION (v.10).**

This is a crucial point and it is clearly seen. Abraham made his decision to follow God at least fourteen years before he was circumcised. The story of Abraham believing the promises of God is a dramatic picture (cp. Gen.15:1-6, esp. 5-6). Scripture clearly says, "He believed in the Lord, and the Lord counted it to him for righteousness" (Gen.15:6). But the story of his circumcision is two chapters and fourteen years later (Gen.17:9f). He was counted righteous long before he underwent any ritual. His righteousness--his being accepted by God--did not depend upon a ritual; it depended upon his faith and his faith alone. God did not count Abraham righteous because of circumcision, not because of...
- a ritual
- an ordinance
- a good deed
- a moral life
- a ceremony
- a good work
- a religious life

God accepted Abraham and counted him righteous because he believed God and His promises.

**QUESTIONS:**
1. What rituals were you tempted to trust in before you gave your life to Christ? What made these rituals or traditions so attractive to you?
2. Is there a ritual in your life now that is keeping you from truly trusting in God and His promises? Do you believe the ritual can save you? If not, why are you waiting to be saved? Why not ask God to save you now?
3. Why is the timing of Abraham's circumcision such an important fact for you to remember as you share the gospel with others?


**4. ABRAHAM RECEIVED CIRCUMCISION AS A SIGN OR SYMBOL ONLY (v.11).**

Circumcision was not the road into God's presence; it was not what made Abraham acceptable to God. Circumcision *did not confer* righteousness on him; it only confirmed that he was righteous. Circumcision did not convey righteousness on him; it only bore testimony that he was righteous.

Note that circumcision was both a sign and a seal. Circumcision was...
- a sign of celebration: it was a picture of the joy that the believer experienced in being counted righteous by God
- a sign of witness: the believer was testifying that he now believed and trusted God
- a sign of a changed life and a separated life: the believer was proclaiming that he was going to live for God, to live a righteous and pure life that was wholly separated to God
- a sign of identification: the believer was declaring that he was now joining and becoming one of God's people
- a sign pointing toward Christ's baptism

Circumcision was a seal in that it stamped God's justification upon Abraham's mind. Abraham had believed God, and God had counted his faith as righteousness. Circumcision was given as a seal or a stamp upon his body to remind him that God had counted him righteous through belief. Circumcision was a seal in that it...

- confirmed
- assured
- substantiated
- validated
- authenticated
- strengthened
- verified

...what God had done for Abraham. Now note. The Bible never says that rites, rituals, or ordinances bestow anything on anyone. They are merely signs of something that has already taken place. They are merely *shadows* not the *substance* (Col.2:16-17).

This is not to take away from the importance of rites and rituals. They are extremely important, for they are the *signs and seals* of the Christian believer's faith. To neglect or to reject a rite given by God is to be disobedient, and to be disobedient is a clear sign that one was never sincere in the first place. A person who believes, who truly trusts God, is ready to *obey* God, to follow Him even in the rites, rituals, and ordinances of the church. We must always remember that Abraham was not saved by the ritual of circumcision, for circumcision had not yet been given by God as a sign.

⇒ But Abraham was *immediately circumcised* after God established circumcision as the sign of "righteousness by faith."

Very simply said, if circumcision had existed when Abraham first believed God, then Abraham would have been circumcised immediately. He would have obeyed God. How do we know this? Because Abraham truly believed God, and when a man believes God, he immediately begins to do what God says.

## APPLICATION 1:
Circumcision and all other rituals are a matter of the heart, not a matter of being spiritually cleansed by physical and material substances.

> **"For he is not a Jew, which is one outwardly; neither is that circumcision, which is outward in the flesh: but he is a Jew, which is one inwardly; and circumcision is that of the heart, in the spirit, and not in the letter; whose praise is not of men, but of God" (Ro.2:28-29).**

## APPLICATION 2:
This is a strong message on baptism for New Testament believers. A true believer should be baptized immediately upon believing. Baptism should be the first step of obedience in the believer's new life in Christ.

> **"Then Peter said unto them, Repent, and be baptized every one of you in the name of Jesus Christ for the remission of sins, and ye shall receive the gift of the Holy Ghost" (Acts 2:38).**

## QUESTIONS:
1. What are some legitimate rites or rituals observed in your church and what is their purpose? How can you be sure of keeping them in the proper perspective?
2. Why is it even necessary for there to be a sign (whether circumcision, baptism, confirmation, church membership, or whatever) of what God has already done in your heart?
3. What lesson can you gain from Abraham's immediate decision to become circumcised when God established it as a sign of faith?

## 5. ABRAHAM WAS CHOSEN BY GOD FOR A TWOFOLD PURPOSE (v.11-12).

Before looking at the purposes, note that Abraham is said to have a unique relationship to the world. He is seen not as a mere private individual, but as a public man, a representative man of the human race, a pivotal figure in human history. He is seen as the "father" of all who believe God, as the head of the household of faith. God chose Abraham for two specific purposes.

1.     Abraham was chosen that he might be the "father" of all believers regardless of ritual and ordinance. Abraham was chosen by God to be the father of faith to all--all the ungodly and heathen of the world--who repent and believe Jesus Christ to be their Lord and Savior. No matter how uncircumcised, unbaptized, irreligious, immoral and unclean a person is, he has a father in the faith, a father to follow. Abraham is...

|   |   |   |
|---|---|---|
| • the pattern | • the example | • the father |
| • the picture | • the standard | |

...of faith to all the lost of the world. A person...
- does not have to begin to go to church before God will save him.
- does not have to get religious before God will accept him.
- does not have to be baptized or *ritualized* before God will forgive his sins.

What he *has to do* is believe God and believe God's promises. When he bows in humble faith and believes, two things happen:
- ⇒ immediately God counts his faith as righteousness.
- ⇒ immediately he arises and is baptized and begins to keep all the commandments and rituals and ordinances of God.

> **"And Jesus answering said unto them, They that are whole need not a physician; but they that are sick. I came not to call the righteous, but sinners to repentance" (Lk.5:31-32).**
>
> **"For the Son of man is come to seek and to save that which was lost" (Lk.19:10).**

2.     Abraham was chosen that he might be the "father" of the circumcised, of the religious who "follow in the steps of Abraham's faith." Note: it is not being...

|   |   |
|---|---|
| • circumcised | • ritualized |
| • baptized | • religious |
| • moral | • good and virtuous |

...that justifies a religious person. It is "walking in the steps" of Abraham's faith that causes God to accept the religious person.

The religionist cannot earn, merit, or work his way into God's presence and righteousness. He can only trust God for the righteousness of Jesus Christ.

> **"Many will say to me in that day, Lord, Lord, have we not prophesied in thy name? and in thy name have cast out devils? and in thy name done many wonderful works? And then will I profess unto them, I never knew you: depart from me, ye that work iniquity" (Mt.7:22-23).**

## ILLUSTRATION:

Abraham was a great man of God, a man whose simple faith in God has affected billions of lives. What kind of legacy will you leave behind for the next generation?

> *"Charlie Waters, former strong safety for the Dallas Cowboys football team, tells a story about Frank Howard, who had been Charlie's college coach. When Frank Howard was head coach at Clemson University, he went out to practice one Monday before a big game with his first-and third-string quarterbacks out with injuries. That left him with his second-, fourth-, and fifth-string QB's to play the coming Saturday. In the first five minutes of practice, his starting quarterback (previously second-stringer) hurt his knee. That elevated the fourth-stringer to first-string position and put the fifth-stringer on the second team. About ten minutes later, that replacement QB hurt his knee. Well, the fifth-stringer was now next in line for the first team.*
> *"Coach Howard blew the whistle and gathered all the players around him. He took the one remaining QB, put his arm around him, and said in his gruff voice, 'Son, do you believe in magic?' The QB said in a halfhearted way, 'Well, sort of.' Coach Howard looked at him, pointed his five fingers at him like a magician, and said, 'Poof! You are now a first-string quarterback.'"[3]*

If you leave a godly legacy for the next generation, it will not be because of magic or some work you do, but because of your faith in God, your faith in what God has done for you. The best way to impact the world is with your faith. Do you believe God? Really believe Him, believe what He says?

## QUESTIONS:

1. Why did God chose Abraham? Could He have chosen just any man?
2. If God were to choose one person today to carry on the great work of spreading the gospel, could He call on you? Do you strive to be worthy of God's calling through your obedience? What is your responsibility toward God and His promises?

## SUMMARY:

God's Word tells you how to be right with God, how to be justified. Rituals, rules, and ordinances are the wrong way for a man to seek justification. No one can improve on God's way--the way of faith and belief. The faith of Abraham shows us this:

1. Who receives the blessing of forgiveness.
2. Abraham was counted righteous when he believed.
3. Abraham was counted righteous before circumcision, that is, before the ritual.
4. Abraham received circumcision as a sign or symbol only.
5. Abraham was chosen by God for a twofold purpose.

---

[3]   Michael P. Green. *Illustrations for Biblical Preaching*, p.320-321.

# ROMANS 4:9-12

## PERSONAL JOURNAL NOTES
### (Reflection & Response)

1. The most important thing that I learned from this lesson was:

2. The area that I need to work on the most is:

3. I can apply this lesson to my life by:

4. Closing Statement of Commitment:

| | E. Law: The Wrong Way for a Man to be Justified, 4:13-16 | none effect:<br>15 Because the law worketh wrath: for where no law is, there is no transgression. | the promise<br>b. Law works wrath<br>c. Law means transgression |
|---|---|---|---|
| 1. The unmistakable statement: The promise is not through the law but through faith | 13 For the promise, that he should be the heir of the world, was not to Abraham, or to his seed, through the law, but through the righteousness of faith. | 16 Therefore it is of faith, that it might be by grace; to the end the promise might be sure to all the seed; not to that only which is of the law, but to | 3. The argument for faith<br>a. Faith brings grace<br>b. Faith makes the promise sure<br>c. Faith assures the promise for everyone: It is available to all |
| 2. The argument against the law<br>  a. Law voids faith & erases the hope of | 14 For if they which are of the law be heirs, faith is made void, and the promise made of | that also which is of the faith of Abraham; who is the father of us all, | |

## Section III

## FAITH AND JUSTIFICATION: THE WAY FOR THE WORLD TO BE RIGHT WITH GOD
### Romans 3:21-5:21
Study 5: Law: The Wrong Way for a Man to be Justified

**Text:** Romans 4:13-16

**Aim:** To understand why the law cannot save you, why faith in God alone can save you.

**Memory Verse:**
> "For the promise, that he should be the heir of the world, was not to Abraham, or to his seed, through the law, but through the righteousness of faith" (Romans 4:13).

## INTRODUCTION:

Every person has been tripped up by the law. From the habitual criminal to the Sunday school member with the perfect attendance pin, all have failed to keep the law perfectly.

*Henry was a model citizen. He was a father who spent quality time with his kids. He was a good husband who was faithful to his wife. And he was a really good policeman. One night when he was off-duty, he drove by a house and noticed fire coming out of the roof. Henry beat on the locked door and was able to awaken a woman and her children from a sound sleep. As the house was burning to the ground, he went from bedroom to bedroom to ensure that each child was taken out of harm's way. If not for Henry's heroic act, the family probably would have perished. Henry did everything by the book. It was a perfect story about the actions of a perfect citizen.*

*But Henry's story does not end on this happy note. Two weeks later, in a moment of weakness, Henry was caught shoplifting a twenty dollar item from the local department store. Fortunately, the merchant did not press charges because he knew Henry. But Henry was severely reprimanded by his supervising officer and word of his misdeed somehow spread through the small town. His one 'small' mistake cost*

*Henry and his family much pain and embarrassment in the community. His one 'small' mistake ruined a seemingly perfect citizen.*

Thank God a man is not justified by the law and its works, because no man is perfect. The law is the wrong way for a man to seek acceptance and justification by God.

**OUTLINE:**
1. The unmistakable statement: the promise is not through the law but through faith (v.13).
2. The argument against the law (v.14-15).
3. The argument for faith (v.16).

## 1. THE UNMISTAKABLE STATEMENT: THE PROMISE IS NOT THROUGH THE LAW BUT THROUGH FAITH (v.13).

Note several things.
1. The promise involves inheriting the whole world. This is clear from several facts.
   a. Canaan was the *promised land*, a type of heaven and a type of the new heavens and earth God is to recreate for Abraham and his seed (the believer).

   > **"These all died in faith, not having received the promises, but having seen them afar off, and were persuaded of them, and embraced them, and confessed that they were strangers and pilgrims on the earth. For they that say such things declare plainly that they seek a country....But now they desire a better country, that is, an heavenly: wherefore God is not ashamed to be called their God: for he hath prepared for them a city" (Heb.11:13-14, 16).**

   b. Abraham was promised that he would be the "father" of many nations. He is said to be the father of all believers from all nations of the earth (v.11-12). He and his seed (believers) are promised a new world when Christ returns.
   c. Christ is to inherit the world and be exalted as the Sovereign Majesty of the universe, ruling and reigning forever and ever.
   ⇒ Abraham and his seed (believers) are said to be heirs of God and joint heirs with Christ.

   > **"The Spirit itself beareth witness with our spirit, that we are the children of God: and if children, then heirs; heirs of God, and joint-heirs with Christ; if so be that we suffer with him, that we may be also glorified together" (Ro.8:16-17).**

   ⇒ They shall all reign with Christ through all eternity. (See Mt.19:28; Lk.16:10-12; Rev.14:13; 21:24-27.)

   > **"When the Son of man shall come in his glory, and all the holy angels with him, then shall he sit upon the throne of his glory: and before him shall be gathered all nations: and he shall separate them one from another, as a shepherd divideth his sheep from the goats" (Mt.25:31-32).**

2. The "seed" of Abraham refers to *all believers*. This is clear from the promise that is said to be "sure to <u>all the seed</u>" (v.16). Every true believer is an heir of the promise. If a man believes, he receives the most glorious promise: he will inherit the world.

"Blessed are the meek: for they shall inherit the earth" (Mt.5:5).

"And if ye be Christ's, then are ye Abraham's seed, and heirs according to the promise" (Gal.3:29).

3. God does not give the promise through the law, but through the righteousness of faith.

a. A man will not receive an inheritance in the *new world* because he...
   * tried to keep the law
   * did some great works
   * lived by good deeds
   * was baptized and joined a church
   * was moral and very religious

b. A man will receive an inheritance in the *new world* because he...
   * believed God for righteousness, and God took his belief and *counted* it for righteousness.

The point is clearly seen, and it is unmistakable:

"For what saith the scripture? Abraham believed God, and it was counted unto him for righteousness" (Ro.4:3).

"To him that worketh not, but believeth on him that justifieth the ungodly, his faith is counted for righteousness" (Ro.4:5).

"The promise, that he should be the heir of the world, was not...through the law, but through the righteousness of faith" (Ro.4:13).

**ILLUSTRATION:**

Have you ever thought that God's promises are just too good to be true? Many men have thought that very thing--and have suffered the consequences.

"Peter Eldersveld tells of a rich Christian who had a large company of employees, and many of them owed him money. He was constantly trying to teach them something about Christianity, and one day he hit upon a plan. He posted a notice for his employees to see that said, 'All those who will come to my office between eleven and twelve o'clock on Thursday morning to present an honest statement of their debts will have them canceled at once.' The debtors read the notice with a great deal of skepticism, and on Thursday morning, although they gathered in the street in front of his office, not one of them went to the door. Instead they gossiped and complained about their employer, and ridiculed the notice he had posted. They said it didn't make sense.

"But finally, at 11:45, one man jumped forward, dashed up the steps into the office, and presented his statement. 'Why are you here?' the rich man asked him. 'Because you promised to cancel the debts of all those who come as you instructed,' the other replied. 'And do you believe the promise?' 'Yes, I do.' 'Why do you believe it?' persisted the employer. 'Because, although it was too much for me to understand, I know that you are a good man and would not deceive anyone.'

"The rich man took the bill and marked it 'Paid in full,' at which time the poor man, overcome, cried out, 'I knew it! I told them so! They said it couldn't be true, and now I'm going out to show them.' 'Wait,' said his benefactor, 'it's *not quite twelve o'clock. The others are not entitled to any special proof of my sincerity.'*

*"When the clock struck twelve, the forgiven debtor ran out waving his receipt in the face of his fellows. With a mad rush they made for the door, but it was too late. The door was locked."*[1]

God has also promised to cancel your debt of sin--not because of your righteousness but because of His. Have you believed Him?

**QUESTIONS:**
1. What would become of God's promises to you if they were all based upon the law? How good would you have to be?
2. Are you a part of the seed of Abraham? How can you know for sure?
3. All God wants from you is belief. Why are so many men tempted to offer God their works instead? What kinds of things have you offered God?

## 2. THE ARGUMENT AGAINST THE LAW (v.14-15).

The promise of the inheritance does not come through the law. Three facts about the law show this.

1. Law voids faith; it erases any hope of ever receiving the promise. The reason can be simply stated: law demands perfection; law insists that it be obeyed. Law cries out, "Violate and break me and you become guilty and condemned and are to be punished."

No man can live perfectly righteous before God; no man can keep from coming short and breaking the law of God at some point. Therefore every man is a lawbreaker, imperfect and short of God's glory, and is to be condemned and punished.

   a. If the promise of God's inheritance is by law, then no man shall inherit the promise, for the promise is given only to the righteous; and no man is perfectly righteous. This, of course, means something. If the promise is by law, then no man has hope of ever receiving the promise, for he does not and cannot keep the law. The law erases the promise, makes it of no effect or value whatsoever.
   b. If the promise of God's inheritance is by law, then faith is voided and has absolutely nothing to do with securing the promise. A man would have to keep his mind and eyes and, most tragic of all, his heart upon the law, for it would be the law that would determine whether or not the man received the promise. Faith would not be entering the picture; it would be voided, irrelevant, having nothing to with receiving the promise.

   **"For what the law could not do, in that it was weak through the flesh, God sending his own Son in the likeness of sinful flesh, and for sin, condemned sin in the flesh" (Ro.8:3).**

   c. This point is often overlooked. If the promise of God's inheritance comes by the law, then receiving the promise would have nothing to do with faith, nothing to do with...
   • trusting the love of God
   • learning and knowing the love of God
   • focusing one's mind and thoughts upon God
   • knowing God's Son, the Lord Jesus Christ

---

[1] Spiros Zodhiates, Th.D. *Illustrations of Bible Truths*, p.73.

If God accepted us and gave us the promise of inheritance because we kept the law, then we would have to focus our lives upon the law. Believing and loving God and knowing God's Son would have nothing to do with our salvation. The law would force us to seek God by keeping the law. Faith would have nothing to do with the promise. The law would void faith and make useless and ineffective the love of God and the Son of God.

> **"Casting down imaginations, and every high thing that exalteth itself against the knowledge of God, and bringing into captivity every thought to the obedience of Christ" (2 Cor.10:5).**

2. Law works wrath in three terrible ways.
   a. Law shouts out at a man, "Break me and you become guilty, condemned, and are to be punished." Such is antagonistic and stirs and aggravates anger and wrath. When God is seen as a legalistic Person who hovers over us, watching every move we make, there is a tendency to view God as stringent, demanding, condemnatory, upset, angry, vengeful and full of wrath against us. Why? Because we fail and come short ever so often. Therefore if God is legalistic, then He is hovering over us, and not a single one of us is going to inherit the promise. We are guilty and to be judged, and we are not going to be rewarded with an inheritance. Therefore, law works wrath between God and man; it keeps a man from being acceptable to God and from ever receiving the promise of God.
   b. Law works wrath in that it keeps a man tied up in knots, under pressure and tension, in a strain. The man who works to do the law struggles to do the right thing and guards against doing the wrong thing. He fights to avoid all the evil he can, wondering and worrying if he is ever doing enough to be acceptable to God.
   
   Such a life is not full of love and joy and peace. There is no sense of purpose, meaning, and significance, no sense of completeness and fulfillment. Such a life is filled with uneasiness and turmoil, uncertainty and insecurity. Such a life of legalism works wrath: it keeps tension between God and man, establishing and building a strained and uneasy relationship.
   c. Law works wrath in that it causes a man to focus his life upon the law and not upon God. His mind, attention, and thoughts are upon...
      * keeping the rules, not upon trusting God
      * watching where he steps, not upon drawing near God
      * avoiding errors, not upon learning the truth of God
      * observing certain rituals, not upon fellowshipping with God
      * practicing religion, not upon worshipping God

> **"And the commandment, which was ordained to life, I found to be unto death. For sin, taking occasion by the commandment, deceived me, and by it slew me" (Ro.7:10-11).**

**QUESTIONS:**
1. God wants you to obey the law. But if your salvation were dependent upon your complete obedience to the law, how long would you stay saved? What hope would you have when you disobeyed the law? What would the hopelessness do to the quality of your life?
2. Why is your faith such an important ingredient in receiving God's promises?
3. The law works in a very subtle way. It takes a person's focus off the Lord and puts it on the law. What is the key to keeping your focus on God?

3. Law means transgression. There are three reasons for this.
   a. If no law exists, there is no law to break; therefore, there is no transgression. But if there is a law, then breaking the law begins to exist; transgression becomes a reality, a living fact. Where there is no law, there is no transgression; where there is law, there is transgression. The point is this: the man who seeks God's acceptance by keeping the law lives in a world of transgression, of breaking the law and coming short of God's glory. The law means transgression, that a man fails and comes short of God's acceptance; therefore, it means that the legalist is guilty and condemned and is not to receive the promise of God.
   b. When a law exists, there is an urge within man to stretch it to its limits and to break it. This is one of the paradoxes of human nature. Man has that within himself, an *unregulated urge*...

   | | |
   |---|---|
   | • not to be regulated | • to seek his own desires |
   | • not to be ordered around | • to do as he pleases |
   | • not to be restricted | • to fill his fleshly passions |
   | • not to be governed | • to fulfill his urges |
   | • not to be ruled | • to see, have, hold, and get more |

   When a law exists, it *tells* a man he can go this far and no further. He must not go beyond this limit or he becomes a lawbreaker, a transgressor (cp. a speed limit sign). The law actually pulls a man to go that far. It is within his nature to go to the limit, to do as much as he can. The urge within his nature even stirs him to stretch the law and to go beyond its limits.
   ⇒ The grass on the other side looks greener.
   ⇒ The melon on the other side of the fence is juicier.
   ⇒ The stolen fruits are sweeter.
   ⇒ The forbidden is more appealing.
   ⇒ The unknown is more exciting.

   When the law exists, there is transgression. Every man becomes guilty and is to be condemned and punished, not rewarded with the promise.

   > **"For when we were in the flesh, the motions of sins, which were by the law, did work in our members to bring forth fruit unto death" (Ro.7:5).**
   > **"But sin, taking occasion by the commandment, wrought in me all manner of concupiscence. For without the law sin was dead" (Ro.7:8).**

   c. When a law exists, it becomes an accuser, an antagonist. It shouts, "Break me and you become a law-breaker and are to be condemned and punished." Now note: the law has no power to keep a person from transgressing; it can only shout: "Transgression!" The law is...
   • not a power to save but a rule to control and condemn
   • not a savior but a judge

   This is the very problem with the law.
   ⇒ It can only accuse; it cannot deliver.
   ⇒ It can only point out sin; it cannot save from sin.
   ⇒ It can only show a man where he failed; it cannot show him how to keep from failing.
   ⇒ It can only condemn; it has no power to free.

The man who tries to live by law is left hopeless and helpless, for he transgresses and becomes a law-breaker. He is to be condemned, never receiving the inheritance of God's promise.

**"Therefore by the deeds of the law there shall no flesh be justified in his sight: for <u>by the law is the knowledge of sin</u>" (Ro.3:20).**

<u>QUESTIONS:</u>
1. It is natural for people to press the boundaries of the law as much as possible. Whether it be speed limits, tax laws, or labor laws, many people come as close as they can to the edge--and then some. What laws do you press to the limit? If you had no laws, what would you do differently?
2. The law is a very condemning thing, especially if you get caught. Yet God knows your every failure, but you are free of His condemnation. How can you explain that? How can you use this as a powerful testimony to God's love?

## 3. THE ARGUMENT FOR FAITH (v.16).

The promise of the inheritance comes through faith. Three facts about faith show this.
1.    Faith brings grace. *Grace* means a gift, a free·gift, a gift given without expecting anything in return. It means favor, approval, acceptance, goodwill, assistance, help, kindness--all freely given without expecting anything in return.
Picture the scene of a man broken over his sin. He may be a mild sinner or the worst sinner on earth, yet he comes to God. He...
- falls to his knees
- confesses his sin
- confesses his inadequacy to save himself
- cries for God to have mercy and to forgive his sin
- thanks God that He does forgive sin
- praises God for answering his prayer and forgiving his sin

Now, who is the *Savior*, the *Deliverer*, the *Subject* who deserves the praise and the honor and the glory? The answer is obvious: God. God is the center of the picture. This is the very reason salvation and all its promises are by grace through faith. Grace puts God in the center. And when a man makes God the center of his life, casting himself completely upon God and putting all his faith and trust in God, God is bound to hear and answer the man. Why? Because the man is honoring God completely, and the man who honors God is always acceptable and heard by God.
Now note: when a man *really believes* God, his faith brings the grace of God to him. It causes him to focus upon God, to center his life upon the love of God, to see the presence of God, to secure the fellowship and companionship of God, to know the love, joy, peace, care and concern of God. Simply stated, it causes a man to seek a personal relationship with God, a relationship of trust and dependence. Such is the life of grace, the grace that is given to man by faith. It is faith that honors and praises and glorifies God, and because it does, it brings the grace of God to man.

**"Not unto us, O Lord, not unto us, but unto thy name give glory, for thy mercy, and for thy truth's sake" (Ps.115:1).**
**"For by grace are ye saved through faith; and that not of yourselves: it is the gift of God: not of works, lest any man should boast" (Eph.2:8-9; cp. Ro.3:24; 5:15; 11:6; Eph.2:4-10).**

2. Faith makes the promise sure. This is seen in the above point. When God is honored and made the center and focus of one's life and trust, that person can rest assured God will accept him and give him the promise of the inheritance. That man will inherit the earth.

> **"That being justified by his grace, we should be made heirs according to the hope of eternal life" (Tit.3:7).**

3. Faith assures that the promise is for everyone, that it is available to all. The promise is not given to an exclusive club of people, to an exclusive nation or race or class of people. The promise is given to all, to every person on earth. If the promise was by law, then it would be only for those who have the law and are able to keep the law. What then would happen to the heathen who do not have the law and to the handicapped who are unable to do some of the things the law commands? They could never be saved if the promise came by the law. However, when the promise is given by the grace of God through faith, no man is exempt from the inheritance. Every man can be saved and inherit the promise of eternal life in the new heavens and earth, for every man can believe and trust God (the very thing that even a human father wants of his children).

> **"Heaven and earth shall pass away: but my words shall not pass away" (Lk.21:33).**
> **"The works of his hands are verity and judgment; all his commandments are sure" (Ps.111:7).**

### ILLUSTRATION:
Man has tried for thousands of years to find some way to gain eternal life apart from faith in Jesus Christ. But man is doomed to failure apart from Christ.

> *"Ponder the following statements: You may offer like Cain (Gen. 4:3), weep like Esau (Gen. 27:38), serve like Gehazi (2 Ki. 5:20), leave Sodom like Lot's wife (Gen. 19:26), tremble like Felix (Acts 24:25), be zealous for God like Israel (Rom. 10:2), be a disciple like Judas (Acts 1:25), take part in worship like Korah (Num. 16:19), desire to die the death of the righteous like Balaam (Num. 23:10), make long prayers like the Pharisees (Mt. 23:14), prophesy like Saul (1 Sam. 10:10), have lamps like the foolish virgins (Mt. 25:1-13), be a seeking soul like the rich young ruler (Mt. 19:16), be almost a Christian like Agrippa (Acts 26:28), and YET BE LOST!"*[2]

God's grace has made a way for *every* man not to be lost. Have *you* tried it God's way?

> **"For God so loved the world, that he gave his only begotten Son, that whosoever believeth in him should not perish, but have everlasting life" (Jn.3:16).**

---

[2] *INFOsearch Sermon Illustrations* (Arlington, TX: The Computer Assistant, 1-888-868-9029, 1986-1996).

# ROMANS 4:13-16

**QUESTIONS:**

1. The promise of the inheritance comes by faith. How can you be certain this is true for you?
2. How can you make God's grace real in your life every day?
3. Do you think God's promise is just as sure for the person who lives on the other side of the world? The other side of town? The other Christian who goes to a different church? How should this impact your testimony to others?

## SUMMARY:

If the only way to receive God's promise was through keeping the law perfectly, just imagine what life would be like. The first time you made a mistake you would be automatically disqualified you from receiving God's promise. The promise of salvation would never be yours, not if...

- you told a lie
- you stole time from your employer
- you spread a word of gossip
- you lost your temper
- you made things more important than people
- you neglected your relationship with God for the things of the world

Thank God! His precious promise is not bound to laws that no one can keep perfectly. This great truth is reinforced in the Scripture...

1. The unmistakable statement: the promise is not through the law but through faith.
2. The argument against the law.
3. The argument for faith.

## PERSONAL JOURNAL NOTES
### (Reflection & Response)

1. The most important thing that I learned from this lesson was:

2. The area that I need to work on the most is:

3. I can apply this lesson to my life by:

4. Closing Statement of Commitment:

| | F. Abraham: The Example of a Man Justified by Faith Alone, 4:17-25 | Sarah's womb: 20 He staggered not at the promise of God through unbelief; but was strong in faith, giving glory to God; | 2) He was strong in faith—not staggering but giving glory to God |
|---|---|---|---|
| **1. The source of Abraham's faith** | 17 (As it is written, I have made thee a father of many nations,) before him whom he believed, even God, who quickeneth the dead, and calleth those things which be not as though they were. | 21 And being fully persuaded that, what he had promised, he was able also to perform. 22 And therefore it was imputed to him for righteousness. | 3) He was convinced of God's ability & God's power |
| a. It was God Himself | | | |
| b. It was God who quickened the dead | | | |
| c. It was God who created | | | b. His faith was credited as righteousness |
| **2. The strength of Abraham's faith** | 18 Who against hope believed in hope, that he might become the father of many nations, according to that which was spoken, So shall thy seed be. | 23 Now it was not written for his sake alone, that it was imputed to him; 24 But for us also, to whom it shall be imputed, if we believe on him that raised up Jesus our Lord from the dead; | **3. The recording of Abraham's faith** |
| a. His faith was in what God had said: The promise of a seed, a son | | | a. That men might read |
| | | | b. That men might be counted righteous—by believing |
| 1) He was not weak in faith—despite thinking about his own physical inability | 19 And being not weak in faith, he considered not his own body now dead, when he was about an hundred years old, neither yet the deadness of | 25 Who was delivered for our offences, and was raised again for our justification. | 1) That God raised Jesus 2) That Jesus died for our sins & was raised again for our justification |

## Section III

### FAITH AND JUSTIFICATION: THE WAY FOR THE WORLD TO BE RIGHT WITH GOD
### Romans 3:21-5:21

**Study 6: Abraham: The Example of a Man Justified by Faith Alone**

**Text:** Romans 4:17-25

**Aim:** To model your faith after the courageous faith of Abraham.

**Memory Verse:**
> **"He staggered not at the promise of God through unbelief; but was strong in faith, giving glory to God" (Romans 4:20).**

**INTRODUCTION:**
    We live in a society where it seems everyone has a hero. There are many candidates who can command our attention. People look up to and shower praise upon...

- athletes
- musicians
- politicians
- movie and television stars

But there is a much better person for the Christian believer to admire and emulate: it is the person who has developed a solid faith in the Lord Jesus Christ. One of the greatest accomplishments we can make is to live a life of faith that will inspire others to follow Christ more closely.

> *"In order to convince the people of Philadelphia of the advantages of street lighting, Benjamin Franklin decided to show his neighbors how compelling a single light could be. He bought an attractive lantern, polished the glass, and placed it on a long bracket that extended from the front of his house. Each evening as darkness descended, he ignited the wick. His neighbors soon noticed the warm glow in front of his residence. Even those living farther down the street and in the next block were attracted by Franklin's light. Passers-by found that the light helped them to avoid tripping over protruding stones in the roadway. Soon others placed lanterns in front of their homes, and eventually the city recognized the need for having well-lighted streets."*[1]

Faith that is grounded in the truth of God's Word is like a brilliant light that shows others the way. Developing your faith is a critical part of your Christian life. There is no better place to examine where you are on your spiritual journey than to examine the courageous faith of Abraham. Abraham is the prime example or pattern that a person is justified by faith and by faith alone.

**OUTLINE:**
1. The source of Abraham's faith (v.17).
2. The strength of Abraham's faith (v.18-22).
3. The recording of Abraham's faith (v.23-25).

**1. THE SOURCE OF ABRAHAM'S FAITH (v.17).**

Note three points.

1.   It was God Himself whom Abraham believed: "I have made thee a father of many nations" (v.17; cp. Gen.17:1-5, esp. 4-5). Abraham had never had a son, not by Sarah. He was now about one hundred years old, and Sarah was close to the same age. They were both well beyond the years of having a son. Just think about it for a moment and the impossibility is clearly realized. If Abraham was ever to have a son, the son would have to come from God. God would have to be the source, for only God could do such an impossible thing. And note: despite the impossibility Abraham *believed God*. The source of Abraham's faith was God.

> **"Have faith in God" (Mk.11:22).**
> **"But without faith it is impossible to please him: for he that cometh to God must believe that he is, and that he is a rewarder of them that diligently seek him" (Heb.11:6).**

2.   It was the God who quickens the dead whom Abraham believed. The source of Abraham's faith was...
   * the living and true God: the God who is omnipotent, possessing all power, the power to breathe life into *dead matter*

---

[1] *INFOsearch Sermon Illustrations* (Arlington, TX: The Computer Assistant, 1-888-868-9029, 1986-1996).

No matter how impossible the promise seemed, God was able to fulfill it because *He is God*, the One who possesses all power (omnipotent). God is able to quicken and resurrect the dead; therefore, He is able to fulfill His promise.

> **"Verily, verily, I say unto you, He that heareth my word, and believeth on him that sent me, hath everlasting life, and shall not come into condemnation; but is passed from death unto life. Verily, verily, I say unto you, The hour is coming, and <u>now is</u>, when the dead [spiritually dead] shall hear the voice of the Son of God: and they that hear shall live" (Jn.5:24-25).**

3.   It was the God who creates who was the source of Abraham's faith. Because God is God, that is, omnipotent, He is able to create. He can make something *out of nothing*. He needs nothing to create. He can speak things into existence just as He did when He created the world (Gen.1:1, 3). Abraham believed this; he believed that if it was necessary God could create life in the organs of his and Sarah's bodies. Abraham trusted and believed the promise of God. God was the source of his faith.

### ILLUSTRATION:
The circumstances of life often place believers in situations where faith in God is their only hope. If your faith rests in anything or anyone other than God, it is a very shallow faith--to say the least.

> *Leon and Jane were the perfect model of a happy marriage. After successfully raising two daughters, Leon and Jane were ready to settle down and enjoy some time together. But a year later, Leon shocked everyone by taking his life. For no apparent reason, Leon took his gun and abruptly and violently ended his life.*
>
> *Jane's mind flashed back to her wedding day. As she had looked into Leon's eyes, she had taken in every word he had said to her: to be her husband...to protect her and to provide for her...in sickness and in health...for richer or poorer... "until death do us part." But now, questions and doubt flooded Jane's mind. "Lord, I just do not understand. I feel so alone and vulnerable. I trusted Leon for everything. I feel sad...disappointed...confused...angry! He promised to take care of me. What am I going to do?"*

Leon made a promise he did not keep: to take care of Jane. Over the course of time, Jane came to realize a very important principle. No matter how sincere people are, their limitations are numerous. Only God can perfectly keep every promise He has made. God promised to be her Protector and Provider--forever. He alone can keep such a promise. He alone is the source of your faith. He alone should be the object of your faith.

### APPLICATION:
Note a fact often overlooked. Every promise made by God is a promise that only He can fulfill. He is not needed if man can meet and do whatever is needed. Therefore, if a man puts his faith in men, all the hopes and promises that extend beyond this life will not be met. No man can fulfill the hope and promise of salvation from sin, death, and hell. No man can fulfill the promise that we shall be "the heirs of the world," that we shall receive eternal life in the new heavens and earth (cp. v.13). Only God can fulfill the impossible promise of eternal life.

> **"But Jesus beheld them, and said unto them, With men this is impossible; but with God all things are possible" (Mt.19:26).**

**QUESTIONS:**
1. Most people place more faith in themselves and others than they do in God, only calling on God as a last resort. Have you ever fallen into this trap? How can you train yourself to put God in His proper place and keep Him there?
2. When is it easiest for you to believe God's Word? When is it most difficult for you to believe God's Word? Is anything too difficult for God? Do you ever act like it is?
3. From where does *your* faith come? Why is it important to know the source of your faith?
4. Every promise made by God is a promise that only He can fulfill. What will happen if *you try to do* what only God can do?

## 2. THE STRENGTH OF ABRAHAM'S FAITH (v.18-22).

Note two very significant lessons.

1.    Abraham's faith was in *what God said*, the promise of a seed or of a son. He had nothing else to go on but God's Word: "that which was spoken."
The phrase "against hope believed in hope" means that Abraham was past hope, beyond all human help and any possibility of having a son. His situation was beyond hope, yet he believed God; he placed his hope in God and in what God had said.
   a. Abraham was not weak in faith despite thinking about his own physical inability. His body was "now dead"; he and Sarah were about one hundred years old. The word *dead* is a perfect participle in the Greek which means that his reproductive organs had stopped functioning and were dead forever; they could never again function. Abraham could never have a son; it was not humanly possible. He and Sarah were almost one hundred years old, now sexually "dead."
      Abraham thought about the matter. The word *considered* means he fixed his thoughts, his mind, his attention upon the matter. But he did not give in to the thoughts. He was not weak in faith.

   **APPLICATION:**
      Just imagine the *personal relationship* Abraham must have had with God! To know God so well--loving and trusting God so strongly--that God could give him an experience so meaningful that Abraham would believe the promise without even staggering in faith.

   > **"And now, Israel, what doth the LORD thy God require of thee, but to fear [trust] the LORD thy God, to walk in all his ways, and to love him, and to serve the LORD thy God with all thy heart and with all thy soul, to keep the commandments of the LORD, and his statutes, which I command thee this day for thy good?" (Dt.10:12-13).**

   b. Abraham was strong in faith--not staggering at the promise of God. Instead he walked about glorifying and praising God for His glorious promise. The word "staggered" means he did not waiver, did not vacillate, did not question God's ability to fulfill His promise.
   c. Abraham was fully convinced of God's ability and God's power. He knew God could overcome the difficulty of his body being "dead," and he believed God could and would either...
      • quicken his body, or
      • recreate his reproductive organs (v.17).

He did not know what method God would use, but he knew God was able to do what He had promised. Abraham believed God; he was fully persuaded that the promise would be fulfilled.

> **"Commit thy way unto the LORD; trust also in him; and he shall bring it to pass" (Ps.37:5).**

2. Abraham's faith was credited (counted) as righteousness. Abraham *deposited* his faith with God, and God *credited* Abraham's faith as righteousness.

Remember, when a person *really believes* that Jesus Christ is *his Savior*, God takes that person's faith and counts it for righteousness (Ro.4:3, 5, 9, 11, 22, 24). The person is not righteous; he has no righteousness of his own. He is still imperfect, still sinful, still corruptible, still short of God's glory as a sinful human being. But he does believe that Jesus Christ *is his Savior*. Such belief honors God's Son (whom God loves very much), and because it honors God's Son, God accepts and counts that person's faith for righteousness. Therefore, that person becomes acceptable to God.

> **"And be found in him, not having mine own righteousness, which is of the law, but that which is through the faith of Christ, the righteousness which is of God by faith" (Ph.3:9).**

**APPLICATION:**

Imagine someone making a large cash deposit into your bank account for you: you did not work for it, ask for it, or deserve it. You never have to pay it back. You merely have to acknowledge it and accept it to be able to draw upon it. This is what God has done for you in Jesus Christ. He has credited to your account the most valuable deposit possible--the gift of eternal life. You did not work for it, ask for it, or deserve it. You never have to pay it back. But it is yours--just because you believe in His Son and accept Him.

If you knew about the bank deposit, you would not dream of letting the money sit there and go to waste, would you? How many people never bother to draw upon the gift of eternal life that God has offered? How many times have you failed to tell someone about the precious gift that is available to him?

**QUESTIONS:**

1. What was the only thing Abraham had to go on? Given his circumstances, would you have done the same thing? Why?
2. How can you deepen your relationship with God even more--enough so that you would trust Him with the impossible?
3. When you need to claim one of God's promises, how convinced are you that God has the power to give it to you? Do you need to trust God even more than you do?

## 3. THE RECORDING OF ABRAHAM'S FAITH (v.23-25).

The recording of Abraham's faith is for two purposes.

1. That men might read the account. It was not recorded just to honor Abraham as a great man. It was written so that we might read and understand how we are to become acceptable to God.

**"But these are written, that ye might believe that Jesus is the Christ, the Son of God; and that believing ye might have life through his name" (Jn.20:31).**

ILLUSTRATION:

What kind of legacy will you leave behind when your life on this earth is done? In Abraham's case, his faith became an unmistakable sign for others to note and then follow.

> *"The great preacher F. B. Meyer said that his thoughts always turned to Titus 2:12 as he walked down 'Godliman Street' in London. He assumed that the unusual name was evidently a combination of the two words 'godly' and 'man,' and he often asked himself, 'Did some saintly Christian once reside here whose life was so holy that the entire community was affected by his influence?'"[2]*

Ask yourself: Is my life so holy that others are affected by my influence?

> **"Teaching us that, denying ungodliness and worldly lusts, we should live soberly, righteously, and godly, in this present world" (Tit.2:12).**

2.    That men might be counted righteous by believing. It is necessary to believe two things. (See **A CLOSER LOOK,** Ro.4:25 for discussion.)

    a.    That God raised Jesus our Lord from the dead (see **A CLOSER LOOK**, Jesus Christ, Resurrection--Ro.4:25; note).

    b.    That Jesus died for our sins and was raised again for our justification.

QUESTIONS:

1. What do you know about how to be acceptable to God? What specific Scriptures come to mind that instruct you on being acceptable to God?
2. In what ways do men attempt (and fail) to become righteous before God? What is the only way you can be counted as righteous?

---

A CLOSER LOOK:

(4:25) **Justification--Jesus Christ, Death; Resurrection--Propitiation**: Christ was delivered to death for our sins and raised again for our justification. He offered Himself as a *propitiation* for our sin. Propitiation means sacrifice, covering. (See note--Ro.3:25.) Christ offered Himself as our sacrifice, as our substitute, as the covering for our sins. God accepted the offering and the sacrifice of His life for us. The resurrection proves it.

1.    The resurrection shouts loudly and clearly that God is satisfied with the settlement for sin which Christ made.

2.    The resurrection declares the believer justified, free from sin, and righteous in God's eyes.

> **"Him, being delivered by the determinate counsel and foreknowledge of God, ye have taken, and by wicked hands have crucified and slain: whom God hath raised up, having loosed the pains of death: because it was not possible that he should be holden of it" (Acts 2:23-24).**

---

[2]   INFOsearch Sermon Illustrations.

# ROMANS 4:17-25

**QUESTIONS:**
1. How would you explain the term "propitiation" to a brand new Christian?
2. Why does the resurrection of Jesus Christ prove God's acceptance of His sacrifice?

## SUMMARY:

God has given you, the Christian believer, the perfect example of how to develop your faith. The faith of Abraham should challenge you to never be satisfied with a mediocre faith. A personal relationship with Jesus Christ requires that you be justified, a justification that comes only through believing faith.

Will you accept the challenge today and strive to match your faith with Abraham's? His example to you is clear. It is seen through...

1. The source of Abraham's faith.
2. The strength of Abraham's faith.
3. The recording of Abraham's faith.

## PERSONAL JOURNAL NOTES
### (Reflection & Response)

1. The most important thing that I learned from this lesson was:

2. The area that I need to work on the most is:

3. I can apply this lesson to my life by:

4. Closing Statement of Commitment:

| | **CHAPTER 5**<br><br>**G. God's Unbeliev-<br>able Love (Part I):<br>The Results of<br>Justification, 5:1-5** | joice in hope of the<br>glory of God.<br>3 And not only so, but<br>we glory in tribula-<br>tions also: knowing<br>that tribulation work-<br>eth patience; | **4. There is hope for the<br>glory of God**<br>**5. There is glory in<br>trials & sufferings**<br>a. Trials stir patience<br>b. Patience stirs char-<br>acter |
|---|---|---|---|
| **1. There is justification<br>by faith**<br>**2. There is peace with<br>God** | Therefore being jus-<br>tified by faith, we<br>have peace with God<br>through our Lord Je-<br>sus Christ: | 4 And patience, ex-<br>perience; and experi-<br>ence, hope:<br>5 And hope maketh<br>not ashamed; because | c. Experience stirs<br>hope<br><br>d. Hope never shames |
| **3. There is access into<br>the grace & the pres-<br>ence of God** | 2 By whom also we<br>have access by faith<br>into this grace where-<br>in we stand, and re- | the love of God is<br>shed abroad in our<br>hearts by the Holy<br>Ghost which is given<br>unto us. | **6. There is the constant<br>experience of God's<br>love--all through the<br>indwelling presence<br>of His Spirit** |

## Section III
## FAITH AND JUSTIFICATION:
## THE WAY FOR THE WORLD TO BE RIGHT WITH GOD
### Romans 3:21-5:21

**Study 7:** GOD'S UNBELIEVABLE LOVE (PART I): THE RESULTS OF JUS-
TIFICATION

**Text:** Romans 5:1-5

**Aim:** To sharpen your focus on the results of justification: the unbelievable love of
God.

**Memory Verse:**
**"Therefore being justified by faith, we have peace with God
through our Lord Jesus Christ" (Romans 5:1).**

## INTRODUCTION:

Have you ever thought about what life would be like as a caterpillar? You might as-
sume it would be uneventful and boring. The caterpillar plods along until he spins a cocoon and then he waits. But after a period of time, a transformation occurs and out of the
cocoon flies a beautiful butterfly.

Like this slow-moving creature, we sometimes tend to look at our current situation and
wrongly conclude that we are going nowhere, that all is lost. Far too many people tend to
think there is no way out, that the grass is always 'greener on the other side.' Why? Because...

- they suffer set-back after set-back
- they never seem to get a break in life
- they lose hope that anything will ever change for the better

But God still has a plan for the believer. In fact, He comes to us while we are still
caterpillars and declares us to be beautiful butterflies--a new creation. This is the wonder
of justification: God declares dead men to have new life in His Son. Only God has the

power to justify. Only God has the power to transform us from death to life. Only God has the love that will do such a wonderful thing.

Man is blessed by God through justification, blessed beyond all imagination. Justification and its results are gloriously covered in this passage of Scripture.

**OUTLINE:**
1. There is justification by faith (v.1).
2. There is peace with God (v.1).
3. There is access into the grace and the presence of God (v.2).
4. There is hope for the glory of God (v.2).
5. There is glory in trials and sufferings (v.3-5).
6. There is the constant experience of God's love--all through the indwelling presence of His Spirit (v.5).


## 1. THERE IS JUSTIFICATION BY FAITH (v.1).

Justification means to count someone righteous. It means to reckon, to credit, to account, to judge, to treat, to look upon as righteous. It does not mean to make a man righteous. All Greek verbs which end in "oun" mean not to make someone something, but merely to count, to judge, to treat someone as something.

There are three major points to note about justification.
1. *Why justification is necessary*:
   a. Justification is necessary because of the sin and alienation of man. Man has rebelled against God and taken his life into his own hands. Man lives as he desires...
   - fulfilling the lust of the eyes and of the flesh
   - clinging to the pride of life and to the things of the world

   Man has become sinful and ungodly, an enemy of God, pushing God out of his life and wanting little if anything to do with God. Man has separated and alienated himself from God.
   b. Justification is necessary because of the anger and wrath of God. **"God is angry with the wicked every day" (Ps.7:11)**. Sin has aroused God's anger and wrath. God is angry over man's...
   - rebellion
   - hostility
   - sin
   - ungodliness
   - unrighteousness
   - desertion

   Man has turned his back upon God, pushing God away and having little to do with Him. Man has not made God the center of his life; man has broken his relationship with God. Therefore, the greatest need in man's life is to discover the answer to the question: How can the relationship between man and God be restored?
2. *Why God justifies a man*: God justifies a man because of His Son Jesus Christ. When a man believes in Jesus Christ, God takes that man's faith and counts it as righteousness. The man is not righteous, but God considers and credits the man's faith as righteousness. Why is God willing to do this?
   a. God is willing to justify man because He loves man that much. God loves man so much that He sent His Son into the world and sacrificed Him in order to justify man (Jn.3:16; Ro.5:8).

b. God is willing to justify man because of what His Son Jesus Christ has done for man.

⇒ Jesus Christ has secured the *Ideal* righteousness for man. He came to earth to live a sinless and perfect life. As Man, He never broke the law of God; He never went contrary to the will of God, not even once. Therefore, He stood before God and before the world as the Ideal Man, the Perfect Man, the Representative Man, the Perfect Righteousness that could stand for the righteousness of every man.

⇒ Jesus Christ came into the world to *die* for man. As the *Ideal Man,* He could take all the sins of the world upon Himself and die for every man. His death *could stand* for every man. He exchanged places with man by becoming the sinner (2 Cor.5:19). He bore the wrath of God against sin, bearing the condemnation for every man. Again, He was able to do this because He was the Ideal Man, and as the *Ideal Man* His death could stand for the death of every man.

⇒ Jesus Christ came into the world to *arise from the dead* and thereby to conquer death for man. As the *Ideal Man*, His resurrection and exaltation into the presence of God *could stand* for every man's desperate need to conquer death and to be acceptable to God. His resurrected life could stand for the resurrected life of the believer.

Now, as stated above, when a man believes in Jesus Christ--really believes--God takes that man's belief and...

• counts it as the righteousness (perfection) of Christ. The man is counted as *righteous in Christ*.

• counts it as the death of Christ. The man is counted as having already *died in Christ*, as having already paid the penalty for sin *in the death of Christ*.

• counts it as the resurrection of Christ. The man is counted as already having been *resurrected in Christ*.

Very simply, God loves His Son Jesus Christ so much that He honors any man who honors His Son by *believing in Him*. He honors the man by taking the man's faith and counting (crediting) it as righteousness and by giving him the glorious privilege of living with Christ forever in the presence of God.

3. *How God justifies a man*: the word justify is a legal word taken from the courts. It pictures man on trial before God. Man is seen as having committed the most heinous of crimes: he has rebelled against God and broken his relationship with God. How can he restore that relationship? Within human courts if a man is acquitted, he is declared innocent, but this is not true within the Divine Court. When a man appears before God, he is anything but innocent; he is utterly guilty and condemned accordingly.

But when a man sincerely trusts Christ, then God takes that man's faith and counts it as righteousness. By such, God counts the man--judges him, treats him--as if he was innocent. The man is not made innocent; he is guilty. He knows it and God knows it, but God treats him as innocent. "God justifies the ungodly"--an incredible mercy, a wondrous grace. (See Ro.4:1-3; 4:1-25; 4:22.)

How do we know this? How can we know for sure that God is like this? Because Jesus said so. He said that God loves us. We are sinners, yes; but Christ said that we are very, very dear to God.

**"Knowing that a man is not justified by the works of the law, but by the faith of Jesus Christ, even we have believed in Jesus Christ, that we might be justified by the faith of Christ, and not by the works of the law: for by the works of the law shall no flesh be justified" (Gal.2:16).**

**QUESTIONS:**
1. In practical terms, what does it mean to be justified by faith? Why is it so important to understand this?
2. What is the difference between being *counted* as righteous and *being* righteous? Can you ever *be* righteous?
3. What was your position before God as an unbeliever--before you believed in God's Son? What is your position now that you are a believer? How can you demonstrate your love for God in return for what He has done for you?

## 2. THERE IS PEACE WITH GOD (v.1).

The first result of justification is peace with God.

1. The meaning of peace with God is striking. Peace with God does not mean escapism, a quiet atmosphere, the absence of trouble, the control of situations by positive thinking, the denial of problems, the ability to keep from facing reality. Peace *with* God means the *sense and knowledge...*

- that one has restored his relationship with Godyou
- that one is no longer alienated and separated from Godyou
- that one is now reconciled with Godyou
- that one is now accepted by Godyou
- that one is freed from the wrath and judgment of Godyou
- that one is freed from fearing God's wrath and judgmentyou
- that one is now pleasing Godyou
- that one is at peace with Godyou

2. The source of peace is Jesus Christ. Men can have peace with God only because of Jesus Christ. It is He who reconciles men to God. He has made peace by the blood of His cross. (See Ro.3:25.)

> **"For he is our peace, who hath made both one, and hath broken down the middle wall of partition between us; having abolished in his flesh the enmity, even the law of commandments contained in ordinances; for to make in himself of twain one new man, so making peace" (Eph.2:14-15).**

3. The reason we have peace is the glorious truth of justification (see Ro.5:1 for discussion).

**QUESTIONS:**
1. What does it mean to you personally to be at peace with God?
2. Why is the source of peace such an important thing to know?
3. Can you have peace without God, without the justification He offers? Why or why not?

## 3. THERE IS ACCESS INTO THE GRACE, THE FAVOR, AND THE PRESENCE OF GOD (v.2).

The second result of justification is access into the grace of God.

1. Grace means a gift or a favor, an *unmerited* and undeserved gift or favor. In the present passage grace is looked upon as a place or a position. Grace is a place to which

we are brought, a position into which we are placed. It is the place of God's presence, the position of salvation. The person who is justified...

- stands in God's presence
- stands before God saved
- stands in the favor of God
- stands in the privileges of God
- stands in the promises of God

2.     Note it is *through Christ* that we have access into this grace. The word "access" means to bring to, to move to, to introduce, to present. The thought is that of being in a royal court and being presented and introduced to the King of kings. Jesus Christ is the One who throws open the door into God's presence. He is the One who presents us to God, the Sovereign Majesty of the universe.

> **"I am the door: by me if any man enter in, he shall be saved, and shall go in and out, and find pasture" (Jn.10:9).**

### APPLICATION:

Note we "stand" in God's grace, in His presence.
1) We are not bowed down, intimidated, stricken with fear, and humiliated. Christ has justified us, removed our guilt and shame, and given us great confidence before God. Therefore, we take a stand of honor and dignity before Him, standing in the perfect righteousness of the Lord Jesus.
2) We are not sitting or lying down, but we are standing. This pictures our service and labor for God. We are brought into His presence for the purpose of service; therefore, there is not time for sitting and lying around. We stand before Him justified, yes, but we stand to receive our orders from Him. (Cp. 1 Cor.15:58; 2 Cor.5:18-21.)

Just imagine! Because of what Jesus Christ did, you are able to stand in the presence of the God of universe, the Creator of all mankind, the only true and living God. You can know God as your Father; you can be loved and treated as a precious child. You can be a joint heir with Jesus Christ. God could not have made a greater sacrifice nor given a greater gift--all because He loves you!

### QUESTIONS:
1. How would you explain the meaning of God's grace to an unbeliever? Why is it crucial for you to be able to explain the meaning of grace to others?
2. Jesus Christ provides the only access to the grace of God. Why was Christ God's choice to do this? Could anyone else have qualified?
3. What is the significance of your *standing* in God's presence?

## 4. THERE IS HOPE FOR THE GLORY OF GOD (v.2).

The third result of justification is hope, hope for the glory of God. Note that the hope of the believer is for *the glory of God*.
1.     When Scripture speaks of the believer's hope, it does not mean what the world means by hope. The hope of the world is a *desire*, a *want*. The world hopes--wants, desires--that something will happen. But this is not the hope of the believer. The hope of the believer is a *surety*: it is perfect assurance, confidence, and knowledge. How can hope be so absolute and assured? By being an *inward possession*. The believer's hope is based upon the presence of God's Spirit who dwells within the believer. In fact, the believer possesses the *hope of glory* only by the Spirit of God who dwells within him.

> **"For the hope which is laid up for you in heaven, whereof ye heard before in the word of the truth of the gospel" (Col.1:5).**

2.      The glory hoped for by the believer is to abundantly exceed the most wonderful experience we can ask or think. Glory means to possess and to be full of perfect light; to dwell in the perfect splendor and magnificence of God.

> **"Then shall the righteous shine forth as the sun in the kingdom of their Father. Who hath ears to hear, let him hear" (Mt.13:43).**

## APPLICATION:

Note how far short we often come. Instead of rejoicing in the glorious hope God has given...

- we moan, groan, and complain, living a discouraged and defeated life.
- we slip back into the ways of the world: the lust of the flesh and the eyes, pursuing the pride of life and the things of the world. (Cp. 1 Jn.2:15-16.)
- we become discouraged and defeated, no longer conscious of the glorious hope for the glory of God.

> **"Wherein he hath abounded toward us in all wisdom and prudence; having made known unto us the mystery of his will, according to his good pleasure which he hath purposed in himself" (Eph.1:8-9).**

## QUESTIONS:

1. What is the difference between the world's view of hope and the Christian's view of hope?
2. When life is difficult, in what ways do you struggle to keep hope alive?
3. Does your everyday life reflect a true hope for the glory of God, or would people be surprised to know that you have a priceless treasure at your disposal?

## 5. THERE IS GLORY IN TRIALS AND SUFFERING (v.3-5).

The fourth result of justification is glory in trials and sufferings. When a man is truly justified, he is no longer defeated by trials and sufferings. Trials and sufferings no longer discourage and swamp him, no longer cast him down into the dungeon of despair and hopelessness. The very opposite is true. Trials and sufferings become purposeful and meaningful. The *truly* justified man knows...

- that his life and welfare are completely in God's care and under His watchful eye.
- Therefore, whatever events come into his life--whether good or bad--they are allowed by God for a reason. The justified man knows that God will take the trials and sufferings of this world and work them out for good, even if God has to twist and move every event surrounding the believer.

This passage explains the great benefits of trials and sufferings; it shows exactly how the trials and sufferings of life work good for us. The word *trials* or *tribulations* means pressure, oppression, affliction, and distress. It means to be pressed together ever so tightly. It means all kinds of pressure ranging from the day to day pressures over to the pressure of confronting the most serious afflictions, even that of death itself.

**"In the world ye shall have tribulation: but be of good cheer; I have overcome the world" (Jn.16:33).**

1.   Trials stir patience: endurance, fortitude, stedfastness, constancy, perseverance. The word is not passive; it is active. It is not the spirit that just sits back and puts up with the trials of life, taking whatever may come. Rather it is the spirit that stands up and faces life's trials, that actively goes about conquering and overcoming them. When trials confront a man who is truly justified, he is stirred to arise and face the trials head on. He immediately sets out to conquer and overcome them. He knows that God is allowing the trials in order to teach him more and more patience (endurance).

**"My brethren, count it all joy when ye fall into divers temptations; knowing this, that the trying of your faith worketh patience. But let patience have her perfect work, that ye may be perfect and entire, wanting nothing" (Jas.1:2-4).**

2.   Patience stirs experience: character, integrity, strength. The idea is that of proven experience, of gaining strength through the trials of life; therefore, the word is more accurately translated character. When a justified man endures trials, he comes out of it stronger than ever before. He is a man of much stronger character and integrity. He knows much more about the presence and strength of God.

**"Blessed be God, even the Father of our Lord Jesus Christ, the Father of mercies, and God of all comfort; who comforteth us in all our tribulation, that we may be able to comfort them which are in any trouble, by the comfort wherewith we ourselves are comforted of God" (2 Cor.1:3-4).**

3.   Experience stirs hope: to expect with confidence; to anticipate knowing; to look and long for with surety; to desire with assurance; to rely on with certainty; to trust with the guarantee; to believe with the knowledge. Note that hope is expectation, anticipation, looking and longing for, desiring, relying upon, and trusting. But it is also confidence, knowledge, surety, assurance, certainty, and a guarantee. When a justified man becomes stronger in character, he draws closer to God; and the closer he draws to God, the more he hopes for the glory of God.

4.   Hope never shames: never disappoints, deludes, deceives, confounds, confuses. The believer, the person who is truly justified, will never be disappointed or shamed. He will see his hope fulfilled. He will live forever in the presence of God inheriting the promises God has given in His Word.

**"Whosoever believeth on him shall not be ashamed" (Ro.9:33).**

**ILLUSTRATION:**
    Some people retreat at the first sign of trial or tribulation. They give up all hope of overcoming and learning from the experience. People who live for comfort and for the pleasures of the world see trials as a thing to be avoided at all costs. God wants believers to glory in their trials and sufferings, that is, tro grow and become stronger because of the experience. Here is an example of a man who refused to allow trials to defeat him in life.

    *"What do you do when faced by a closed door in life? A young boy from Missouri named Harry had to answer that question. He gave evidence of brilliance on the piano even as a child. In addition to being gifted, Harry had such discipline that at the age of seven he was at the keyboard by five each morning.*

*He practiced faithfully for hours each day. Under the tutelage of Mrs. E.C. White, he produced each day stronger hope that he would eventually reach greatness.*

*"When Harry was 15, Mrs. White brought news to her star pupil. Paderewski, the greatest pianist of the day was coming to town. The young boy was thrilled as he listened to Paderewski play. Mrs. White took her pupil backstage after the concert to meet Paderewski. With trembling voice, the young boy told the world-renowned pianist that he played his minuet. 'There is a part of it,' young Harry explained, 'that I do not know how to execute.'*

*"Paderewski walked back with the boy to the empty stage and to the piano. The boy sat at the same piano where Paderewski had played only a few minutes before. As the student played, Paderewski gave a smile of approval to the boy's teacher. A bright future seemed to loom before him.*

*"Then ensued the closed door. The next year Harry's father lost everything in the Kansas City grain market. Harry had to go to work, and his dreams of the concert stage were shattered.*

*"Did the boy give up on life? Did he let this closed door stop him?*

*"Not at all, for this young, gifted, promising pianist would become world famous before his life was over, as President of the United States. His name was Harry S. Truman."*[1]

## QUESTIONS:

1. Believers are not immune from trials and tribulations. How is it possible to glory in trials and suffering during difficult circumstances?
2. Relate an example of how trials stir patience; how patience stirs experience; how experience stirs hope.
3. How does the hope that God gives help you to live daily for Christ?

## 6. THERE IS THE CONTINUOUS EXPERIENCE OF GOD'S LOVE THROUGH THE INDWELLING SPIRIT (v.5).

1.     The love of God is demonstrated in His justifying the man who truly believes in His Son Jesus Christ.

> **"For God so loved the world, that he gave his only begotten
> Son, that whosoever believeth in him should not perish, but have ev-
> erlasting life" (Jn.3:16).**

2.     The Holy Spirit sheds the love of God abroad in our hearts. He grows and matures us in the love of God, increasing our understanding of what God has done and is doing for us. He helps us learn more and more about our justification and more and more of the glorious salvation He promises.

The Holy Spirit...

- makes us *conscious* and *aware* of God's love, and gives us a *deep* and *intimate* sense of God's love.
- makes us *conscious* and *aware* of God's presence, and of His care and concern for all that is involved in salvation.

It is the sense and intimacy of God's love that is being stressed: a personal manifestation, a personal experience of the presence and love of God, of His justification and care for us as we walk through life moment by moment.

---

[1]     Ted Kyle & John Todd. *A Treasury of Bible Illustrations*, p.347-348.

# ROMANS 5:1-5

> "He that hath my commandments, and keepeth them, he it is that loveth me: and he that loveth me shall be loved of my Father, and I will love him, and will manifest myself to him" (Jn.14:21).

Note: the Holy Spirit is "given unto us." He enters our hearts and lives for the very purpose of sealing or guaranteeing us. He seals or guarantees our justification, and He seals the fact that God loves us and cares for and looks after us. It is because of His indwelling presence that we have the continuous and unbroken experience of God's love. But remember: this glorious intimacy with God is a result of justification. *Only the person who is truly justified experiences the love of God.*

Note another fact: the love of God is a gift, a gift deposited in the believer by the Holy Spirit. (Cp. the divine nature which is *deposited* within us when we truly trust Jesus Christ as our Savior, 2 Pt.1:4.)

> "For ye have not received the spirit of bondage again to fear; but ye have received the Spirit of adoption, whereby we cry, Abba, Father. The Spirit itself beareth witness with our spirit, that we are the children of God: and if children, then heirs; heirs of God, and joint-heirs with Christ; if so be that we suffer with him, that we may be also glorified together" (Ro.8:15-17).

### ILLUSTRATION:

God has given the Holy Spirit to you, the Christian believer. How much of your life do you allow the Holy Spirit to enter?

> *"Mendelssohn [the great composer] once visited a cathedral containing one of the most priceless organs in Europe. He listened to the organist, then asked for permission to play. 'I don't know you,' was the reply, 'and we don't allow any chance stranger to play upon this organ.'*
>
> *"At last the great musician persuaded the organist to let him play. As Mendelssohn played, the great cathedral was filled with such music as the organist had never heard. With tears in his eyes he laid his hand upon Mendelssohn's shoulder. 'Who are you?' he asked. 'Mendelssohn,' came the reply. The old organist was dumbfounded. 'To think that an old fool like me nearly forbade Mendelssohn to play upon my organ!'*
>
> *"If we only knew what wonderful harmonies the Holy Spirit can draw out of our lives, we should not be content until He has complete possession and is working in us and through us to do His will."*[2]

### QUESTIONS:

1. Can you honestly say that you are aware of the presence of the Holy Spirit in your life? Always? Frequently? Occasionally? Never?
2. How can you become more conscious of the Holy Spirit in your life? Why do you need to be more conscious of the Holy Spirit?
3. What are the benefits of having the Holy Spirit in your life? Are the benefits worth making more of an effort on your part?

---

[2] *From Senior Teacher, S. B. C.* Walter B. Knight. *Knight's Master Book of 4,000 Illustrations.* (Grand Rapids, MI: Eerdmans Publishing Company, 1994), p.290.

# ROMANS 5:1-5

## SUMMARY:

God loves you beyond all belief. His love for you cannot be easily measured. It is greater than the highest mountain and deeper than the deepest ocean. God's love stretches from finger tip to finger tip, from hands that were held secure by the piercing nails of the cross. The same love that held Christ on the cross is available to you today, available to justify you. What are the results of God's justification of your life?

1. There is justification by faith.
2. There is peace with God.
3. There is access into the grace and the presence of God.
4. There is hope for the glory of God.
5. There is glory in trials and sufferings.
6. There is the constant experience of God's love--all through the indwelling presence of His Spirit.

## PERSONAL JOURNAL NOTES:
### (Reflection & Response)

1. The most important thing that I learned from this lesson was:

2. The thing that I need to work on the most is:

3. I can apply this lesson to my life by:

4. Closing Prayer Of Commitment: (put your commitment down on paper).

| | H. God's Unbeliev-able Love (Part II): The Great Depth of Justifi-cation, 5:6-11 | died for us.<br>9 Much more then, being now justified by his blood, we shall be saved from wrath through him. | a. By Christ's death<br>b. By justification<br><br>c. By saving us from wrath |
|---|---|---|---|
| 1. We were ungodly & without strength, yet Christ died for us<br>a. In God's time<br>b. Was an uncommon, unbelievable love | 6 For when we were yet without strength, in due time Christ died for the ungodly.<br>7 For scarcely for a righteous man will one die: yet peradven-ture for a good man some would even dare to die. | 10 For if, when we were enemies, we were reconciled to God by the death of his Son, much more, being reconciled, we shall be saved by his life.<br>11 And not only so, but we also joy in God | 3. We were enemies, yet God reconciled and saved us<br>a. We are reconciled by Christ's death<br><br>b. We are saved by Christ's life<br>c. We are given joy by Christ's atone-ment (reconcilia-tion) |
| 2. We were sinners, yet God demonstrated His love for us | 8 But God commen-deth his love toward us, in that, while we were yet sinners, Christ | through our Lord Je-sus Christ, by whom we have now received the atonement. | |

## Section III
## FAITH AND JUSTIFICATION:
## THE WAY FOR THE WORLD TO BE RIGHT WITH GOD
### Romans 3:21-5:21


**Study 8:** **GOD'S UNBELIEVABLE LOVE (PART II): THE GREAT DEPTH OF JUSTIFICATION**

**Text:** **Romans 5:6-11**

**Aim:** To become gripped with God's love--so gripped that it influences your every thought and action.

**Memory Verse:**
> **"But God commendeth his love toward us, in that, while we were yet sinners, Christ died for us" (Romans 5:8).**

**INTRODUCTION:**
If you had to come up with a list, who would you be willing to die for?  Would you die for...
- your country?
- your children?
- a close friend?
- a poor man?
- a hardened criminal?
- a murderer?
- a convicted drunk driver?
- a drug addict?
- a person infected with the aids virus?
- an atheist who hated you and your God?

Jesus Christ did. He died for everyone, even for those who are on the bottom rung of society's ladder. He died for the person who has never missed a day of church. He died for the person who has never been to church. He did not wait for us to improve our lives. He died for us while we were stuck in sin's lethal grasp. Unbelievable? In a way, yes. Impossible? In a word, no.

This passage discusses God's unbelievable love. It shows the great depth of justification. The passage also gives one of the clearest definitions of *agape* love. It actually shows the meaning of *agape love. Agape love* goes much farther than *phileo love. Phileo love* is brotherly love, a love that gives itself for a brother. But *agape love* is a new kind of love: it is a godly love, a sacrificial love, a love that gives itself for those without strength (Ro.5:6), for the ungodly (Ro.5:6), for sinners (Ro.5:8), and for enemies (Ro.5:10).

**OUTLINE:**
1. We were ungodly and without strength, yet Christ died for us (v.6-7).
2. We were sinners, yet God demonstrated His love for us (v.8-9).
3. We were enemies, yet God reconciled and saved us (v.10-11).

## 1. WE WERE UNGODLY AND WITHOUT STRENGTH, YET CHRIST DIED FOR US (v.6-7).

God's great love is seen in this unbelievable act.

1. We were *without strength*: weak, worthless, useless, helpless, hopeless, destitute, powerless. We were spiritually worthless and useless and unable to help ourselves.

> **"I sink in deep mire, where there is no standing: I am come into deep waters, where the floods overflow me" (Ps.69:2).**

2. We were *ungodly*: not like God, different from God, profane, having a different life-style than God. God is godly, that is, perfect; man is ungodly, that is, he is not like God; he is imperfect.

> **"Knowing this, that the law is not made for a righteous man, but for the lawless and disobedient, for the ungodly and for sinners, for unholy and profane, for murderers of fathers and murderers of mothers, for manslayers, for whoremongers, for them that defile themselves with mankind, for menstealers, for liars, for perjured persons, and if there be any other thing that is contrary to sound doctrine" (1 Tim.1:9-10).**

3. It was in *due time* that Christ died for us. It was in God's appointed time: His destined time, appropriate time. Men had to be prepared for Christ before God could send Him into the world. Men had to learn that they were without strength and ungodly, that they needed a Savior. (This was the purpose of the Old Testament and the law, to show men that they were sinful. See Ro.4:14-15.)

> **"But when the fulness of the time was come, God sent forth his Son, made of a woman, made under the law, to redeem them that were under the law, that we might receive the adoption of sons" (Gal.4:4-5).**

4. Christ died *for* us. The word *for* means for our benefit, for our sake, in our behalf, in our stead, as our substitute.

a. Christ died as our sacrifice (as our substitute).

> **"And that he died for all, that they which live should not hence-forth live unto themselves, but unto him which died for them, and rose again" (2 Cor.5:15).**

b. Christ died as our ransom (for our release).

> **"Who gave himself for us, that he might redeem us from all iniquity, and purify unto himself a peculiar people, zealous of good works" (Tit.2:14).**

c. Christ died as our propitiation (to redeem us).

> **"Whom God hath set forth to be a propitiation through faith in his blood, to declare his righteousness for the remission of sins that are past, through the forbearance of God" (Ro.3:25).**

5. God's love is an uncommon and an unbelievable love. Just think about the illustration given in Scripture. Some people will attempt to save a person caught in a desperate tragedy, and others might offer their lives to represent leaders in their great purpose.
   ⇒ A few will die for a just and upright man (righteous).
   ⇒ Some will even *dare* to die for a "good" man.

But this is not what Christ did. Christ did not die for the righteous and godly man nor for the good and pure man. He went well beyond what men do. Christ...
- died for the ungodly, for those who were the very opposite of righteous and good.
- died for those "without strength": the useless, destitute, worthless, and those without value to society and men.

Christ died for those for whom no other man would die, for those who were of no value and of no good. He died for those who were diametrically opposed to God, the very opposite from all that He is. Such is the unbelievable love of God; such is the depth of justification.

**ILLUSTRATION:**
What if you were poor, a social outcast, an unlovely person? How would you want to be treated by other people? You would want to be treated with dignity and with respect. You would want to be loved because of who you are, not because of what you are not. Jesus Christ loves everyone with a love that is unconditional. It is not a love that is based upon performance or status but upon need--a need that everyone shares.

> *The late shift at the hospital's emergency room was busy as usual. People from all walks of life were in desperate need of its services. Freddy was brought in because of his latest drug overdose. A pathetic figure, Freddy's only success in life was that he had failed to kill himself--at least up to this point. Terri fell into the trap of basing her popularity on how many boys she sexually pleased. Eventually, one of her boyfriends passed on a sexually-transmitted disease that would be with her for the remaining years of her life. She was here to get some relief, again. John, on the other hand, was a model father and husband--a good and faithful man. John's life was now hanging in the balance because of a terrible car accident.*

*The doctor on call that night was equipped to handle any type of medical emergency. He moved from room to room, giving the same quality of care to each of his patients: to Freddy, to Terri, and to John. He did not look at the bank accounts of his patients before he treated them. He did not notice the color of their skin. He did not judge them for the reason they had come to the emergency room. He was there to care for them, to comfort them, to help them recover. The doors to the emergency room were opened to anyone who had an emergency.*

The sole reason for the emergency room is to have a place where people who need care can receive it. In the same way, God is there for all of us--men, women, boys, and girls--who are not just sick with sin, but who are dead in sin, who are in need of a doctor who can save and give us eternal life. Jesus Christ did not die for the good man, but He died for those who could not help themselves. He died for those whom no one else could or would die for. He died for you.

**"But he *was* wounded for our transgressions, *he was* bruised for our iniquities: the chastisement of our peace *was* upon him; and with his stripes we are healed" (Is.53:5).**

**QUESTIONS:**
1. How would you characterize your life before Christ saved you? What special qualities did you have that caused Christ to save you?
2. God loves the unlovely as much as He does the lovely. What challenges do you face in loving the unlovely?
3. How can you go about expressing the love of God to others so they will have a desire to know His love personally?

## 2. WE WERE SINNERS, YET GOD DEMONSTRATED HIS LOVE FOR US (v.8-9).

The word *commendeth* means to show, prove, exhibit, demonstrate. It is the present tense: God is always showing and proving His love to us. The word *sinners* refers to a man who is sinful, the man who sins...
- by disobeying God's Word and will (cp. Ro.1:29-31)
- by living selfishly
- by ignoring God's commandments
- by doing his own thing
- by the lust of the flesh, the lust of the eyes
- by pursuing the pride of life and the things of the world

The point is this: it is "while we were yet sinners" that God proved His love to us. This is the unbelievable love of God, that He stooped down to save sinners. We would expect Him to save righteous and good men, but it catches us completely off-guard when it is stated that He saves sinners. Such is the unbelievable love of God.
Now note how God proved His love.
1.    God proved His love by giving up His only Son to die *for* us. Some earthly fathers would be willing to give up their sons for a "good" man or for a great cause. But how many would be willing to give up their sons for a man who committed treason or for a man who murdered one of the greatest men living? Think of the enormous price God paid in proving His love: He gave up His Son to die for the unworthy and useless, the ungodly and sinful, the wicked and depraved--the worst sinners and outcasts imaginable.

Just think what God Himself must have gone through: the feelings, the suffering, the hurt, the pain, the terrible emotional strain. Just think what is involved in God giving up His Son:

⇒ God had to send His Son *out of* the spiritual and eternal world (dimension) *into* the physical and corruptible world (dimension).

⇒ God had to humiliate His Son by stripping Him of His eternal glory and insisting that He become clothed with corruptible flesh and die as a man.

⇒ God had to watch His Son walk through life being rejected, denied, cursed, abused, arrested, tortured, and murdered. God had to sit back and watch His Son suffer being murdered by the hands of men; He had to sit back when He knew He could reach out and deliver Him.

⇒ God had to destine His Son to die upon the cross for the sins of men.

⇒ God had to lay all the sins of the world upon His Son and let Him bear them all.

⇒ God had to judge His Son as the sinner and condemn Him to death for sin.

⇒ God had to turn His back upon Christ in death.

⇒ God had to cast His wrath against sin upon Christ.

⇒ God has to bear the pain of His Son's sufferings eternally, for He is eternal and the death of His Son is ever before His face. (Just imagine! It is beyond our comprehension, but the eternal agony is a fact because of the eternal nature of God.)

As stated, God proved His love. He has given up His Son to die for us. We do not deserve it--we never have and we never will--but God loves us with an unbelievable love. Therefore, He has given His Son to die <u>for</u> us, as our substitute, in our behalf.

> **"But he was wounded for our transgressions, he was bruised for our iniquities: the chastisement of our peace was upon him; and with his stripes we are healed" (Is.53:5).**

## APPLICATION:
God showed the greatest example of sacrifice when He gave us His Son to die for our sin. We are a society that needs to learn the value of real sacrifice.

⇒ Parents need to sacrifice in order to raise their children as true Christian believers.

⇒ Young people need to sacrifice in order to remain pure.

⇒ Christian businessmen need to sacrifice in order to keep a Christian witness.

Sacrifice does not come easily. If we want to be more like Jesus, we must be willing to count the cost. We must look at the cost He paid.

> *"Gary Player for years was a great competitor in national and international golf tournaments. People would constantly come up to him and make the same remark: 'I'd give anything if I could hit a golf ball like you.'*
>
> *"Player, on one occasion, lost his patience when a spectator made that comment, and replied, 'No you wouldn't. You'd do anything to hit a golf ball like I do if it were easy! Do you know what you have to do to hit a golf ball like I do? You've got to get up at 5:00 every morning, go out to the golf course, and hit a thousand golf balls! Your hands start bleeding, and you walk to the clubhouse and wash the blood off your hands, slap a bandage on it, and go our and hit another thousand golf balls! That is what it takes to hit a golf ball like I do!'*
>
> *"Playing the game of life like that will cost you something."*[1]

---

[1] *Biblical Preaching Journal*, Spr. 1992. INFOsearch Sermon Illustrations (Arlington, TX: The Computer Assistant, 1-888-868-9029, 1986-1996).

2.    God proves His love by justification through the blood of Christ.

> **"And, having made peace through the blood of his cross, by him to reconcile all things unto himself; by him, I say, whether they be things in earth, or things in heaven" (Col.1:20).**

3.    God proves His love by saving us from wrath.

> **"For the wages of sin is death; but the gift of God is eternal life through Jesus Christ our Lord" (Ro.6:23).**

**QUESTIONS:**
1. Think carefully: What sins did you have to overcome *before* Christ saved you? What lesson does this teach you about loving and forgiving others?
2. God willingly gave His only Son to die for sinners. (Imagine yourself in that position!) What do you think God was feeling as His Son died on the cross? What does this tell you about God's love for you?


## 3. WE WERE ENEMIES, YET GOD RECONCILED AND SAVED US (v.10-11).

God reconciles and saves us by doing three things.
1.    God *reconciles us (restores us)* by Christ's death (see **A CLOSER LOOK-- Ro.5:10** for discussion).
2.    God *saves us* by Christ's life. "His life" means the life of the *living Lord*. Christ stands before God as our great Intercessor and Mediator. Standing before God, He stands as the Sinless and Righteous Son of God, as the Ideal and Perfect Man. When we believe in Christ, God takes our belief and counts it as righteousness. The Ideal Righteousness of Christ covers us, and God accepts and saves us because we *trust* Christ as the living Lord, as our Intercessor and Mediator before God.

> **"For there is one God, and one mediator between God and men, the man Christ Jesus" (1 Tim.2:5).**

3.    God *gives us joy* through the atonement or reconciliation of Christ. A person who receives so much from God is bound to be filled with joy and rejoicing.

> **"These things have I spoken unto you, that my joy might remain in you, and that your joy might be full" (Jn.15:11).**

**QUESTIONS:**
1. Christ's death restores you to God. Christ's death saves you. How can you explain this in simple terms to an unbeliever?
2. Why is it important for you to have a personal relationship with Jesus Christ?
3. What is the source of the believer's joy? What is the key to experiencing this joy daily?


---

**A CLOSER LOOK:**

(5:10) **Reconcile--Reconciliation**: to change, to change thoroughly, to exchange, to change from enmity to friendship, to bring together, to restore. The idea is that two persons who should have been together all along are brought together; two persons who had something between them are restored and reunited.

Three points should be noted about reconciliation.

1. The thing that broke the relationship between God and man was sin. Men are said to be enemies of God (Ro.5:10), and the word "enemies" refers back to the sinners and the ungodly (Ro.5:6, 8). The "enemies" of God are the sinners and ungodly of this world. This simply means that every man is an enemy of God, for every man is a sinner and ungodly. This may seem unkind and harsh, but it is exactly what Scripture is saying. The fact is clearly seen by thinking about the matter for a moment.

The sinner cannot be said to be a friend of God's. He is antagonistic toward God, opposing what God stands for. The sinner is...

- rebelling against God
- rejecting God
- cursing God
- ignoring God
- disobeying God
- fighting against God
- denying God
- refusing to live for God

When any of us sin, we work against God and promote evil by word and example.

⇒ When the sinner lives for himself, he becomes an enemy of God. Why? Because God does not live for Himself. God gave Himself up in the most supreme way possible: He gave His only Son to die *for* us.

⇒ When the sinner lives for the world and worldly things, he becomes an enemy of God. Why? Because he chooses the temporal--that which passes away--over God. He chooses it when God has provided eternal life for him through the death of His Son.

This is the point of God's great love or reconciliation. He did not reconcile and save us when we were righteous and good. He reconciled and saved us when we were enemies, ignoring and rejecting Him. As stated above, it is because we are sinners and enemies that we need to be reconciled.

2. The way men are reconciled to God is by the death of His Son, Jesus Christ. Very simply stated, when a man believes that Jesus Christ died for him...

- God accepts the death of Jesus Christ for the death of the man.
- God accepts the sins borne by Christ as the sins committed by the man.
- God accepts the condemnation borne by Christ as the condemnation due to the man.

Therefore, the man is freed from his sins and the punishment due his sins. Christ bore both the sins and the punishment for the man. The man who truly believes that God loves that much--enough to give His only begotten Son--becomes acceptable to God, reconciled forever and ever.

3. God is the One who reconciles, not men. Men do not reconcile themselves to God. They cannot do enough work or enough good to become acceptable to God. Reconciliation is entirely the act of God. God is the One who reaches out to men and reconciles them unto Himself. Men *receive* the reconciliation of God.

**"And all things are of God, who hath reconciled us to himself**
**by Jesus Christ, and hath given to us the ministry of reconciliation"**
**(2 Cor.5:18; cp. v.19-21).**

### ILLUSTRATION:

Do you love your enemies? Do you love them enough to die for them? Relating to your enemies is one of life's greatest challenges. The old nature says to retaliate against them, but the new nature--the one that has been born again--is commanded to love our enemies. The Lord Jesus did this very thing.

*"In Context, Martin Marty retells a parable from the Eye of the Needle newsletter:*
   *"A holy man was engaged in his morning meditation under a tree whose roots stretched out over the riverbank. During his meditation he noticed that the river was rising, and a scorpion caught in the roots was about to drown. He crawled out on the roots and reached down to free the scorpion, but every time he did so, the scorpion struck back at him.*
   *"An observer came along and said to the holy man, 'Don't you know that's a scorpion, and it's in the nature of a scorpion to want to sting?'*
   *"To which the holy man replied, 'That may well be, but it is my nature to save, and I must change my nature because the scorpion does not change its nature?'"*

Have you allowed God's loving nature to change your sinful nature?

## SUMMARY:

There are a lot of things in this world that are beyond belief. Some things seem too good to be true, while even more are too appalling to believe. The world has no concept of God's great love for the sinner. Who can comprehend Christ's unconditional love? Who can begin to explain how much He loves people, how much He loves you?

The great composer Charles Wesley captured the essence of this truth as he penned the words to this classic hymn, "And Can It Be?"

*"And can it be that I should gain an int'rest in the Savior's blood?*
*Died He for me, who caused His pain?*
*For me, who Him to death pursued?*
*Amazing love! How can it be that Thou, My God shouldst die for me?"*

In this splendid passage of Scripture, the apostle Paul explained this great truth:

1.   We were ungodly and without strength, yet Christ died for us.
2.   We were sinners, yet God demonstrated His love for us.
3.   We were enemies, yet God reconciled and saved us.

## PERSONAL JOURNAL NOTES:
### (Reflection & Response)

1. The most important thing that I learned from this lesson was:


2. The thing that I need to work on the most is:


3. I can apply this lesson to my life by:


4. Closing Prayer Of Commitment: (put your commitment down on paper).

---

[2]   Craig B. Larson. *Illustrations for Preaching and Teaching*, p.141.

**I. Adam and Christ: The Two Focal Points of History, 5:12-21**

**1. The entrance of sin & death through Adam**
a. Sin came by one man—Adam
b. Adam's nature of sin & death passed to all
c. The proof: Sin & death existed before the law; sin & death came from & through Adam
d. Adam's real importance: A type of Christ, cp. 1 Cor. 15:22, 45-49

**2. The counteraction—the reversal—of sin & death by Christ**
a. Adam's sin brought death; God's gift brought righteousness
b. Adam's sin brought condemnation; God's gift brought justification

c. Adam's sin brought the reign of death; God's gift brought the reign of life

d. Adam's sin brought condemnation to all men; God's gift brought justification & life to all men

**3. Conclusion**
a. Adam's disobedience made many sinners, but Christ's obedience made many righteous

b. The law was given to point out & magnify sin, but God's grace was so much greater

c. Sin results in death, but God's grace results in eternal life—through Christ's righteousness

12 Wherefore, as by one man sin entered into the world, and death by sin; and so death passed upon all men, for that all have sinned:
13 (For until the law sin was in the world: but sin is not imputed when there is no law.
14 Nevertheless death reigned from Adam to Moses, even over them that had not sinned after the similitude of Adam's transgression, who is the figure of him that was to come.
15 But not as the offense, so also is the free gift. For if through the offense of one many be dead, much more the grace of God, and the gift by grace, which is by one man, Jesus Christ, hath abounded unto many.
16 And not as it was by one that sinned, so is the gift: for the judgment was by one to condemnation, but the free gift is of many offenses unto justification.
17 For if by one man's offense death reigned by one; much more they which receive abundance of grace and of the gift of righteousness shall reign in life by one, Jesus Christ.)
18 Therefore as by the offense of one judgment came upon all men to condemnation; even so by the righteousness of one the free gift came upon all men unto justification of life.
19 For as by one man's disobedience many were made sinners, so by the obedience of one shall many be made righteous.
20 Moreover the law entered, that the offense might abound. But where sin abounded, grace did much more abound:
21 That as sin hath reigned unto death, even so might grace reign through righteousness unto eternal life by Jesus Christ our Lord.

**Section III
FAITH AND JUSTIFICATION:
THE WAY FOR THE WORLD TO BE RIGHT WITH GOD
Romans 3:21-5:21**

**Study 9:      ADAM AND CHRIST: THE TWO FOCAL POINTS OF HISTORY**

**Text:      Romans 5:12-21**

**Aim:      To mark the sharp contrast between the life of Adam and the life of Christ: To understand exactly what Christ has done for you.**

**Memory Verse:**

> "For if by one man's offence death reigned by one; much more they which receive abundance of grace and of the gift of righteousness shall reign in life by one, Jesus Christ" (Romans 5:17).

## INTRODUCTION:

The challenge for every Christian believer is to follow a straight and narrow path of holiness. Life provides many forks in the road where decisions must be made: to love God or to love self, to follow God or to follow the world. It was the great devotional writer Oswald Chambers who wrote:

> *"Am I becoming more and more in love with God as a holy God, or with the conception of an amiable being who says, 'Oh, well, sin doesn't matter much?'"*[1]

The believer must decide to follow either the path of death and destruction as introduced to the world by Adam, or to follow the path of holiness and life as introduced to the world by Jesus Christ, by His life, death, and resurrection.

This passage deals with two of the focal points of human history. It deals with Adam and Christ, the two chief representatives and figureheads of the human race. It tells how sin and death entered the world and how Jesus Christ counteracted sin and death.

## OUTLINE:

1. The entrance of sin and death through Adam (v.12-14).
2. The counteraction--the reversal--of sin and death by Christ (v.15-18).
3. Conclusion (v.19-21).

## 1. THE ENTRANCE OF SIN AND DEATH THROUGH ADAM (v.12-14).

1. The fact is very simply stated: sin and death entered the world through one man, Adam. God had said:

> "Of the tree of the knowledge of good and evil, thou shalt not eat of it: for in the day that thou eatest thereof [disobey God] thou shalt surely die" (Gen.2:17).

Adam sinned and corrupted himself; therefore, he died.

2. Adam's nature of sin and death was and still is passed on to all men. His corruptible nature was passed on to his children and on down through history to all men. It is a well known fact that the child inherits the nature of his parents. Therefore, if the parent's nature is bent toward sin and is corruptible, so will the child's nature be. Nature is like an *infectious blood line*: whatever the nature is, it is passed on down to the next generation.

Now note a significant fact: a man is not condemned to death because of Adam's sin. Scripture clearly says this: **"Death passed upon all men, for that <u>all</u> have sinned"** (v.12). A man dies because of his own sins, not because of his father's sins. Every man is personally responsible to God.

> **"For all have sinned, and come short of the glory of God"** (Ro.3:23).

---

[1]    Edward K. Rowell, Editor. *Quotes & Idea Starters for Preaching & Teaching*, p.80.

3.    The proof that we inherit Adam's nature is that sin and death existed even before the law (v.13). The law of God does charge men with sin; it does show men that they are sinful and condemned to die. But *something* caused men to sin and die before the law was ever given to Moses in a written form. The people before Moses were not charged with sin by the law, for they did not have the law in a permanent and written form. What was it then that was causing the people between Adam and Moses to sin and die? It was nature, the sinful, corruptible nature of man, the nature that every child inherited from his father; and the process began with Adam. Adam was the first man created by God, and he was the first to sin, to become corruptible, and to bear the punishment of death.

> **"In the sweat of thy face shalt thou eat bread, till thou return unto the ground; for out of it wast thou taken: for dust thou art, and unto dust shalt thou return" (Gen.3:19).**

4.    The importance of Adam is critical. He was "the figure [type, picture] of Him that was to come," that is, of Christ. Adam and Christ are pictured as the two pivotal points of human history, as the two *figureheads or representatives* of the human race. (Cp. 1 Cor.15:20-28, 45-49.) Adam stands at the head of the human race, as *the first* to bring sin and death to man: **"Thy first father hath sinned" (Is.43:27).** Christ stands at the head of the human race...
- as the first to live a sinless and perfect life, securing a perfect righteousness
- as the first to conquer death by literally arising from the dead
- 

Now note the difference between Adam and Christ. Adam was made a "living soul"; Christ a "quickening spirit" (1 Cor.15:45). What man needs and has always needed is a "quickening spirit," a spirit that has the power to infuse life into his soul, life that is both abundant and eternal.

> **"Therefore as by the offense of one judgment came upon all men to condemnation; even so by the righteousness of one the free gift came upon all men unto justification of life. For as by one man's disobedience many were made sinners, so by the obedience of one shall many be made righteous" (Ro.5:18-19).**

5.    Note that sin is *the cause of death*, and that Adam was the cause of sin. He was the author of apostasy, of withdrawal from God. Whatever theories may say, one thing is clear: *Adam was the cause of sin in the very same way in which Christ is the cause of righteousness.*
- a. Note v.13. Since Adam, sin has been universal. But sin was not charged against a person because there was no law. There has to be a law for there to be a charge.
- b. Note v.14. Nevertheless, death was still the judgment and experience of man. Why? Why did man die if he was not charged with personal sin? Because Adam was the figurehead and the representative man for all who would be born with his nature. What does this mean? He sinned, took on a corruptible nature, therefore, he died (Ro.5:12f). So death *was passed on* to all men because all inherited the corruptible nature of Adam (Ro.5:12f).

Some argue that this is unjust--to be condemned to die because the father of the human race, Adam, sinned. But the argument is not familiar with the facts, for the truth is, the way to eternal life is now clearer and much more positive. God has now made a greater provision for life and salvation.

a. This is clearly seen in three facts. A man now has a clearer choice than Adam had. A man can now live forever by simply choosing to take Christ into his life, and the positive choice of choosing Christ is greater and has more pull than Adam's choice. Adam was to remain incorruptible if he did not eat of the fruit of the tree. Note his choice was a negative command and it had no pull and no power to enable him to obey. Man's choice today is positive. Adam was *forbidden to do something*. We are instructed *to do something*--a positive command. These two facts, the fuller and clearer revelation in Christ and the stronger pull of the positive, show that every man has an equal chance at immortality; and in reality, man today has more of a chance than Adam had, more than an equal chance.

b. There is no human life apart from being born to corruptible human beings. It is a matter of being born and privileged with life or not being born and never having the privilege of life. In order to have the privilege of living, a person has to be born of corruptible parents.

c. The way of salvation and the way for man to live forever is now much clearer. Man could never know the love of God apart from being born into a corruptible world and experiencing the love of God demonstrated in Christ Jesus. Therefore, the birth of a person, his entrance into the world, is the greatest imaginable blessing. Being born into this depraved and corruptible world is the only way a person can ever know the love of God and experience eternal life with God.

> "That in the ages to come he might show the exceeding riches of his grace in his kindness toward us through Christ Jesus" (Eph.2:7).

**QUESTIONS:**
1. Can you justify your sin by blaming it on Adam? Why or why not? If you had been the first man, do you think you could have remained sinless?
2. What is the ultimate cause of death? What have you done to keep yourself from spiritual death?
3. What advantages do you have that Adam did not have? Imagine having to live each day with your salvation depending on your complete obedience! Would you *ever* be saved? Would you *remain* saved?
4. Do you live in such a way that you show your gratitude to God for making your salvation truly accessible and eternal?

**A CLOSER LOOK:**

(5:12) **Sin--Death**: Adam sinned and corrupted himself; therefore, he died. Why is there such an awful penalty for sin? Is not death an awful price to pay for sin? Such questions overlook the awfulness and seriousness of sin. Sin is the most heinous, vulgar, uncouth, abominable, outrageous, shocking, and hateful thing that can exist. Two things show the evil nature of sin.

1. Sin is the ultimate thing that can be done *against God*. Sin is *disobeying God* and *rebelling against God*. Sin acts against God, fights and struggles against God. Sin goes against all that God is. Sin is insurrection against God; it is the crime of high treason against God. To turn away from the Supreme Being of the universe is to commit the *ultimate offense* (disobedience), and the ultimate offense deserves the ultimate judgment: death. (Keep in mind the glorious love of God. The only way to truly see the love of God is to see man committing the ultimate offense against God [disobeying Him] and having to bear the ultimate punishment of death. Seeing this is the only way a man can see how God paid the ultimate price in giving His Son to die *for us*. His love is the supreme love, the

love that sacrificed the greatest thing in all the world, that gave His Son to die for sinners. See Ro.5:6-11.)

2. Sin cost God the ultimate price, the supreme sacrifice of His Son. God, being God, is perfect love. As perfect love He is bound to prove His love by providing a way for man to be forgiven his sin and to be saved. And the way chosen to save man had to be the perfect salvation, the perfect expression of His love.

> **"Greater love hath no man than this, that a man lay down his life for his friends" (Jn.15:13).**

But note, Christ did not give His life just for friends. He went well beyond; He loved perfectly: He gave His life for those who were without strength, for the ungodly, the sinners, the enemies of God (Ro.5:6, 8, 10).

> **"God demonstrated [proved] His love toward us, in that while we were yet sinners, Christ died for us" (Ro.5:8).**

Sin cost God the ultimate price, the supreme sacrifice, even the death of His own Son.

> **"But he was wounded for our transgressions, he was bruised for our iniquities: the chastisement of our peace was upon him; and with his stripes we are healed" (Is.53:5).**

QUESTIONS:
1. Many people feel the penalty of death is much too harsh for sin. What makes this argument false?
2. What is sin? Who sins? Why do they sin? What is God's solution for the problem of sin?
3. Think of an average day. Given the definition of sin (anything that displeases God), how often in a day do you think you sin? By sins of commission? By sins of omission? Multiply that by the day and years of your life. How should that make you feel about the sacrifice Christ made for you? Do you need to stop and thank Him right now?

## 2. THE COUNTERACTION--THE REVERSAL--OF SIN AND DEATH BY CHRIST (v.15-18).

Jesus Christ has counteracted and reversed what Adam did. He has made it possible for man to live righteously and to conquer death. Note the descriptive contrast between what Adam did and what God did through Christ.

1. Adam's sin brought death; God's gift brought righteousness. The gift is righteousness (cp. v.17). God's gift of righteousness differs entirely from the sin of Adam. Adam sinned and brought sin and death to "many" (to the human race). But Adam was only one man and God is far greater than one mere man, even if that man has influenced the whole human race. God was able to do *"much more"* good than Adam was able to do bad. In fact, God has counteracted and reversed all the bad Adam did.

    a. God has showered the grace of God, His glorious favor, care, and love, upon man.

> **"But God, who is rich in mercy, for his great love wherewith he loved us, even when we were dead in sins, hath quickened us to-gether with Christ, (by grace ye are saved;) and hath raised us up**

together, and made us sit together in heavenly places in Christ Jesus: that in the ages to come he might show the exceeding riches of his grace in his kindness toward us through Christ Jesus. For by grace are ye saved through faith; and that not of yourselves: it is the gift of God: not of works, lest any man should boast" (Eph.2:4-9).

b. God has made the gift of God (righteousness) available to man.

"But for us also, to whom it [righteousness] shall be imputed, if we believe on him that raised up Jesus our Lord from the dead; who was delivered for our offenses, and was raised again for our justification" (Ro.4:24-25).

2. Adam's sin brought condemnation; God's gift brought justification. God's gift differs entirely from what Adam did. Adam doomed the human race, but God's gift justifies the human race. And note how glorious God's justification is: when Adam sinned, his one sin was judged and brought condemnation to men; but what God did is so glorious, it explodes the human mind.
⇒ God's gift not only dealt with Adam's offense and condemnation, it dealt with "*many*" offenses. God's gift of righteousness justifies us from *all our offenses*, not only from Adam's one offense. God's gift justifies us from all the corruption we have inherited from our fathers and from all the corruption of human nature--all the sins we have committed with our own hands.

The man who truly trusts Christ is justified from all things, from all sin and corruption and condemnation...
• inherited from our fathers (Adam)
• committed and caused by our own sinful behavior

"Therefore being justified by faith, we have peace with God through our Lord Jesus Christ" (Ro.5:1).

3. Adam's sin brought the reign of death; God's gift brought the reign of life. Adam sinned and brought the reign of death upon all men. But Adam was only one man, one mere man. No matter what he did, God was able to counteract it and do more, for He is greater; and He is able to do anything.
God has done more, much more. They who "receive" God's grace and God's gift of righteousness "shall reign in life." The term "reign in life" means to dwell and rule in eternal life. But note, the source of righteousness is Jesus Christ.

### APPLICATION:
Note two glorious truths.
1) Believers "reign in life" while on this earth. They receive the abundance of God's grace.
   a) There is the gift of abundant life.

"I am come that they might have life, and that they might have it more abundantly" (Jn.10:10).

   b) There is all sufficiency in all things.

"And God is able to make all grace abound toward you; that ye, always having all sufficiency in all things, may abound to every good work" (2 Cor.9:8).

c)   There is great power.

> **"Now unto him that is able to do exceeding abundantly above all that we ask or think, according to the power that worketh in us" (Eph.3:20).**

d)   There is the supply of all needs.

> **"But my God shall supply all your need according to his riches in glory by Christ Jesus" (Ph.4:19).**

e)   There is an abundant entrance into heaven.

> **"For so an entrance shall be ministered unto you abundantly into the everlasting kingdom of our Lord and saviour Jesus Christ" (2 Pt.1:11).**

f)   There is abundant satisfaction.

> **"They shall be abundantly satisfied with the fatness of thy house; and thou shalt make them drink of the river of thy pleasures" (Ps.36:8).**

2) Believers shall "reign in life" throughout all eternity.

> **"For God so loved the world, that he gave his only begotten Son, that whosoever believeth in him should not perish, but have everlasting life" (Jn.3:16).**

4.   Adam's sin brought condemnation to all men; God's gift brought justification of life upon all men. This is simply a summary of what has already been said.
⇒   "By the offense of one [Adam] judgment came upon all men to condemnation."
⇒   "By the righteousness of One [Jesus Christ] the free gift came upon all men unto justification of life."

> **"He that spared not his own Son, but delivered him up for us all, how shall he not with him also freely give us all things?" (Ro.8:32).**

### ILLUSTRATION:
It is one thing to say that Jesus Christ countered everything that Adam did, everything. It is quite another when we realize that Christ did all of this not for intimate friends but for His enemies. He did it for you.

> *"In The Grace of Giving, Stephen Olford tells of a Baptist pastor during the American Revolution, Peter Miller, who lived in Ephrata, Pennsylvania, and enjoyed the friendship of George Washington.*
> *"In Ephrata also lived Michael Wittman, an evil-minded sort who did all he could to oppose and humiliate the pastor.*
> *"One day Michael Wittman was arrested for treason and sentenced to die. Peter Miller traveled seventy miles on foot to Philadelphia to plead for the life of the traitor.*

> *"'No, Peter,' General Washington said, 'I cannot grant you the life of your friend.'*
> *"'My friend!' exclaimed the old preacher. 'He's the bitterest enemy I have.'*
> *"'What?' cried Washington. 'You've walked seventy miles to save the life of an enemy? That puts the matter in a different light. I'll grant your pardon.' And he did. Peter Miller took Michael Wittman back home to Ephrata--no longer an enemy, but a friend.'"[2]*

Jesus Christ did the very same thing. The lives of His enemies were pardoned by His Father. One day, He will take each believer home--no longer as an enemy but as a friend.

**"Greater love hath no man than this, that a man lay down his life for his friends" (Jn.15:13).**

**QUESTIONS:**
1. Sin and death have been counteracted by Christ. In what obvious ways has Jesus Christ countered the actions of Adam in your life?
2. What does justification mean to you personally?
3. Salvation is more than just waiting for heaven. Salvation is *now* for the believer. What changes have you noticed in your life since you were saved?

## 3. THE CONCLUSION (v.19-21).

The conclusion is one of the most instructive and striking passages in all of Scripture. It includes three points.

1.     Adam's disobedience made many (all men, v.12, 18) sinners, but Christ's obedience made many righteous. Jesus Christ lived a sinless life; He never sinned, never displeased God--not even once. He was perfectly righteous, *securing the Ideal Righteousness.*

Since His righteousness is *the Ideal Righteousness*, it can stand for the righteousness of all men, and that is exactly what happens. When a man believes in Jesus Christ, God takes that man's belief and counts it as righteousness. God lets the *Ideal Righteousness* of Jesus Christ cover the man because the man *believes and honors* His Son, Jesus Christ.

Any man who will so honor God's Son by believing and trusting Him, God will honor by counting his faith as the righteousness of Christ. It is that simple and that profound: "By the obedience of Jesus Christ shall many be made righteous." But note, a person must truly believe--he must have the kind of belief that really trusts Jesus Christ, that really casts his life upon Christ, that casts all that he is and has upon Christ and His keeping.

**"For it became him, for whom are all things, and by whom are all things, in bringing many sons unto glory, to make the captain of their salvation perfect through sufferings" (Heb.2:10).**

2.     The law was given to point out and magnify sin, but God's grace was so much greater. If righteousness is by Jesus Christ, then why did God give us the law? What is the purpose of the law? Very simply. "The law entered [the world] that the offense might abound." The law was given...

- to point out and magnify sin
- to give men a greater knowledge of sin
- to make men more responsible for their sin
- to make men more aware of sin
- to stir more conviction over sin

---

[2]   Craig B. Larson. *Illustrations for Preaching and Teaching*, p.142.

# ROMANS 5:12-21

> "Wherefore the law was our schoolmaster to bring us unto Christ, that we might be justified by faith" (Gal.3:24).

3. Sin resulted in death, but God's grace resulted in eternal life.
   a. By Adam, sin reigns, triumphs, holds authority and leads to death.

   > "The soul that sinneth, it shall die. The son shall not bear the iniquity of the father, neither shall the father bear the iniquity of the son: the righteousness of the righteous shall be upon him, and the wickedness of the wicked shall be upon him" (Ezk.18:20).

   b. By God, grace reigns, triumphs, holds authority, and leads to eternal life.

   > "In him was life; and the life was the light of men" (Jn.1:4).

   But note the source: eternal life comes only through the righteousness of "Jesus Christ our Lord."

**ILLUSTRATION:**
Can you imagine the despair you would feel if Christ had refused to be obedient to His Father? He could have let mankind fend for itself, to go it alone, to fight the power of sin and death alone, to keep the law perfectly. He could have, but He did not. Instead, Jesus Christ came as a righteous man to save you and take the burden and punishment of sin off your shoulders and onto His own.

> "A _Peanuts_ cartoon pictured Lucy and Linus looking out the window at a steady downpour of rain. 'Boy,' said Lucy, 'look at it rain. What if it floods the whole world?'
> "'It will never do that,' Linus replied confidently. 'In the ninth chapter of Genesis, God promised Noah that would never happen again, and the sign of the promise is the rainbow.'
> "'You've taken a great load off my mind,' said Lucy with a relieved smile.
> "'Sound theology,' pontificated Linus, 'has a way of doing that!'"[3]

The facts are simple: God's Word is sure. His grace is greater than our sin.

**QUESTIONS:**
1. Have you acknowledged your sinfulness? Have you accepted God's grace--His gift of salvation through Jesus Christ? What are you waiting for?
2. Why do men still try to achieve righteousness through the law? What is the purpose of the law? Are you still supposed to obey it?

**SUMMARY:**

There is a great contrast between the lives of Adam and Jesus Christ. One man brought death into the world; the other brought life. One man brought sin; the other forgives sin. One man lived for himself; the other gave His life for others. One man had no answers, the other was the Answer. This passage states this in strong terms:

---

[3] Michael P. Green. _Illustrations for Biblical Preaching_, p.113.

# ROMANS 5:12-21

1. The entrance of sin and death was through Adam.
2. The counteraction--the reversal--of sin and death is through Christ.
3. Conclusion: sin results in death; the grace of God results in eternal life.

Adam or Jesus Christ: Whom have you chosen to follow?

## PERSONAL JOURNAL NOTES:
### (Reflection & Response)

1. The most important thing that I learned from this lesson was:

2. The thing that I need to work on the most is:

3. I can apply this lesson to my life by:

4. Closing Prayer Of Commitment: (put your commitment down on paper).

# OUTLINE & SUBJECT INDEX

## ROMANS
### Volume 1, Chapters 1-5

# OUTLINE & SUBJECT INDEX

# OUTLINE & SUBJECT INDEX

# ROMANS

# Volume 1, Chapters 1-5

REMEMBER: When you look up a subject and turn to the Scripture reference, you have not only the Scripture, you have <u>an outline and a discussion</u> (commentary) of the Scripture and subject.

This is one of the <u>GREAT VALUES</u> of the <u>Teacher's Outline & Study Bible</u>. Once you have all the volumes, you will have not only what all other Bible indexes give you, that is, a list of all the subjects and their Scripture references, <u>BUT</u> you will also have...

- An outline of <u>every</u> Scripture and subject in the Bible.
- A discussion (commentary) on every Scripture and subject.
- Every subject supported by other Scriptures or cross references.

<u>DISCOVER THE GREAT VALUE</u> for yourself. Quickly glance below to the very first subject of the Index of Romans Volume 1. It is:

**ABRAHAM**
    <u>A Closer Look</u>. Discussed.               Ro.4:1-25

Turn to the reference. Glance at the Scripture and outline of the Scripture, then read the commentary. You will immediately see the GREAT VALUE of the INDEX of the <u>Teacher's Outline & Study Bible</u>.

## OUTLINE & SUBJECT INDEX

**ABRAHAM**

| | |
|---|---|
| <u>A Closer Look</u>. Discussed. | Ro.4:1-25 |
| And history. Representative man of human race. | Ro.4:11-12 |
| Example. | |
|     Of faith over works. Justification & righteousness. | Ro.4:1-25 |
|     Of great faith. Pivotal point in history. | Ro.4:1-25 |
|     Of justification by faith. | Ro.4:9; 4:17-25 |
| Place in Jewish history. | |
|     Father of believers. | Ro.4:11-12 |
|     Founder of Jewish nation. | Ro.4:1-25 |
| Promises to. Discussed. | Ro.4:1-25 |
| Seed of. | |
|     Christ. | Ro.4:1-25 |
|     Nations of people. | Ro.4:11-12; 4:13; 4:17 |

**ABUNDANCE**
    Spiritual. Of grace & salvation. Six things.      Ro.5:15-18

**ACCEPTABLE**
    How one becomes <u>a</u>.            Ro.2:25-27

# OUTLINE & SUBJECT INDEX

# OUTLINE & SUBJECT INDEX

# OUTLINE & SUBJECT INDEX

# OUTLINE & SUBJECT INDEX

# OUTLINE & SUBJECT INDEX

# OUTLINE & SUBJECT INDEX

# OUTLINE & SUBJECT INDEX

Nature.
- Impartial. — Ro.3:29-30
- Just. Genuine love is j. — Ro.3:5-8
- Love.
  - Genuine love is l. — Ro.2:2-5
  - Is not indulgence & license. — Ro.3:5-8
- One God. Universal Fatherhood. — Ro.3:29-30
Power of. Uses p. in a loving, caring way. — Ro.1:16
Proof of.
- Creation. — Ro.1:19
- Inner sense. Instinctives within man. Conscience. — Ro.1:19
Revelation of. Through nature & creation. — Ro.1:20
Righteousness of.
- Discussed. — Ro.3:21-26
- Revealed in the gospel. — Ro.1:16-17
- Revelation of. — Ro.3:21-26
Witnesses to. Threefold w. within man. — Ro.2:11-15
Wrath of.
- Cause is sin of men. — Ro.5:1
- Gives man up. Reasons. — Ro.1:24
- How God shows w. — Ro.1:24-32
- Meaning. — Ro.1:18
- Misconceptions of. Some think God is too good to judge. — Ro.2:2-5
- Subjects of. Two classes of men. — Ro.1:18
- Why God shows w. Four reasons. — Ro.1:18; 1:18-23

## GODLESS - GODLESSNESS
Caused by. Self-centeredness. — Ro.3:10-12
Result. Cannot save self. — Ro.5:6-7

## GOD'S, FALSE (See IDOLS - IDOLATRY)

## GOSPEL
A Closer Look. Comparison.
The Apostle's Creed & the Apostle Paul. — Ro.1:1-7
Duty toward.
- To be enslaved to the g. — Ro.1:8-15
- To be unashamed of the g. — Ro.1:16-17
Facts. Some are ashamed of g. — Ro.1:16
Message of.
- Outline of. — Ro.1:2
- Reveals the righteousness of God. — Ro.1:16-17

## GRACE
Discussed. — Ro.5:2
Meaning. — Ro.4:16; 5:2

## HARD - HARDNESS (See HEART, Known)

## HATE - HATING
Haters of God. — Ro.1:30

# OUTLINE & SUBJECT INDEX

**HEAR - HEARER - HEARING**
    Duty.
        To be a doer not a <u>h</u>. of the Word.     Ro.2:11-15

**HEART**
    Known, exposed by God.     Ro.2:2-5
    State of - Kinds of. Darkened. Cannot see.     Ro.1:21

**HEATHEN**
    Basis of judgment. Discussed.     Ro.2:11-15
    What happens to the <u>h</u>. who never hear of Christ.     Ro.2:11-15

**HEIRS** (See **INHERITANCE**)

**HELPLESS - HELPLESSNESS**
    Of man. Cannot save himself.     Ro.5:6-7

**HISTORY**
    Christ & history. Adam & Christ, two representatives
        of mankind.     Ro.5:12-21
    Pivotal point of <u>h</u>.
        Abraham.     Ro.4:11-12
        Adam.     Ro.5:12-21

**HOLY SPIRIT**
    Work of.
        Justifies.     Ro.4:25
        Proves Christ is the Son of God.     Ro.1:4
        Saves.     Ro.5:10
        Seals, guarantees believer.     Ro.5:5
        Sheds the love of God abroad in the hearts of believers.     Ro.5:5

**HOMOSEXUAL - HOMOSEXUALITY**
    Discussed.     Ro.1:26-27

**HONOR**
    Meaning.     Ro.2:7
    Of believer. To be rewarded in eternity.     Ro.2:6-10
    Verses. List of.     Ro.2:7

**HOPE**
    Believer's hope. The glory of God.     Ro.5:2
    Comes through.
        Experience through trials.     Ro.5:3-5
    Discussed.     Ro.5:2
    For whom. Depraved man.     Ro.3:9-20
    Meaning.     Ro.5:2; 8
    Verses. List of.     Ro.5:2

**HOPELESS - HOPELESSNESS**
    State - Condition.
        Cannot save self.     Ro.5:6-7
    Verses. List of.     Ro.5:6-7

# OUTLINE & SUBJECT INDEX

**HUMANISM**
    Discussed.                                   Ro.1:22-23;
                                                    1:24-25

**HYPOCRITE**
    Discussed.                                   Ro.2:17-29
    Mistakes of.                               Ro.2:17-29

**IDOLS - IDOLATRY**
    Discussed.                                   Ro.1:22-23; 1:24-
                                                    25; 2:21-24
    Effects. Causes God to give man up to i.         Ro.1:24-32
    Source.
             Man. Creates own "gods" in mind & imaginations.     Ro.1:22-23;
                                                    1:24-25
             Pride. Man's claim to be "wise."         Ro.1:22-23;
                                                    1:24-25

**IGNORANT - IGNORANCE**
    Of God. Cause. Depraved nature.              Ro.3:10-12

**IMAGINATION**
    Described. As vain, empty.                 Ro.1:21

**IMMORALITY**
    Results. Causes God to give man up to i.        Ro.1:26-27

**IMMORTALITY**
    Meaning.                                     Ro.2:7
    Verses. List of.                           Ro.2:7

**IMPARTIAL** (See PARTIALITY)

**IMPLACABLE**
    Meaning.                                     Ro.1:31

**IMPUTE**
    Meaning.                                     Ro.4:6-8; 4:22

**INDIFFERENT - INDIFFERENCE**
    Describes. Sinful nature.                   Ro.3:10-12

**INDIGNATION**
    Meaning.                                     Ro.2:8

**INDULGE - INDULGENCE**
    Sin of. Is not love.                         Ro.3:5-8

**INHERITANCE**
    Of Abraham. Promised that he would i. the world.     Ro.4:13
    Of the believer.
             To i. whole world.                   Ro.4:13
    Surety of. Is not by law, but by faith.          Ro.4:13-16

# OUTLINE & SUBJECT INDEX

# OUTLINE & SUBJECT INDEX

# OUTLINE & SUBJECT INDEX

# OUTLINE & SUBJECT INDEX

Wrong way to seek j.

    By law or works.                                   Ro.3:27-31; 4:1-8; 4:13-16

    By ritual.                                  Ro.4:9-12

Verses. List of.                              Ro.5:1

## KNOWLEDGE

Of man. Without understanding of God & reality.     Ro.3:10-12

## LAW

Deliverance from.

    By faith & justification.              Ro.4:13-16

Described as.

    Law of faith. Discussed.           Ro.3:27

    Of works. Discussed.              Ro.3:27

Duty. To be a doer, not a hearer of the l.    Ro.2:11-15

Fulfilled by Christ.                      Ro.3:31

Nature.

    Is established, upheld by faith.      Ro.3:31

    Is spiritual.                        Ro.4:14

Purpose of.

    Discussed.                        Ro.7:7-13

    Fivefold.                         Ro.3:19-20

    To point out sin, transgression.     Ro.4:14-15; 5:19-21; 5:20

    To reveal man's depravity.        Ro.3:9-20

    To stop boasting.              Ro.3:19-20

    To work wrath.                Ro.4:14-15

Relation to man.

    Not charged when there is no law.   Ro.5:13

Results. Voids faith; works wrath; points out sin.   Ro.4:14-15

Vs. faith. Discussed.                  Ro.4:13-16

Weakness & powerlessness of the l.

    Cannot give the reward nor fulfill the promise of God.  Ro.4:13

    Does not produce righteousness.     Ro.3:21-22

    Does not receive an inheritance.     Ro.4:13-16

    Is against man.                 Ro.3:19-20

    Is excluded, voided by faith.       Ro.3:27-31

    Threefold w.                   Ro.4:14-15

    Wrong way to seek justification.     Ro.4:13-16

## LICENSE

Meaning. Is not love.                   Ro.3:5-8

## LIFE

Described as.

    Abundant life. Of grace & salvation.   Ro.5:15-18

## LOGIC

Proves that faith alone justifies a man.     Ro.4:1-8

## LOVE

Misconceptions - Errors of. Thinking God is l. & not just.  Ro.2:2-5; 3:5-8

Nature. Requires justice & judgment.     Ro.2:2-5; 3:5-8

# OUTLINE & SUBJECT INDEX

# OUTLINE & SUBJECT INDEX

# OUTLINE & SUBJECT INDEX

# OUTLINE & SUBJECT INDEX

| | |
|---|---|
| Meaning. | Ro.1:17 |
| Christ Himself is the r. of God. | Ro.3:21-22 |
| Sins are not counted. | Ro.4:6-8 |
| The seal, sign of right standing with God. | Ro.4:9; 4:10 |
| Need for. | |
| Sin. | Ro.3:22-23 |
| The way to be right with God. | Ro.3:21-26 |
| Purpose. To declare God's r., His justice. | Ro.3:25-26 |
| Source. How to secure. | |
| By faith in Christ. | Ro.3:22 |
| By God. Seen in Abraham. | Ro.4:1-25; 4:1-3 |
| By God's r. Is Jesus Christ. | Ro.3:21-22 |
| By Jesus Christ. | Ro.3:21-22 |
| Not by the law. | Ro.3:21-22 |
| Vs. self-righteousness. | Ro.4:9-12 |

**RITUAL** (See RELIGION)

| | |
|---|---|
| Problem with. | |
| Does not make men acceptable to God. | Ro.2:25-27 |
| Does not save. | Ro.2:17-29; 4:11 |
| Signs & symbols only. | Ro.4:11 |
| Wrong way to seek justification. | Ro.4:9-12 |

**RULES & REGULATIONS**

| | |
|---|---|
| Problem with. Wrong way to seek justification. | Ro.4:9-12 |

**SACRIFICE**

| | |
|---|---|
| Of Christ. Died as our s. | Ro.5:6-7 |

**SALVATION - SAVED** (See Related Subjects)

| | |
|---|---|
| A Closer Look. Meaning. | Ro.1:16 |
| Conditions - How one is saved. | |
| By an inward working. | Ro.2:28-29 |
| By God's power. | Ro.1:16-17 |
| By Jesus Christ. | Ro.5:19-21 |
| By the death & resurrection of Jesus Christ. | Ro.4:23-25 |
| By the gospel. | Ro.1:16-17 |
| By the life of the living Lord, the Intercessor, the Mediator. | Ro.5:10-11 |
| Not by religion or ritual. | Ro.2:28-29 |
| Not by heritage, parents, race, or institution. | Ro.3:1-2 |
| Discussed. | Ro.1:16; 1:16-17 |
| Need for. How to be right with God. | Ro.3:21-26 |
| Purpose. Are s. to obey & to lead others to obey. | Ro.1:5 |
| Results. | |
| Abundance of six things. | Ro.5:15-18 |
| Fivefold. | Ro.1:16 |

**SCRIPTURES** (See **WORD OF GOD**)

| | |
|---|---|
| Inspiration of. Discussed. | Ro.1:1-4 |
| Message of. Discussed. | Ro.1:1-4 |
| View of. Paul's v. | Ro.1:1-7 |

# OUTLINE & SUBJECT INDEX

# OUTLINE & SUBJECT INDEX

# OUTLINE & SUBJECT INDEX

# OUTLINE & SUBJECT INDEX

# OUTLINE & SUBJECT INDEX

# ILLUSTRATION INDEX

## ROMANS
Volume 1, Chapters 1-5

# ILLUSTRATION INDEX

# ILLUSTRATION INDEX

# ILLUSTRATION INDEX

# ILLUSTRATION INDEX

# ILLUSTRATION INDEX

# PURPOSE STATEMENT

## LEADERSHIP MINISTRIES WORLDWIDE

exists to equip ministers, teachers, and laymen in their
understanding, preaching, and teaching of God's Word
by publishing and distributing worldwide
*The Preacher's Outline & Sermon Bible*®
and related *Outline* Bible materials,
to reach & disciple men, women, boys, and girls for Jesus Christ.

# •MISSION STATEMENT•

1. To make the Bible so understandable - its truth so clear and plain - that men
   and women everywhere, whether teacher or student, preacher or hearer,
   can grasp its Message and receive Jesus Christ as Savior; and...
2. To place the Bible in the hands of all who will preach and teach God's Holy
   Word, verse by verse, precept by precept, regardless of the individual's
   ability to purchase it.

The *Outline* Bible materials have been given to LMW for printing and especially
distribution worldwide at/below cost, by those who remain anonymous. One fact,
however, is as true today as it was in the time of Christ:

**• The Gospel is free, but the cost of taking it is not •**

LMW depends on the generous gifts of Believers with a heart for Him and a love and
burden for the lost. They help pay for the printing, translating, and placing *Outline*
Bible materials in the hands and hearts of those worldwide who will present God's
message with clarity, authority and understanding beyond their own.

LMW was incorporated in the state of Tennessee in July 1992 and received IRS 501(c) 3 nonprofit status in March 1994. LMW is an international, nondenominational mission organization.
All proceeds from USA sales, along with donations from donor partners, go 100% into under-
writing our translation and distribution projects of *Outline* Bible materials to preachers,
church & lay leaders, and Bible students around the world.

5/97

PO Box 21310 - Chattanooga, TN 37424 • (423) 855-2181 • FAX (423) 855-8616
• E-Mail 74152.616@compuserve.com — Web site: http://www.outlinebible.org •

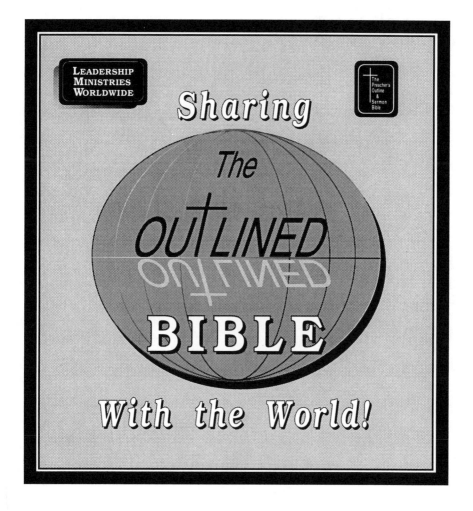